The three-time Winston Cup champion and Daytona 500 winner shares his memories of a life in racing—and a knowing look at the evolution of the sport and its greatest drivers and personalities.

"Waltrip's wild-child, run-from-the-police teenage beginnings, his cocky, say-anything attitude as a race car driver, and his true love for his family and sport make this autobiography a fun ride ... entertaining and amusing."
—*Fort Worth Star-Telegram*

"I would have loved to race against guys like David Pearson and Bobby Allison, but I really wish I could have raced against Darrell in that green Mountain Dew car."
—Dale Earnhardt Jr.

"Possibly the most popular guy in motor racing, Darrell Waltrip, or DW, as he's known, tells his life story with humor and good timing. There's never a slow moment and the book is made more credible by comments from other drivers about DW and the sport....A nitty-gritty, behind-the-scenes peek at the personalities and peculiarities of racing."
—*The Charlotte Observer*

"I wanted to hire him as a driver because he was the guy who changed the whole sport. Until he came along, it was like all of the drivers were out of one mold, and he broke the mold. He was outspoken, but he could back it up on the track. He was great with people.... He was great with a crowd ... and that was a huge leap for our sport."
—Rick Hendrick

continued ...

DW

A Lifetime Going Around in Circles

DARRELL WALTRIP

WITH JADE GURSS

A SIGNET BOOK

SIGNET
Published by New American Library, a division of
Penguin Group (USA) Inc., 375 Hudson Street,
New York, New York 10014, USA
Penguin Group (Canada), 10 Alcorn Avenue, Toronto,
Ontario M4V 3B2, Canada (a division of Pearson Penguin Canada Inc.)
Penguin Books Ltd., 80 Strand, London WC2R 0RL, England
Penguin Ireland, 25 St. Stephen's Green, Dublin 2,
Ireland (a division of Penguin Books Ltd.)
Penguin Group (Australia), 250 Camberwell Road, Camberwell, Victoria 3124,
Australia (a division of Pearson Australia Group Pty. Ltd.)
Penguin Books India Pvt. Ltd., 11 Community Centre, Panchsheel Park,
New Delhi - 110 017, India
Penguin Group (NZ), cnr Airborne and Rosedale Roads, Albany,
Auckland 1310, New Zealand (a division of Pearson New Zealand Ltd.)
Penguin Books (South Africa) (Pty.) Ltd., 24 Sturdee Avenue,
Rosebank, Johannesburg 2196, South Africa

Penguin Books Ltd., Registered Offices:
80 Strand, London WC2R 0RL, England

Published by Signet, an imprint of New American Library, a division of Penguin
Group (USA) Inc. Previously published in a G. P. Putnam's Sons edition.

First Signet Printing, February 2005
10   9   8   7   6   5   4   3   2   1

Like all things I've done, this book has been a labor of love! It's composed of good times, bad times, fun times, and sad times!

Through it all, I've had the Red Head by my side, and then later, Jessica and Sarah were with us as well.

For Mom and Dad and all my family for the sacrifices they all made so I could pursue my dream.

—*Darrell Waltrip*

Contents

An autobiography? That's a book about cars, right?

Introduction

This is not another book about racing. This is a love story. A love story about me and my wife, Stevie; my daughters, Jessica and Sarah; my faith; my family; my friends; my fans; and, of course, racing.

OK ... *mostly* it's about racing. It's the story of a guy who knew what he wanted, and was willing to do whatever it took to get it. I lived my dream every time I climbed into a race car, and those dreams got better every time I climbed out in Victory Lane.

And the story got better, as well.

The key word is *story*. Jeff Hammond, my crew chief when I won a lot of races and championships, likes to remind me that my stories get a little better every year. If we won a race at Darlington, South Carolina, by an entire lap over the field, it might become a *two-lap* victory after a few years of embellishing. He says my career gets more glamorous every time I open my mouth. I hope the stories are ones you'll enjoy. And we're talking about NASCAR, so when did the truth or reality ever enter the picture? Plus, I hit my head pretty hard in a lot of those crashes. So who can blame me if the facts are a little fuzzy?

Even if you don't like racing, or have never even seen a race, I hope you enjoy and learn from what I've been through in my life.

Once I told my mom how hard I was working, and she said—and this is my mom—"Son, you've never worked hard a day in your life."

And I thought, "Mom!? You, of all people! You were there. You should know!"

I was hurt. Insulted. Angry, too . . . at first.

But the more I thought about it, the more I saw it as a compliment. If you can do something with pure love and desire, with the intensity I had, you are lucky. It doesn't matter what that thing is, just so long as you have that love and passion. I had it burning inside, and I succeeded because of it. And I sure had a lot of fun along the way.

Like my mom, sometimes people look at me and say, "You never worked that hard." It especially made me angry after I won a race. I worked my tail off, driving hard every lap, and I'd get out of the car ready to pass out or fall down from the fumes and the heat and the exhaustion, and someone would say, "Hey, DW, that looked pretty easy!"

I'm glad I made it look easy, but it darn sure wasn't.

The best people—whether it is politics, business, or sports—make it look easy. Michael Jordan could score 50 points in a game and make it look easy, but that's because people never saw the thousands of hours of hard work he put in. Or Tiger Woods taking a seven-iron and knocking it 100 yards farther than any other human—it looks effortless. Or our president, George W. Bush (he's one of three U.S. presidents I have had the honor to meet throughout my career)—no matter what you think of his politics, he became a leader when this country came under attack, and he looked as if he had been prepared for that moment all of his life. It must have been the toughest thing he ever had to do, but he rose to the occasion. I look back on those days when it seemed every fan in the grandstand was booing me, but I held my head up and rose to the occasion 84 times.

■■

A lot of new NASCAR fans may know me only as the commentator on the FOX Network. You know—the *Boogity! Boogity! Boogity!* guy. Yet there's a lot more to my story than you might guess. I've always been a great communicator, so it was a natural progression from the cockpit of a race car to the television booth. If *Boogity* is how you know me, then you'll learn a lot from this book and come to know that when I 'splain something on TV, I know what I'm talking about. As I say, it's all about 'sperience. . . .

This book is also for the fans who only saw me compete in my final years in NASCAR Winston Cup and never win a race. I admit it: I retired too late. My struggles at the end of my career didn't do anything to improve my record. But my career speaks for itself, and I'm among the best drivers in NASCAR history. I can say that without bragging, because the numbers prove it. You do the math. I won three Winston Cup championships, and I won more races than anyone else in NASCAR Winston Cup history other than David Pearson and Richard Petty.

I had 84 victories in 809 career Winston Cup starts. Those numbers mean the most to me. That's a victory in one out of every ten races I started. Of course, a lot of those wins were in clusters, and in a perfect world I'd be able to spread those wins evenly across my whole career. It's hard to fathom that I won more poles and races in 1981 and 1982 than most guys do in a career, but then I didn't win a race in the last eight years of my driving career. Go figure.

This book also tells you how as a young driver I feared I might never win a Winston Cup race. Then, once the wins started coming, they seemed as if they were never going to stop. Conversely, as my career wound down, I thought my victory drought was just a slump. I kept waiting for the magic to come back. It's like you wake up one day and it's been two years since you last won a race. There are a lot of reasons why: I coulda, I shoulda, I mighta won, if ... Then it's five years, six years, seven years, and you realize it's never going to happen again. By then, the damage is done and you retire, feeling like you never experienced success.

<hr>

Fans who want to know about the sport "back then" and how it got to where it is today have come to the right place for a slice of NASCAR history. I'm a bridge between the start of what's called "the modern era" of the sport, which I dominated, and the NASCAR of today. I helped make NASCAR one of the most popular sports in the world. As this book is published, a new NASCAR era is beginning, with the departure of Winston and the arrival of new sponsor Nextel and the Nextel Cup for 2004. In addition to the sponsor changes, Bill France Jr. has handed the reins of NASCAR to his son, Brian, making him the third generation of the France family to be the chairman and CEO of NASCAR. It's an exciting time to look forward, but it's also important to look back and reflect on what has happened to the sport in the past 30 years.

In every sport, there are eras where one or two guys (or teams) dominate. Pick a sport, any sport, and you'll see. The numbers show that the 1980s was my era. When NASCAR gathered a select panel to name the top 50 NASCAR drivers of all time, I was voted "Driver of the '80s." I was the man. Later in my career, people said to me, "DW, it looks like your era is over." But I could say, "At least I had my era, and it lasted longer than most."

I was a young, hungry kid when I raced against Petty and Pearson and the other kingpins of the sport in the 1960s and 1970s. I was a three-time champion who raced hard for years with Dale Earnhardt and Jeff Gordon, guys I consider the drivers of the 1990s. And I was the wily ol' veteran who raced against the "young guns" like Dale Earnhardt Jr., Tony Stewart, Matt Kenseth, and the other kids who will be the drivers of the new century.

Through it all, I had my wife, Stevie, by my side every step of the way, even when those steps were racked with pain and heartbreak. She's been my rock, and you'll get used to seeing her name in chapter after chapter.

Most of all, this book is for my longtime fans. Like the woman who walked up to me the other day and told me, "I went to the bookstore to look for your book, and you didn't have one!" So here it is. My story. Like my life, it gets better every year. Just ask me.

—DW
January 2004

Oh, by the way . . .

■ ■ □ ■ □

Oh, by the way (there's always an "Oh, by the way" with my stories), that reminds me of a great story. One time we were . . . Well, OK, let me stop there so we can get started.

1

Good Timing

I t's about time.

Racing is all about time. It can't be described any easier. Finish a certain distance—300 miles, whatever the distance—in less time than everyone else. If you can do that, you win. It's as simple as that.

But the truth is, it's anything but simple. Racing is like a world-title chess match or high-stakes poker game taking place at warp speed, and the stopwatch never lies.

When racers talk about a good lap, we rarely talk about miles per hour or top speed. While the fans might be impressed when they hear 200 miles per hour, to a racer that number really doesn't mean a lot, because no matter what, it's all about the stopwatch. Everything a team does is focused on one thing: getting around the track in less time than anyone else.

The stopwatch is great, because it doesn't take anything into consideration. It doesn't care about big egos or how nice a car may have looked in the garage. If something doesn't make the car go quicker around the track, it's worthless. Improving one-tenth of a second per lap can be huge. It might mean the difference between winning and finishing at the back of the pack. It can mean the difference between a horrible crash and sliding past untouched. You can say "in the blink of an eye," but a normal blink takes about three-tenths of a second. In racing, that's an eternity. And that's way too long.

When I look at my life on and off the track, the same thought keeps coming back to me: *timing*. It defined what I did as a race car driver, but I've also been blessed with great timing all my life (well, most of my life, anyway).

So many things outside of my control fell into place at just the right moment that much of my own good fortune has been about being in the right place at the right time. It's been about getting opportunity after opportunity, and taking advantage of what was available when it was available. Some say it was luck, but I've always been told luck is when your hard work and effort successfully collide. So in the end, you make your own luck.

I grew up watching races with my grandmother, but racing was something I always enjoyed with my whole family. My dad and I raced go-karts on the weekends, and my family came to the track and we always had a great time.

The 1960s were a great time for cars in this country. America has always been car-crazy, but my coming of age coincided perfectly with the "golden era of muscle cars." There were great, American-made monster machines everywhere. And there were no worries about gas shortages or oil embargoes. The louder, the faster, the better was all that mattered.

When I was 16 years old, my dad and I put together my own race car—a 1936 Chevy coupe. "The Wild Child" was painted on the side. The first night out, at a little dirt track in Newman, Kentucky, I was so excited about driving my own race car. Problem was, I didn't know what I was doing on a dirt track, because all I'd ever driven was a go-kart. I didn't realize there was a "slide factor" on dirt. I probably held that accelerator pedal to the floor until the moment I slid right into the wall. Smashed that sucker bad. The Wild Child didn't even make a full lap. My first night was smashing, not a smashing success. I thought my career was over before it had even begun. But in typical Waltrip fashion, Dad and I took the car home and beat it back into shape with a hammer. We returned the next week with a better attitude and better results.

It didn't take us long to realize that we didn't have the finances to keep our own car going. Luckily, there were some guys in my hometown of Owensboro who had a fast race car, and they offered me a tryout. I had learned how to drive smoothly on asphalt in karts, and I soon discovered I could do the same in a full-size race car. I made the most of that chance and got the ride. I was in the right place at the right time, and it was a stepping-stone to bigger things.

P. B. Crowell was one of the best racers in the area then, and he was always helpful to me. When P. B. hurt his back in a crash at Nashville and needed someone to drive his car, he gave me a call. I was there, ready to go and seize another opportunity.

Speaking of opportunities, when Stevie and I were dating, her parents wanted her to go to Southern Methodist University. I knew that if she left for SMU, I might never get her back. So before she could go I asked her to marry me. I must have had the right timing, because she said "Yes" and has been with me ever since.

One night at a cocktail party, the chairman of the board of Texas Gas, where my father-in-law was the president, asked, "What would it take to sponsor a race car at Daytona?" He was a man who could write a check to make it happen, so that question was music to my ears.

Timing was everything, because when I came into Winston Cup, there were no other new or young faces showing up on the scene. I was anywhere from 10 to 15 years younger than the big stars like Cale Yarborough, Richard Petty, and David Pearson. As they were nearing the end of their careers, I was starting mine. I looked at them and said, "You know, time is on my side. I'm not scared of those cats. I guarantee I can wear 'em out." I thought, "When they're gone, I'll still be here." (Of course, the thing I didn't realize is that when I got older, there were going to be a lot of young guys saying the same thing about me!)

Man, I looked at Winston Cup and all I could see were opportunities and possibilities. I wanted to shout, "I've arrived!" I wanted to make an impression.

I'd come to the track, and I'd see these guys in cowboy boots and big ol' belt buckles and chewin' tobacco (and there's not anything wrong with that), but I thought, "What is *this*?! This is supposed to be the big leagues!" I wasn't *GQ*, but I looked at how they dressed and I thought, "Man, the direction this sport is going, with corporate America starting to pay attention, I can blow these guys off the track. All I gotta do is show up in a polo shirt, slacks, and a pair of loafers, and talk with something other than a slow southern drawl. . . . Heck, I'm gonna be something new and improved."

Everywhere I looked: opportunity.

In 1972, NASCAR entered what's been called "the modern era." R. J. Reynolds with its Winston brand of cigarettes came on board as the series sponsor, and they brought well-conceived, coordinated ideas about how to market and promote the sport to a national audience. Best of all, they had the cash to make it happen and introduce Winston Cup to more than a southern audience. The government had banned cigarette advertising on television, so suddenly the tobacco companies had all of this money they needed to spend elsewhere. Winston chose NASCAR, and a great partnership evolved, helping make the sport what it is today.

It was new, almost as if they wiped the slate clean, and here I was about to start my career. Bill France Jr. had just taken over from his father, "Big Bill" France, who had ruled with an iron hand since founding NASCAR in 1949. It was perfect timing for me to make my Winston Cup debut.

When cable television came along, they needed to fill those channels 24 hours a day, seven days a week. A little sports network named ESPN began televising NASCAR races live in the early 1980s, when I was in the prime of my career. In 1981, '82, and '83, I won most of the races and two championships, and ESPN was right there, showing races live across the nation. Now, even if you lived somewhere other than Daytona, Talladega, or Darlington, you could become a Darrell Waltrip fan in your living room. Again, it was perfect timing.

Cale Yarborough won three straight championships for car owner Junior Johnson from 1976 through 1978. Junior is like a folk hero in our sport—the last of the original bootleggers who took their "liquor cars" and started racing them on small tracks in the South. Don't let his backwoods, aw-shucks accent fool you: Junior is a brilliant guy, and this sport would be nowhere near what it is today without people like him.

When Cale decided the time was right for him to quit driving for Junior Johnson, he told me Junior was interested in me, and if I was smart, I'd figure a way to get the ride. I was miserable on the team I was with, and all of a sudden, Junior Johnson wanted me to drive his car. I was able to get out of my contract and go to work with the greatest car owner of the era. Junior taught me how to win more than just races—he taught me how to win

championships. With Junior as my team owner, I won
Winston Cup titles in 1981, 1982, and 1985.

When NASCAR said "We're gonna take our awards
banquet to New York," you can guess who was the first
guy who sat at the head table. Me! Yeah, perfect timing.
NASCAR moved its postseason banquet from the little
Plaza Hotel in Daytona to the Waldorf-Astoria in New
York in 1981. I was the first champion to be honored in
New York City, and it was big time!

The Winston, NASCAR's all-star race, was created in
1985. I won't even give you three guesses about who
won the first one. They're still talking about that one,
because the engine in my car exploded as soon as I
crossed the finish line. I'll tell you the rest of that story
a little later. As I mentioned in the introduction, there's
always an "oh, by the way" to every story.

The examples of great timing in my life are almost
endless. Many of the stories behind the stories are in the
following pages. Stories about how I signed to drive for
Rick Hendrick, who is still one of my closest friends and
the man who taught me about the business of racing.
Stories about how I decided to leave Hendrick to start
my own team, how I signed a deal with Western Auto as
a sponsor, even though I was hurt so badly from a crash
at Daytona that I couldn't stand up or move out from
behind my desk. They said "Yes," and we were off and
running.

I retired as a full-time driver in 2000, and I stepped right
into the TV booth in 2001 when FOX TV began its network contract to televise NASCAR races. Timing is everything, because I went from one perfect job to another.

I look back at all of it and I think how fortunate I am.
Whatever it took, I was doing the right things at the
right time. And I had a good time doing it. And that's an
important thing. Was I lucky? Yes. But what is luck?

When Jeff Gordon came to Winston Cup, there was a

lot of talk about how lucky he was to come in at a young age and win so many races and championships. They said it had to be the equipment he was in, or the sponsorship he had, or his crew chief, or . . . They wanted to point to every variable in that equation except Jeff.

"I agree with you," he said. "I have been lucky. But the last time I looked around, I'm the only driver in the car that keeps winning all of the races."

I feel the same way. It may have looked easy, but I can assure you, it wasn't.

I always wonder how to define luck. I have driven into Victory Lane more than once with a tire going flat. One more lap, and I would have been rolling on the rim. When the engine blew at The Winston, it could have blown up going down the back straightaway just as easily as it blew crossing the finish line. After 17 tries, I finally won the Daytona 500 in 1989, with no gas left in the tank. We won on strategy and fuel mileage, and people said we were lucky.

I won my first superspeedway race in 1977 at Darlington, the grand ol' track with a glorious history. I took the lead by driving like a madman through the debris of a crash to beat Bobby Allison, David Pearson, and Richard Petty to the line. The race finished under caution, and I had my first superspeedway win.

I believe there are angels among us, but you make your own luck. I was able to take advantage of those situations. That's what luck is: Something is presented to you and you are able to take advantage of it. You have to put yourself in a position to capitalize on what's been given to you. When I look back on things that happened, good and bad, I was in a good position more often than not. But, my 'sperience has taught me, if you go to the Luck Bank too many times, you'll be overdrawn. So I always tried to use my luck sparingly.

It's like buying stock. If you pay attention to Wall

Street, and you buy stock for $2, then it goes up to $200, is that luck? The stock market is where a lot of people think they can get rich quick. Most of them don't. Racing holds much of the same allure: Victory! Riches! Checkered flags! Pretty girls in the Winner's Circle!

The dream of winning big is what keeps people in racing. Drivers, owners, and even sponsors who have never won a race think they're going to win the next one because they've seen it happen to other people. It's like the lottery. One guy is going to win, and millions of people who thought they were going to win go home unhappy.

So many elements go into a winning race team. It's like a huge puzzle: If any piece of that puzzle is wrong or doesn't fit, you'll never win. If you think you can't, you won't. But if you are committed to doing whatever it takes to win, if you surround yourself with people who believe the same thing and are willing to work just as hard, you just might hit the lottery like I did. Oh yeah—and a little luck along the way doesn't hurt, either.

2

The Wild Child

I had to hold Granny's hand, but at least it meant I could go to the races. I first saw an auto race at Legion Park, an old half-mile dirt track in Owensboro, Kentucky, when I was six years old. It was the most magical thing I had ever seen. How could I not get hooked?

I can close my eyes and still smell the hot dogs and the popcorn and the fuel the cars were burning. I can see the people climbing trees along the backstretch so they wouldn't have to pay to get in. I can see the pond in the middle of the track. The whole place was dusty, and the wooden grandstands weren't very comfortable. I can hear the roar of the engines as they slid and strained around the track, slinging mud and dirt into and over the stands. I was enchanted. I was enthralled. I was in love with racing. It was like the state fair, but ten times more exciting.

Granny was like a feisty rooster, smoking cigarettes and always scratching around. She was a little ol' thing, full of energy and spirit, and not shy about standing up at the races and yelling at someone if she didn't agree with something they did.

My grandfather, Lee Phillips, was a deputy sheriff in

Owensboro, and he would direct traffic at the tracks on weekends. My grandmother, Oda Palestein (dontcha love that name? Now you know why we just called her "Granny"!), liked going to the races when he worked, but she didn't like going by herself, so she would take me. I could go, but only if she called to invite me. In order to ensure the invitation, I'd get up early before anyone else and crawl to the phone to dial her house.

"Granny, don't forget to call me today," I'd tell her.

"You little brat," she'd say, and laugh. "You know I'm gonna call you!"

The cars were so colorful, belching flames out of the pipes as they slid into the turns. Then I'd walk across the track and into the pit area at the end of the night. The cars looked like they were from outer space, what with the big tires and huge steering wheels. All of this was overwhelming to my six-year-old eyes.

The drivers wore white pants and T-shirts, and they all seemed larger than life—guys like G. C. Spencer, Pete Oliver, Stokey Hamburg, and Gene Coons. The cars and the drivers had great nicknames. G. C. had "The Flying Saucer," and Coons was called "The Brute." Spencer was my hero, and I remember getting upset if the Brute beat him. The Flying Saucer had a unique and mysterious sound, so much so you could close your eyes and still tell when the car went past each lap.

I didn't realize how lucky I was to have so many tracks in and around my little hometown. I loved going, and I sat by the phone each weekend waiting for Granny Oda to call.

"I'm going to do that one of these days! That's what I want to be!" I'd tell her. I had no idea the chances were pretty slim I'd make a living driving a race car. But, like any little boy who dreams of being a football player, fireman, or astronaut, it became my goal and my mission in life to make it in racing. I wanted to be a race car driver when I grew up, and I was determined that nothing was going to stop me.

◼◻◼

I was a firebug. I loved the Fourth of July when I was young. I just loved setting stuff on fire. I even set my sister Carolyn on fire once. Well, sort of. She was only three or four years old, and somehow I convinced her to step into some hot ashes from a fire we had been burning in our backyard. There were no flames, but as soon as she stepped on the ashes, she started screaming! I carried her to her room and put her under the covers.

"Shhhhhh . . . be quiet," I told her. "Mom will hear ya crying and I'll get in trouble!"

I've always been a storyteller, and I began to understand the benefits of that talent when I was seven years old. The whole family went to a party at my aunt and uncle's home in Henderson, Kentucky, which is an hour drive from Owensboro. There were firecrackers, cherry bombs, and sparklers at the party.

Before leaving the party, my dad told me, "Once we leave here, no more fireworks. You're not old enough. You don't know how to use them, so no more fireworks."

On the way home, all I could talk about was fireworks. He said, "You didn't take any, did ya?"

"Oh no, Daddy," I said. "You told me not to."

Little did he know I had a cherry bomb burning a hole in my pocket. I was so anxious to set it off that once we got home I snuck out behind the house, struck a match, and lit the thing. As I was getting ready to throw it, I noticed it was just kind of fizzing.

"Darn it," I thought. "The one cherry bomb I get and it won't work."

Kaboom! It went off right in my hand.

I took off running with my fingernails blackened and my hand bleeding. I was screaming my head off as I ran into the house.

"Boy, I told you not to bring any of those fireworks home!" Daddy said as he grabbed me. "I'm going to wear you out."

"No, Daddy, no, no, no!" I pleaded. "You don't understand."

"What is it that I don't understand?" he said, scowling.

"There was a little boy out back, and he threw a firecracker at me and I caught it," I said between sniffles. "He bought it! I caught it! It was the kid down the street!"

<hr>

That was always my dad, Leroy's, favorite story. He was a character, a great personality. He's the one from whom my brothers and sisters and I inherited our sense of humor and outgoing personalities. My mom, Margaret, was really witty, even though she didn't think so. She would say things not intended to be funny, but which were hilarious. They were both wonderful people who got along with everyone.

My parents instilled in me my work ethic. If you wanted something, you had to work for it. I got that from them. Dad dropped out of school in the fourth or fifth grade to work in the coal mines. Strip mining was a big industry around Owensboro, and my dad drove a truck delivering coal. It was brutal, but during that era it was common for kids to go to work as soon as they were old enough to help put food on the table.

My mom was the same way. She worked as a cashier. While I was growing up, both my parents worked hard. My dad drove a truck for the local Dr Pepper bottler. So each summer, as soon as I was out of school, I'd ride in the truck and help load and unload cases and bottles of Dr Pepper.

I was the oldest child, followed by Carolyn, Bobby, Connie, and my youngest brother, Michael. Some of you might have heard of Michael. I've been in a couple of TV commercials with him in the past few years. I'd like to set the record straight: He's my brother, not my son. I was 16 years old when he was born, so I didn't live at home while Michael was growing up, but he's done all right for himself in a race car. He likes to remind me, he's the only one in the family who has won the Daytona 500 more than once. He was a late bloomer as a driver, but once I retired from NASCAR, he became the star of the family and continues to get better every year.

My sister Carolyn, who works in the office at my shop, is afraid to talk to anybody about me, because she doesn't want to tell them anything I don't want them to know. And that's always a possibility, because she knows a lot! She will rarely do an interview or talk about me. She always says, "I don't know what you told them!"

We never had much money, but we always had what we needed to get by as a family, mainly because Mom and Dad worked hard, and it seemed as if they worked all the time.

A lot of today's Winston Cup stars grew up around the racetrack, watching their fathers, many of whom were either drivers or mechanics. I didn't have that luxury. I mean, my dad drove for a living, but he drove a delivery truck, not a race car.

My dad and I never did a lot of fun things together, but I liked riding with him delivering Dr Pepper. We delivered to a hardware store twice a week, and I looked forward to going there, because they sold go-karts. I'd stare at them every time we'd enter the store. Man, I wanted one of those cars so bad. The owner of the store told us about a group who got together on Sundays in a shopping center parking lot to race their karts, and that increased my desire to own a go-kart even more.

I must have been 12 years old when I got the guts to say, "Dad, we should get one of those!" I wore him out, constantly debating the merits of owning a go-kart. Finally, he at least agreed to go watch the action on Sunday afternoon. It was a cool deal, and it seemed like a great family-oriented event. Everyone was racing: moms, dads, sisters, and brothers. That only fueled the intensity of my lobbying. I'd try anything I could think of to convince him.

I made a few dollars a week mowing lawns in our neighborhood with a small push mower. It hit me one day: The hardware store sold power mowers. If I could convince Dad to buy a power mower, I could mow more yards and save the extra money to buy a kart. Then, I figured, why not shoot for the whole thing? So I tried to convince Dad to buy the mower and the kart. I don't remember the brilliant logic I concocted to win him over, but somehow, someway, it worked. Dad bought the power mower and the kart.

The whole family headed to the parking lot the following Sunday. I drove the kart, and Dad drove it as well. That's all it took: We were hooked. Addicted. Every weekend it became a family outing. It was the first time we did something like that together—you know, something fun. Mom would make a basket of food, and we'd load the kart into the trunk of the car.

Imagine the sight of the Waltrip family—Mom, Dad, me, my sister Carolyn, and brother Bobby—piling out of the family sedan Sunday morning at church, with the kart sticking out of the trunk. I'd sit and stare out the window there during the services. I couldn't wait to get out of there and go racin'.

Unfortunately, we learned immediately how expensive it could be. The first day we raced it, we brought the kart home and the tires were junk: all chewed up and worn out. We had to buy a new set of tires, plus the fuel and oil. After a few weeks, the costs began adding up.

But by then Dad had been promoted to management at the plant, which was now owned by Pepsi, so we were able to go every Sunday. I discovered I could drive the living daylights out of a kart. We started going to towns across Indiana and Kentucky, anywhere they were racing. They had different racing classes based on age groups. I'd race in the junior class and Dad would race in the adult class. Dad would win occasionally, but I'd win nearly every time out. The ol' console TV at home became pretty crowded with all of my trophies.

We spent just about every cent on the kart, constantly upgrading and making it faster. Then we met a man, Hoover Maglinger, from Owensboro. He had a fleet of karts and a trailer, and I eventually started driving for him.

Oh, by the way, if you're wondering about the power mower, I probably mowed less than ten yards total. Who has time to mow lawns when there was work to be done on the kart or when we were traveling somewhere to race? I told you I was a pyro, a real firebug. Heck, I'd rather burn the yard than mow it any day!

■ □ ■

I loved racing for a lot of reasons, but one of its greatest benefits was that it gave me an identity. It was something I was good at, and as a result people knew who I was. I wasn't a very good student. I wasn't awful—

rather, I just wasn't motivated. I had only two other interests: I wanted to play basketball at the University of Kentucky, or I wanted to be a singer/performer. I loved basketball, and I would have been a star if the three-point line were in place back then, but as it was I was mediocre at best. And my singing career, it never had a chance. I couldn't play any instruments, so that kind of limited my options, ya know?

Almost by accident, I discovered something else I was able to do well. I was too small to play football, so when they had a tryout for the track team, I decided to check it out. The coach said, "OK. We're gonna run laps around the gym. I'll tell ya when to stop." Off we went, until it was just me and one or two other boys. Everyone else was wheezing alongside the court.

The track at Daviess County High School was smaller than the standard track, so instead of the 880 or half-mile, my event was the 660-yard run. Man, I could haul butt. It suited me. I was undefeated until my junior year, and I set the city and state record at that distance. Like racing, it gave me an identity, something I was good at and known for.

My track career didn't last, though, because I started to develop other interests—mainly girls and hanging out with my buddies. Plus, I didn't like all of the training required for track. And after four years of winning almost every week in karts, I was getting bored with that as well. I was 16 years old, and it was time to move up. I wanted to race a real car.

Dad and I found a 1936 Chevrolet with a roll cage. We bought it for $300 and spent every nickel we had to rebuild that sucker. Every part we bought was used, because that was all we could afford. Harry Pedley owned a local garage, and he offered me a job along with his help fixing that race car. It probably didn't hurt that my dad was the Pepsi plant manager and Harry could do some good business maintaining all of the delivery trucks.

When the car was finally ready to run, we still needed to paint it. We didn't have enough paint of any color to cover the whole car, so we mixed all of the paint together and came up with some sort of awful flat brown color. Oh man. It was ugly. It looked like someone had vomited all over the thing after a few too many beers. It was number 6, in honor of G. C. Spencer and the Flying Saucer (and because it had a six-cylinder engine). I painted "The Wild Child" on the side. That was gonna be my nickname.

There was a dirt track called Ellis Speedway in Newman, Kentucky, and that was where we decided to get started. I hitched the race car behind my 1953 Ford coupe and headed to the track with my brother Bobby. As we drove down the street, the car started to shimmy back and forth. The perfect solution was to have Bobby, who was around 10 years old at the time, sit in the car and hold the steering wheel so it wouldn't flop around.

I took off again, and as it started raining I looked in my mirror and saw Bobby getting tossed around like a rag doll. The poor kid was too small to hold the wheel steady, and it was throwing him back and forth inside the car. The rain got heavier, and before we knew it, the cars jackknifed and we slid into the ditch. It was a mess. A muddy, muddy mess. Thankfully, we managed to dig out and finally made it to the track.

I won almost every go-kart race I ran, so I figured I would get in the car and it would be a piece of cake. All of my karting experience was on pavement, so how was I to know driving on dirt was an entirely different animal?

The pit area was outside of the track. Cars would pull out of the pits in the fourth turn and head down the front straightaway, and then come back into the pits from the third turn. It had finally stopped raining, but the track was slick and muddy when I went out for the warm-up laps. I went down the front straightaway, headed into the first turn . . . and kept going straight off the track. I didn't even make the turn. I went straight up and over the top of the track. I turned the steering wheel to the left and the car plowed ahead in the mud. Fortunately, there was no wall there for me to hit.

"Oh man," I thought. "There's something wrong here."

I got back on the track in turn two and barreled down the back straightaway.

I thought to myself, "I know what I gotta do! I gotta gas it real hard and then throw it sideways, 'cause I've seen the sprint cars do it."

I made it to the third turn, gassed that darned thing, and threw it sideways. It went into a slide. All of a sudden, it stopped sliding, straightened up, and went head-on into the wall in front of the grandstands. It knocked out my radiator and knocked off the right-front tire. I was crushed. I didn't get to race that night. Never even made one lap. I was out of action before Dad and the rest of the family had even made it to the track.

"Well, this ain't going to cut it," Daddy told me. "Next week, we're going to come down early in the day, before anybody gets here."

We got there early the next week, and I practiced before they watered the track. I knew what I was doing this race, and every week I got a little better. I finally started to master it, but it wasn't as easy as I thought it would be. I grew discouraged, often thinking, "The heck with it, I'm gonna go be something else." I'd sell cars or something, anything where I'd have more control.

As I've said, success is often all about being in the right place at the right time. Case in point: There were two dirt tracks in Owensboro, but one of them had shut down. Lucky for me, somebody bought it and decided they'd pave it. For me, this may have been the thing that saved my career before it even began.

We started racing there Sunday nights, and I had instant success. The car drove a lot lighter on asphalt, just like a go-kart, so I had an advantage. The dirt guys couldn't drive with me.

But even with success came a setback. I ran a couple of races in my car, but we didn't have the money to continue. Daddy was doing all he could, and I was doing what I could, but we were broke. We didn't have the money to race, especially after I killed the car while leading the feature one night. I had bought a used right-front tire, and it blew out, sending me into the wall. The car was toast.

Fortunately, several weeks later I got a call from some guys who had a race car. Their driver was a dirt-track racer and didn't do well on asphalt. Having heard about my success, they gave me a tryout and I never looked back. I ended up winning race after race in Owensboro and Whitesville with their car.

If I won a feature at Whitesville, my share of the winnings would be $150 and two cases of beer. Lemme tell ya, in Owensboro, 150 bucks and two cases of beer was big time! It only increased my apathy in school, but it cemented what I wanted to do with my life.

Oh, by the way . . .

■■■□□

As I mentioned earlier, I've been known on occasion to embellish a bit. But no matter what, I always try to tell the truth. "I've always been a good storyteller," I once said. "No, you've always been a good liar," my wife, Stevie, interjected. That hurt my feelings, and she apologized. She didn't realize what she had said. Later on, she reassured me, laughing, "I didn't really mean it *that* way."

3

■■■■■■■

Santa Crashes
in Stevie's Yard

I owe my life with Stevie to the coil wire on an Olds-mobile 442.

There wasn't much for a restless teenager to do grow-ing up in Owensboro. This was long before computers, cable TV, video games, or anything like that, so we would all cruise to the Dairy Drive-In—or the DDI, as we liked to call it. That was the hangout, our own little playground. You probably had a similar place to go if you grew up in any small town in America. Just like the kids in the movie *American Graffiti*, we were short on money but had tons of free time.

I was a regular at the DDI, and I drove the 1953 Ford I had run into the ditch with my brother Bobby on the way to my first race. It was such a piece of junk, but I thought it looked cool regardless. All of my bud-dies would crack up whenever I tried to get the engine to start up—inevitably, five minutes before I was ready to leave. It would crank . . . rrrrr . . . rrrrr . . . rrrrr . . . and it seemed like forever before the car finally sputtered to life. Sometimes I'd need a push to get started. The only thing for certain was my buddies yelling, "Give it up!" as I desperately tried to get the engine to turn over.

I went to Daviess County High School with Carol Rader, Stevie's older sister. And that's how I always thought of Stevie, as Carol's baby sister—that is, until I spotted her one night at the DDI. Her parents had sent her to Holton Arms, a very exclusive boarding school in Bethesda, Maryland, and she had just recently returned to Owensboro. I quickly noticed that Carol's little sister had matured. Stevie was gorgeous—her red hair shining under the neon lights—and I went over and chatted with her. I could tell immediately that even at that tender age she was a strong-willed and independent woman. I was impressed that she seemed so much more mature and beautiful than when I had seen her last. This girl had class. We made plans to get together and went out once or twice.

A few weeks later, just like any other night, we were hanging out in the DDI parking lot when Stevie drove up in a drop-dead gorgeous Olds 442—maroon with a black top. The car and she were stunning. Ohhhh . . . this was the kind of car all of the guys on the west side of town dreamed about. I almost dropped my cheeseburger and vanilla Coke.

My buddies noticed she had a boy with her, so they were razzing me pretty hard.

I hadn't noticed him at first, because I had been admiring her and the car. She and I had gone out a couple of times, and since I thought I was *the* man, hoping to be *her* man, I strutted over to the car, trying to be as cool as could be. Smooth, ya know?

"Hey, Stevie, can I lift the hood on this baby and take a look at that engine?" I asked her.

"Sure, go ahead. Knock yourself out, big guy!"

I took a slow stroll around the car to check out the guy with her. He was a real preppy with a dark tan and some funky sandals. Not the kind of guy you'd usually see on this side of the tracks in Owensboro. I opened the hood of the Oldsmobile and started poking around. It really was a sweet piece. I played it up pretty good, showing my boys and making a little scene. But before I closed the hood, I slipped the coil wire off the engine and into my pocket.

Her parents were pretty strict with her, and she had a 10 P.M. curfew, so at about 9:45 or so, she tried to start the car. *Whiiiirrrrrrrr . . . whiirrrrr . . . whirr* . . . Nothing. She was pumping that gas pedal for all it was worth.

"Watch this, boys," I muttered as I swaggered over. I leaned in her window and asked, "Can I take a look at it for you?" Mr. Preppy hadn't moved. He probably couldn't have opened the hood if his life depended on it.

Stevie was frantic. I opened the hood and slipped the coil wire out of my pocket and back into place.

"Let me try it for you," I said.

She hopped out of the car and I slipped behind the wheel. One twist of the key and that thing roared to life. *Vvroooooom! Vvroooooom!* It was a magical sound, and you could feel the ground rumble.

I was *golden*! Man, she was grateful, and all of a sudden I was "in." She thought I had saved her from breaking curfew, and that was the turning point for us. I called her the next week, and we were soon dating regularly. Sure, I was impressed with the car, but I had eyes only for her. The fact that she had a wealthy father didn't have anything to do with it either. At the time, I was getting along just fine with what I was making at the local racetracks.

(Oh, by the way, Stevie never knew the coil wire details until after we were married!)

■□

That winter I was working at Don Moore Chevrolet, a car dealership in Owensboro. I was hired solely because

I was the local hotshot at the racetrack. I had talked my way in the door with the owner.

I told him, "Look, Mr. Moore, I know a lot about cars. I'm a race car driver. I'd like to become your high-performance expert." This was when Chevrolet had some wonderful cars like the Z28 Camaro, the SS 396, and all the good muscle cars. He gave me a job, and it was so cool. I told him I might need a few days off to race, especially on the weekends, and even though I was probably gone from the dealership four days a week during race season, thankfully no one seemed to mind.

I worked with some great guys, and after geting off work we'd hightail it to Petie's Spotlight Inn. We always ended up at Petie's, playing shuffleboard and drinking beer. If you showed up with five dollars in your pocket, you were a big spender at Petie's. We got paid every Friday, so that was always the big night.

One December evening I was supposed to pick up Stevie at seven for a date. This was during the Christmas season, when Petie's always had these big boxes of candy with a big chocolate heart—I mean, the biggest box of candy you've ever seen. They had a number punch, kind of like a raffle, and if you punched the winning number, you won the big box of candy. Each ticket was a dollar, and if you didn't win the big prize, they'd give you a jar of hard rock candy as consolation.

I had been at Petie's all afternoon, because we had taken off for lunch and never gone back to the dealership. I was determined to win that big box of candy for Stevie, imagining her delight when I showed up for our date. I really thought it would endear me to her. The more beer I had, the more tickets I bought. This was no good, because all I won were the little bottles of hard rock candy. In my quest for chocolate, I lost track of time. By the time I looked at my watch, it was already ten minutes past seven.

I ran out of the bar and threw the armload of rock candy into the backseat of my car. I had upgraded my wheels since the summer, because Don Moore had provided me with a Chevelle SS 396. Talk about the perks of my job: It was a special factory-edition with a 375-horsepower engine. That baby had a chambered exhaust, and it sounded like a B-51 taking off. I loved nothing more than roaring down the street, rattling windows along the way. I'm certain all of my neighbors loved it just as much.

I took off across town to pick her up at her home on Old Hartford Road in a fancy neighborhood called Stone Creek. I was late, so I was really hauling butt. On the open road, I bet this Chevelle could have run at least 150 mph. I wasn't going that fast, but I was sure putting my driving skills to the test on this little two-lane road going to Stevie's parents' house. Just at the city limits, wouldn't you know it, a cop was rolling out of a subdivision as I went flying by. I heard the siren, then I saw the blue lights start to flash. The chase was on.

■□

This was not the first time the cops had chased me. It wasn't like I was a thug or a criminal, but the ol' cat-and-mouse chase scenes had become a fairly regular thing. I mean, it was almost like a game, as the cops would chase me all over town. It seemed like every other week I'd get them to chase me, and they could never catch me. I thought it was cool, and I would use any excuse to polish my driving or show off for the guys. They couldn't catch me, but they certainly knew who I was, so eventually I'd come home or stop somewhere, and they'd find me. My grandfather was the deputy sheriff, so he'd have to go plead my case each time.

Even with my grandfather on my side, I had some things working against me. I raced each weekend at the little tracks in Owensboro, Whitesville, and Ellis, and some of my competitors at those tracks were cops. Three of them had race cars, and I'd beat them almost every week. Even if I didn't win, I might have wrecked each of them a few times. (Accidentally, of course. "Whoops! Sorry, Officer...."). It didn't sit too well when this punk would beat them, and it especially made them mad when I crashed them. They couldn't wait to give me a ticket any chance they could.

One of the cops caught me one day as I went through a school zone. It was the weekend and school was out, but I was speeding, so he gave me a ticket for going too fast in a school zone, which meant a bigger penalty. "I'll show that jerk!" I vowed. I went to the same school zone the next day, and I had traffic backed up for a block. I was going two mph, just chugging along in the Chevelle, just to show him. But he gave me another ticket! This time for "obstruction of traffic."

They'd take any opportunity they could: They gave me a ticket for no turn signal, another for no taillight. It seemed like every time I turned around, they were towing my car. But I didn't let it slow me down.

It finally got so bad that I lost my license. I had to figure out how I was going to get around. A buddy of mine had a motorcycle, so I got a helmet and borrowed the bike. I rode everywhere on that thing for weeks. One night, I had a girl on the back, giving her a ride all around town, and I ran a stop sign. One of the officers saw it and pulled us over. The minute I took off the helmet, he knew it was me and knew I didn't have a driver's license. He took the motorcycle, and he took me. They had to take the poor girl home in a police car.

Soon after, a few of us were out in a buddy's 1969 GTO. He wasn't an accomplished driver, so I agreed to drive. While we were at a stoplight, one of the guys in the backseat threw a beer can at a police car, and the chase was on. It was like Buford T. Justice from *Smokey and the Bandit*! We had every cop in Owensboro after us. We made it to a quiet area called Barn Harbor Hills, but one of the cops turned around in the same driveway and saw us. I fired up the car and slid through the grass as the cop came out with his gun blazin'!

The fun got real serious, real fast. He put six big bullet holes in the side of the GTO! We called Bill, the body man at Harry Pedley's garage, and he said he'd fix the car to cover the evidence. But Harry showed up early and found a strange car with bullet holes behind his shop, and he called the police.

At the trial, the officer who shot at us identified the kid who owned the car as the one who was driving. But my buddies panicked under oath and said I was driving. As the prosecutor started his final argument, imagine my surprise when he told the jury, "These boys have lied to pin the blame on the young Mr. Waltrip because of his reputation. He has no license and nothing to lose, so they are lying to pin the rap on him." I had fought the law, and I had won.

■□

All of this history with the police was in the back of my mind as the cop raced after me on the way to Stevie's house. I was two miles from her house along this country road, but I had a big lead, because I was going at least 100 mph when he saw me. I slid around a curve, throwing the car sideways. Did I lose him? Nope. He slid through the corner and I still saw blue lights. Fueled by beer, adrenaline, and panic, I devised a brilliant plan. I was approaching an intersection, so I turned off my lights, hoping the cop would think I had taken a side road.

Her house sat up on a big hill, and the driveway was beyond another curve in the road. As soon as I turned back around and turned my headlights on, I knew I wasn't going to make the turn. Man, it was like the Joie Chitwood thrill show. I was Evel Knievel in a Chevelle. I shot off the road and up an earth bank at the bottom of the hill. The car went airborne, and all I saw were stars in the sky. It was like it was happening in slow motion inside the car. "Ohhhhhh," I thought. "This ain't gonna be good."

The car flipped over and came down on its roof. It looked like Santa Claus had crashed in Stevie's front yard. Presents, hard rock candy, and car parts were everywhere. I was thrown into the backseat of the car, so I had to crawl out of the back window. The car's lights were still on, the horn was blowing, and the AM radio was blasting. I climbed out of the car without a scratch, but here comes Johnny Law, spotlight on, speeding up the driveway.

Cop cars appeared out of nowhere, surrounding me. I had crawled to the earth bank, so they didn't see me at first. I heard one of them say, "I know he's gotta be around here somewhere!" I wasn't trying to hide, I was just trying to catch my breath, when finally a spotlight glared right into my eyes.

Stevie already had her coat on, waiting for me, when she and her sister, Carol, looked out the window and saw all of the police lights.

I can only imagine how it looked. There I am, handcuffed, my car upside down, with cops and lights and sirens everywhere.

They arrested me and took me downtown to what they call the holdover. That's a little place at City Hall where they put you until you see a judge. There's no court on Saturday or Sunday, so I was convinced I was stuck there until Monday. I knew I did not have enough cash to bail myself out, and I knew my mom and dad didn't have any money. I had one phone call, so I called my friend Johnny Newman. He's the one person I knew I could turn to. He and I were drinkin' buddies, and we always tried to help each other get out of jams when we had a few too many.

It was like a scene out of an old prison movie: I was standing there, holding on to the bars on the door, looking out of a tiny, dirty window. A long, sad face. I was sharing this small space with a bunch of drunks. Iron beds, no mattresses or anything. People lying everywhere. Vomit on the floor.

"Oh God, if I can just get out of here," I prayed. "Please get me out of here."

Like a vision from heaven, through the dirty window I saw a red head! My angel Stevie had come to get me. I raised my hand to wave at her through the window. Then, storming in the door behind her, was her father. He didn't look quite as angelic.

"Ohhhhh no!" I thought after seeing his face. "I don't want out! Leave me in here. I'll just stay here. Forget it!"

He was so angry, but he still bailed me out. The policeman at the desk was one of the guys who hated me because he'd chased me so many times.

"Mr. Rader," he asked. "Is this your daughter?"

My father-in-law-to-be had a tremor, and his head bobbled when he got nervous. He said, "Yes, yes . . . yes it is. Why?"

"Let me tell you something," the cop growled. "If I were you, I wouldn't let her ride with this troublemaker right here, because the next time I get him in my sights, I just might blow his head off."

Mr. Rader grabbed Stevie by the arm and scowled at me. "Come on, we're getting out of here," he told her.

It was ugly. Stevie was forbidden to ride with me from that point on. She had to drive me. I could get in the car with her, but she couldn't get in the car with me behind the wheel.

I was her parents' worst nightmare. I guess I can't blame them. I laugh about it now, but sometimes I wonder if what goes around comes around for what I put them through. I know my daughters, Jessica and Sarah, will end up with boyfriends or husbands who will drive me crazy. Hopefully, Stevie and I will be prepared to deal with it, knowing we've learned a lot from our own mistakes.

Stevie was the classiest woman I ever met, and I didn't want to lose her. Yet her parents did everything they could to keep us apart. She was very independent, and I think it strengthened her resolve to be with me. The reason she had come home from the boarding school was that they hadn't asked her back! She hadn't done anything awful, but it seemed she was always involved in pranks or some minor mischief. In that regard, we were meant for each other.

Unfortunately, her mom and dad didn't share that view. They had planned a very proper education for Stevie. She had an early acceptance to attend Southern Methodist University, and I'm sure they believed she would meet the perfect man there: a doctor or lawyer or oil baron or something.

In their eyes I was from another world—a blue-collar kid from the other side of town. Someone who made a living driving race cars several nights a week? Not for their daughter!

I never forgot Mr. Preppy-Tan-Guy-with-Sandals who was in her car that night at the DDI. I was terrified that if she left me to attend SMU it was over. There were thousands of tanned preppies she could go out with in Dallas. If I didn't do something, she'd be gone forever, and I'd regret it the rest of my life.

So I asked her to marry me.

She called it a "full-court press," but I made a constant, compelling plea for her to marry me and forget about SMU (similar to convincing my dad to buy the mower and the kart). Somehow, my persistence won out, and we planned to get married in August of 1969.

Before the wedding, Stevie's parents decided she needed a vacation, so they sent her to Hawaii for a three-week break. It was a last-ditch effort to try and get her to change her mind, but Stevie returned a week early because she missed me.

One month after Neil Armstrong became the first man to walk on the moon, Stevie and I were married. One small step for man, one giant leap for Mr. and Mrs. Darrell Waltrip.

Oh, by the way . . .

■■■■□

Stevie Waltrip

In 1965, at Thanksgiving, my grandparents died in a car accident. They were my two favorite people on earth. The loss was so great and the pain so intense, I asked my parents if I could go away to school. I thought somehow this would help. It was a great opportunity, but I didn't make the most of it. I didn't take all of the rules and studying very seriously, so my senior year, I came back to Owensboro.

Darrell and I had known each other as friends for a couple of years. I thought he was very cute—those blue eyes, you know—and he was a lot of fun. At this point

CONTINUED

in my life, I wanted some innocent, just-have-a-good-time kind of fun. I ran into DW one afternoon, and he asked me out in early November. We went out and had a lot of fun together.

What he didn't know at the time was that I had already invited the "tan preppy with sandals" to visit for Thanksgiving. He was from Connecticut. Then came the "coil wire incident," and we all know *that* story. . . . But, from that point on, until we were married in August, we were almost inseparable.

Darrell might have been the first person to recognize something in me that no one else did. There was something about him that made me feel appreciated. I think it was the same way with him: Maybe I recognized or appreciated things about him no one else had.

He was so much fun, but he really appealed to me because he was so focused, so driven. He was on his own from a young age. He knew what he wanted to do. It didn't matter to me that he wanted to drive race cars. I know Mom and Dad wanted me to meet someone who was in law school or something, but those kinds of things never meant anything to me. That's not what I admire or look for in a person. Let's just say I like a story that starts with an underdog.

4

The Honeymoon?

I married Stevie when she was only nineteen. It was a small church wedding, and it wasn't one of the happiest ceremonies in history. Her family wasn't pleased, but we were in love. Here she is, the beautiful daughter of a prominent businessman, and the only thing I had to my name was $69 and a bad credit card. That combination may be the makings of a good country-and-western song, but they were little consolation to my in-laws.

We drove a 1966 Ford Galaxy with 127,000 miles on it that used to be one of her dad's company cars. It was all we had, because I had flipped the Chevelle, my ol' Ford had died, and Stevie had lost her Olds 442. She wasn't supposed to let anyone else drive it, but a friend borrowed it and crashed it. Her dad was so mad, he fixed it and then sold it. That was the last we saw of Stevie's 442.

I thought I was going to be fine, because $69 was plenty of money back then. For our honeymoon, we kicked off a weekend in Louisville and then we were headed to a race at Salem, Indiana, on Sunday night. I was confident I could win, and we planned to spend those winnings in French Lick, Indiana, at the French Lick Resort—it was going to be our romantic getaway.

We arrived at the hotel in Louisville the night before the race. Stevie sat in the car while I checked in. I handed the man my credit card and he went into the back office to get it approved. I knew I was over my limit, so I was sweating a little bit. He refused to give the card back to me.

"This credit card has a hold on it," he said.

"It's a little overdrawn," I pleaded. While Stevie was in Hawaii I couldn't stop calling her, and I had rung up a phone bill of several hundred dollars on the card.

"I can't give it back to you," he said. Apparently my reputation as a race car driver hadn't reached him yet, and the whole "I just got married" speech didn't get me anywhere.

"Do you have another method of payment?" he asked.

Ohhhh man, I now knew I had to pay cash for the hotel room. That left almost nothing for food and everything else we'd need for two days. The next morning, I finally had the nerve to tell Stevie I had almost no cash left.

"So what are we going to do?" she asked.

"I . . . I don't know," I answered.

We bought a cheeseburger and split it.

"Mom and Dad are coming to Salem for the race," I told her, trying to sound calm and confident. "We'll meet them on the side of the road and I'll borrow some money."

My parents were in the same financial boat as we were. They didn't have a lot of money, and they sure wouldn't be traveling with a lot of cash to the race. We sat and waited on the side of the road, hoping to see them. We got lucky and were able to flag them down.

"Dad, I need to borrow twenty-five dollars."

"You've got to be kidding," he said. "That's all the money I got."

"How much can you let me have?"

"I can let you have . . . ten dollars," he said, digging through his wallet.

"I'll take it."

I had no choice; I needed that much just to get Stevie and me in the pit gate. I was driving a 1957 Chevrolet for some guys from Owensboro, and the feature paid $1,000 to win. My share would be $500.

I have always had the focus to perform when I was under pressure, so I knew I could win. Salem is a high-banked, fast track, and I was driving the wheels off of the little Chevy. I was leading as the white flag came out, just in front of Les Snow, who was driving a brand-new Hemi-powered Dodge. Snow was one of the factory-backed drivers in the ARCA series, and as we went down the back straight, he got a good run with the power from the huge Hemi engine. He absolutely laid all over me going into the third turn. He slid under me and then drove me up the track. He flat-out put me in the fence, and as I was scraping along the wall with a crushed car, he went on to win the race.

Whoooo, I was fit to be tied. I needed that money. I had visions of winning the race, getting my share of the purse, and taking my new bride on our honeymoon. A romantic time in French Lick . . . it didn't get any better than that.

He was already on the front stretch for the trophy presentation by the time I climbed out of the car. It reminded me of my high school track days as I was running down the track toward him.

"I'm gonna wear this guy's head out!" I thought.

Snow slowly crawled out of the Dodge. He had an old open-face helmet, and as he turned around, it was like his face and all of those scars were struggling to get out of that thing. He looked like he played hockey or something. His face had seen a lot of fights or a lot of bad wrecks. Or both. Attached to that mug was a big, burly man. I mean *big*.

It was too late to turn back now.

"Um . . . um . . . Mr. Snow," I said, sounding less macho than I had intended. "You wrecked me!"

"Son, you need to move on," he said, looking down at me.

"I was leading the race and you flat run over me!" I countered.

"Let me tell you something," he drawled. "You wasn't going fast enough. Do you have any idea how long it's been since I've been outrun by a '57 Chevy?"

"No," I said, "but I just don't think that was fair!"

"Let me tell ya," he said, "the way I drive, I'll go over ya, under ya, around ya, or through ya. And you were in my way."

"Well . . . well . . . ," I stammered, feeling outmuscled and outnumbered. "Okay . . ."

I made less than $30. We had enough to pay for the gas to get home, so we drove back to my apartment that night. When I tried my key, it wouldn't fit. I hadn't told Stevie I was more than three months behind on my rent, and apparently while we were gone the locks had been changed. Here I stood with my brand-new bride and all of our suitcases on the porch of my apartment house—locked out.

There was a sign on the door: "Pay the rent or move out."

The next morning, I called the man who owned the apartment house.

"Look, son," he scolded. "I've worked with you and I've done everything I could to help you, but you know you're almost four months behind on your rent. There's just nothing else I can do. If you can't pay up, you'll have to move."

Eventually we found another apartment for $85 a month. When we moved in, all we had—literally—was a hot plate and an ice chest. Remember those phone calls to Hawaii? We didn't have a phone for months and months until that debt was paid off.

I don't know how my wife has put up with all she's had to put up with. Amazingly, she always believed in me. She always believed I was capable of doing better than I'd shown. She had a lot of faith and belief in me. To this day, she sees things in me that other people don't. I swear, if it wasn't for Stevie, I never would have succeeded. She was the kind of quality person I needed in my life. I needed her, but she sure didn't need me.

Hard work helped get me to where I am, but getting married helped me more than anything. Her steadying influence was what I needed to settle down and get focused. I admit it took me a few years to become a good husband, namely because I didn't immediately understand that it now wasn't always about me, nor would it ever be again.

We were the classic example of "opposites attract." My lifestyle fascinated her. Here she was, a rich girl just back from an exclusive boarding school, being dragged along to Whitesville and Ellis Speedway. She's at these dirty little places, watching the races, seeing all of the fights, and then going home with me to an empty apartment.

Her father found out we were sleeping on an old mattress on the floor, so he got me a job working on the loading docks for a little more than $60 per week. Stevie was making less than that working at the local hospital. I would drive three hours from Owensboro to Nashville each weekend to race, hoping to supplement our income. We finally got our finances in order, so we bought a used stove and a refrigerator, plus a mattress and box spring. We also had a kitchen table, and that table is in our house to this day as a reminder of when we slept on the floor.

The next year, P. B. Crowell decided to give me a chance to race full-time in one of his cars. My career went forward from that moment. I won the 1970 championship at Nashville, and I was soon on my way. It also meant a change of address for Stevie and me, and we moved out of Owensboro to Franklin, Tennessee, just outside of Nashville.

∎

As much of a hard time as I got from Stevie's parents when we were dating, after we were married things started to change. Once they were convinced Stevie and I were gonna stick together, they slowly welcomed me into their family. They held marriage in high esteem, and eventually accepted the fact that their daughter was married to the Wild Child. They were not necessarily DW fans. I can't blame 'em, especially after the big crash in their front yard. I mean, here's this crazy kid that almost gave them both heart attacks before marrying their daughter, so why would they be fans? But let's just say our relationship improved.

The real turning point came at the same Salem track where Les Snow crashed me out of my French Lick honeymoon. Stevie's dad was a big race fan—he had been to Indy and Daytona a number of times—and one weekend, a bunch of guys he worked with at Texas Gas were going to Salem for a race, and they talked him into going with them. They didn't tell him I was racing. While Frank sat in the grandstands with his friends and co-workers, he was forced to watch as I went out and won the feature. I pulled the car into Victory Lane, which was right in front of the grandstand. Stevie was there with me for the big trophy presentation, and Frank got caught up in the moment.

"That's my son-in-law! That's my daughter down there!" he bragged to his friends and anyone else in earshot, nearly the entire grandstand. "That's my daughter! That's my son-in-law!"

All the way back to Owensboro, he kept telling his buddies, "That Darrell's really quite a race car driver. I think he's going to make it."

Until that point he hadn't shown an interest in my racing career or a belief in me, but this was the beginning of a great friendship between Stevie's parents and me. Her dad started coming over to see if he could do anything to help us. It took about a year for him to realize I was committed to making something of myself. He always admired someone who worked hard at what they did, regardless of what it was. He was a lot like my mom and dad in that hard work was very important. He saw my zeal for racing, and he became one of my biggest supporters—and more important, my friend.

Oh, by the way . . .

■ ▨ ▢ ■ ▢

Stevie Waltrip

When I think back on those days, who we were and who we weren't, I am amazed and grateful for the goodness of the Lord. He must have loved us a lot, because we

CONTINUED

didn't make any good decisions for any of the right reasons. He stayed with us and helped us and helped us overcome some tremendous obstacles.

We had been married only a month when I thought I had made the biggest mistake of my life. I wanted to leave, but I didn't want to go back home and have to admit failure, so I stuck it out. Thankfully, we didn't believe in divorce, and neither Darrell nor I could imagine our lives devoid of the other.

I loved how competitive he was. I think I'm a risk taker too. I guess I took a risk with our relationship in the same way he took risks in the race car.

I believed in him, and our marriage was helpful for him. It made him more focused. Once we were married, he took things more seriously. It was like an old TV: You'd change the channel, and the picture was a little fuzzy until you'd fine-tune it a little bit. That's how Darrell was. I saw the loyalty and dedication in him before we were married. I saw glimpses of who he could be, and he's become that.

Together, we knew we weren't going to let go. We were going to make it, even if I did have to cook on an old hot plate. It wasn't easy, but we stayed together.

He eventually became so close with my parents that he'd joke, "If we ever split up, I'm going to stay with *your* parents."

5

Nashville

When Stevie and I moved to Franklin, right outside of Nashville, it was the realization of something I had imagined for a long time. It's a little more than 155 miles between Franklin and Owensboro, but I felt a thousand miles closer to my goals. I struggled living in Owensboro, but I believed I was born to drive a stock car, and always assumed I was going to be a success.

Owensboro is a super place. I loved growing up there, but I knew if I really wanted to succeed, I had to move on. Hit the road, Jack, if you get my drift. That's the sad fact about growing up in a small town with big dreams. No matter how much I loved it, I had to make my way out. I caught the fever for racing in Owensboro, and I found the cure in Nashville. Or maybe the fever became worse and I got sicker? Some would agree with that assessment.

When I was starting out, I raced what we called modified coupes. Eventually, I moved up to late-model stock cars. But the truth is, it didn't matter what kind of car it was. Whatever I drove, I could go to any racetrack, and in a matter of laps, I was as fast or faster than anyone there. I'd show up at a new track, scope it out, give it the once-over, and away I'd go. It was like I'd been racing there forever. It made the other drivers mad when the new kid would show up and go fast right away. Call it instinct or natural ability, call it whatever you want, because I can't explain it otherwise. I just had the knack for running fast at any track I visited.

When I was driving late models, I wouldn't say I was the smartest guy, but I knew enough to make the right changes to ensure that the car would do what I wanted it to do. I learned most of that from Bobby Allison and P. B. Crowell. I was always a Bobby Allison fan, long before he became a Winston Cup champion in 1973. P. B. was a team owner who would occasionally let me race his cars. He was a good driver, and won the Nashville championship in 1968, but he was an especially talented chassis guy. He taught me a lot about setting up the front end of the car so it would handle on almost any track.

Crowell taught me about the springs and how a chassis reacts in the corners. He bought cars from Allison, who built them in his Hueytown, Alabama, shop. These cars were built right, and when a car is right, all the driver has to say is "OK, these are the numbers and the settings that I want." After running well or winning at a particular track, I took that set of springs and tagged 'em. I had a system to keep up with what I needed. The next time we raced at that track, I'd roll into town, pull out that set of springs, and away I went.

I had total focus on getting to the top level of the stock car world. I truly believed someone was going to see the brilliance in this "Waltrip kid" and hand me a ride. But for some reason it never happens that way.

In the late 1960s when I was starting my career, there was a woman named Betty Lilly in Savannah, Georgia, who was a car owner but had trouble keeping a driver. Bobby Allison was one of the guys who drove for her, but for only a short time. I read a newspaper interview where she said she had trouble with all of these "professional" drivers and wanted to give someone young and hungry a chance to drive.

The reason this is so funny now is that through the years kids have sent me their résumés, and I've always wondered "What am I supposed to do with this?" But I sent her my résumé, a big stack of small-town newspaper clippings, and a letter telling her about the great things I had done.

I never heard from her.

I'm sure she got the package and thought, "What am I supposed to do with this?"

The Indianapolis 500 was a huge event, bigger than the Daytona 500, when I was growing up. It had been around since 1911, while the speedway at Daytona didn't open up until the late 1950s and hadn't had time to establish itself as "the Great American Race" in the minds of most race fans around the world. Indianapolis is two hundred miles from Owensboro, while Daytona is more than eight hundred miles away, but Indy was never a serious option for me. It's simple: I wasn't brave enough to drive an open-wheel car.

When I was seventeen, I drove a sprint car at Tri-State Speedway—a dirt track near Owensboro. Sprint cars are tiny beasts with big motors, and they were considered the best training ground for Indianapolis. I drove them for a few weeks, but these cars scared me to death. I wanted to drive something I controlled, not something that controlled me.

I was born to drive a stock car on asphalt. I never liked

the feel of dirt, because I never felt in control. Asphalt was for me; it fit my smooth style. Plus, I never enjoyed getting my uniform dirty or my shoes muddy.

Later in my career, I had several opportunities to drive an Indy car. I never accepted, because every time I saw them race, those little rockets would crash into the wall and catch fire. The drivers were great guys, and I got to know a lot of them, but they would walk around with their hands turned around backwards, their legs broken, bent the wrong way, limpin' all over the place. They looked pitiful. Burns and all . . . oooh, just pitiful. Not for me. Too dangerous. One year, the International Race of Champions (IROC) invited Indy winner Bobby Rahal to compete in the series. "He must be a good ol' boy," I told someone, because I thought his name was Bobby Ray Hall. Imagine my surprise when he showed up in these smart-looking eyeglasses, carrying a brief-case that said "RAHAL."

■□

My cars looked brand new every time I went to the racetrack. Sometimes it was overkill, but I insisted my race car was immaculate. I wanted it to look new. *Slick.* I didn't have a lot of extra stuff hangin' on my car—just exactly what I needed, and only what I needed. I went to great detail to make it look like it was fresh off the showroom floor. That's how I am. I am the guy who walks into a room with a clean, freshly painted white wall and sees the one tiny smudge. When I walk into my shop, it's beautiful, but I see the dust in the corner. I'm the guy who will get a broom and dustpan and clean it up myself. Being on my hands and knees is maybe not the coolest thing for an owner, but my shop needs to be immaculate. I am obsessed to a fault. My cars are spot-less to this day. There's no excuse to drive a dirty car.

How you take care of your car is a reflection of who you are, and that's how I've felt from the very first race I ever ran.

◾◽

Racing is not only about what happens on the track. Sponsors are absolutely necessary to help pay the bills, because it is such an expensive sport. Sponsors expect a lot of people to see their logo on a fast-moving billboard-on-wheels. I learned how to grab those eyes and draw those fans. Love me or hate me, every one of those folks in the stands couldn't help but watch me.

I learned this was show business while racing at the Nashville Fairgrounds. It's also where I learned how to race aggressively. I drove for P. B. Crowell, and I won the season championship in 1970. I won fifty-five feature races at Nashville in my career. I won my first Winston Cup pole position there, and most important, it is where I grabbed my first Winston Cup victory. It was where I established myself as a consistent race winner, and where I gained recognition.

When I first started racing, the track was an odd-shaped place. It had been built in 1958 as a half-mile track with relatively low banking. They had a big NASCAR race the first year, and it became a regular stop in what would become the Winston Cup series. I really liked that track, but they dug it all up in 1969 and put in a high-banked oval that was five-eighths of a mile. I liked that configuration even more.

It was *so* steep and *so* fast, but I loved it. It was called a "killer oval" because of its speed, and a lot of drivers were killed or injured there. You could go almost flat-out the entire way around the track in a late-model stock car, but it was too much speed for the weekly warriors: inexperienced drivers with less-than-top-notch equipment. The track intimidated them.

In 1973, they cut the angle of the banking in half, down to 18 degrees, because of all the injuries and driver complaints about the track being too fast and too dangerous. The change didn't slow me, because I won my second season championship that year.

The Nashville Fairgrounds promoter was Bill Donoho, and he was as tight as a fiddle string. He either liked you, or else. Luckily, he liked me and my sense of humor. More important, he knew I could make him a lot of money.

He would always call me on Monday morning and tell me to come down to the track.

I'd show up at his office and he'd slip me a couple hundred dollars. It was a big deal, because Stevie and I had just moved to Franklin, and we needed every penny to put something in the house besides a used stove and refrigerator.

"Ya did a good job this weekend," Donoho would say. "We sold a lot of tickets because of you, so I wanna take care of you." I guarantee he never did that for anybody else.

Donoho was a real old-school guy. Sometimes he'd be like a second father, insisting I had to get a haircut before I could go to an appearance. He'd pay for the haircut, but then he'd turn right around and be anything but fatherlike. He'd drive around like he was possessed, with me hanging on for my life in the passenger seat. He was crazy. He kept his right foot stomped down on the accelerator, going about 90 miles an hour. It didn't matter if we were on the highway or a side street: He drove wide open. I was in more danger riding with him than I ever was in one of my race cars. He'd pass cars on the wrong side of the road, on the shoulder, wherever he could find enough pavement. To top it off, he never drove anywhere without his pistol! He would sit on that thing wherever he went. He was crazy. (Luckily, I never found out if the pistol was loaded.) It was this flair for the dramatic that helped him promote races and keep the fans buying tickets every week.

Joe Carver, who would later become my manager during my Winston Cup days, and Hope Hines, the local sportscaster, had a racing show on Saturday mornings called *Pit Stop*. It was on Channel 5 in Nashville, but none of the drivers wanted to be on the show. They were scared to do it! There were a lot of great drivers at Nashville, but they were all terrible with the media.

I loved it. And I didn't mind saying things about the other drivers—for example, Coo Coo Marlin, Sterling's father.

"Coo Coo? Coo Coo?!" I'd say, laughing. "What kind of a name is THAT!?"

Clifton "Coo Coo" Marlin won the season title four times, still a track record, so I was looking to get under the skin of the guy at the top of the heap. I usually picked on the guy I knew was going to be my toughest challenger that week. I had to use every trick I could, because at the time the weekly racing at the Nashville Fairgrounds was better than anywhere else in the country. They would run special late-model events that paid big money to win, and the starting lineup on those nights looked like a Winston Cup race. The competition was that good.

"Flookie Buford?!" I'd chuckle. "Awwww, he's just a backhoe driver, he's not a race car driver!"

Flookie, whose real name was James, was no slouch, and his son Joe still races there. (In fact, Joe Buford is the only guy with more wins than me at Nashville.)

Every time I'd say that sort of thing the grandstands would fill a little closer to capacity. I'd promise I was going to lap the entire field or, like Muhammad Ali predicting what round he was going to knock out his opponent, I would predict what lap I was going to take the lead. Half the people in the stands would be cheering for me, hoping I would do what I had predicted, and the other half would be rooting against me. I loved it, because it meant all of them were watching me.

I became close with Ralph Emery, an overnight DJ on WSM radio. Music has always been a big part of my life, and I grew up listening to the Grand Ole Opry on WSM. A lot of people across the country know Ralph from his years on The Nashville Network, but back then he was a local radio guy who befriended me. I'd hang out with him at the radio station, and when he got his own morning television show, I'd hang out there as well. I was always ready to go when they needed a guest. Show me the mike and I was ready to talk.

Ralph was instrumental in helping me develop my personality for the camera, and he was the reason I was asked to guest host *Nashville Now* on TNN in the '80s. At the time I appeared, it was huge. A NASCAR driver hosting a national music talk show was a big deal for both me and the sport.

When I was just getting started in Nashville, it was all about having fun. I was 23, and I found a way to get the attention I wanted. I'd say something crazy or funny, and it nearly always got my competitors and the race fans fired up. The television camera became a good friend. The medium matched my personality. All the other drivers would say, "The car run good." I thought that was pathetic, so I worked on having more to say.

I also learned it was hard to get those tongue-in-cheek comments to come across the same way in print. I could be funny on camera or behind the radio microphone, but I'd see it in the newspaper the next morning and it sounded awful or mean—certainly not funny. It's hard to hear the tone of voice or see the wink of an eye when it's written. That's why I loved television, because the tone of what I said made a big difference. It gave me a way to say these things and make sure people knew I didn't think Flookie Buford was *really* a backhoe driver.

I thought it was all fun, but I knew a lot of people (especially the people I was talking about) thought I was being mean. At times I would take it too far. I'd make fun of someone or I'd point out the obvious just to be colorful. Maybe I shouldn't have. Pointing things out and then exploiting them for my own fame was really over the top, but that's who I was, and it sure helped me throughout the rest of my career.

I knew if I dominated at Nashville, I was ready to move up. If you couldn't win at your local track, how could you think you could win anywhere else? It's like a ladder. I did well at Whitesville and Owensboro, and when I reached the point where I dominated, I was ready to step up to the next rung. My next stop was Nashville. When you raced there, you saw the best competition in the country, and you knew where you stood. Once I felt I had proven myself there, like I had the place in my control, I was ready for the big leagues.

Oh, by the way . . .

■■■■■

Larry Woody, sportswriter,
The Nashville Tennessean

What I remember about Darrell is how much interest he brought to the sport in Nashville. Back then, just like later in Winston Cup, he enjoyed "stirring the pot," as he called it. If anyone in the media needed a good story, we would call Darrell. If there wasn't any news, he'd create some.

Waltrip was unique, because he was wise enough back then to realize the value of publicity. Most drivers didn't pursue it, but Darrell sought it out. I recall thinking how shrewd he was. He would play the media like a violin, and he received tons of coverage.

He had a sharp wit, a good sense of humor, and a depth most other drivers lacked. When you had a conversation with Waltrip, it was apparent that his world didn't start and stop with his carburetor.

After one of his wins at the Fairgrounds, his car was protested by Sterling Marlin's crew. The entire team was composed of Marlin family members: Sterling; his dad, Coo Coo; an uncle; and two or three cousins. Darrell was asked how the postrace inspection was going. "I don't know, because I can't see my car," he said. "It's covered with Marlins."

Waltrip was a great racer, clearly the best ever to come through Nashville. Given that combination—charisma, racing talent, and self-promotion—I knew then Darrell was destined for greatness in this sport.

6

The Mercury and Daytona

I was winning everything at Nashville. I knew I had the talent; now all I needed was the opportunity.

Stevie's father, Frank, who had become a fan the night I won at Salem, was an executive with Texas Gas. Occasionally the company would commission barges, and the company decided to name one of the new barges *The Frank Rader*. Texas Gas threw a big christening party in Louisville to celebrate. Bill Elmer, the CEO, was there, and he was a huge race fan. He and his wife would travel each year to watch the Daytona 500 as guests of Unocal, the official gasoline of NASCAR. Elmer was talking to Stevie and me about how well it had been going at the local tracks.

"Darrell," he said, completely out of nowhere, "what do you think it would cost to sponsor one of those race cars in the Daytona 500?"

I had no idea.

"I . . . I have no idea. I don't know . . . ," I stammered. "Probably a lot, I guess!" Not one of my better answers.

"Why don't you find out," he said. "And if it's a reasonable amount of money, maybe we can work something out with you."

Stevie and I looked at each other, wide-eyed and speechless. We couldn't get out of the party fast enough and find out how much it would cost to race at Daytona.

The first thing we did was find a car. There was one for sale at Holman-Moody's shop in Charlotte. Holman-Moody was a top-of-the-line team in those days, like what a Hendrick, Childress, or Roush team is today. They were a good, reputable race team with a car available for $12,500.

It was a 1969 Mercury, which meant it wasn't eligible for Winston Cup events like the Daytona 500, but it was eligible for the NASCAR Sportsman division (which has become today's Busch Series). The Sportsman cars were similar to what I had been driving, so I thought it was the best way to go.

Plus, this car had some magic in it. Mario Andretti had driven it to victory in the 1967 Daytona 500 with a Ford Fairlane body; David Pearson had driven it after that with a Mercury body. In that era, a chassis (the basic frame of a race car) could be competitive for years. In today's Winston Cup series, each team has fifteen or more race cars sitting in the shop, each one built for a specific purpose. They build cars to race only on flat, short tracks or to race only at the superspeedways. Each one is very specialized and very unique. It was different in 1971, because you could race with the same car every week, even a car that had been around for years. This little Mercury had a history with great drivers and great teams. It was like going into a pet store and knowing immediately which dog was the right one for you. Do you believe in love at first sight? This car was the one for me.

It was completely prepared and ready to race, including a spare engine. Even though $12,500 seemed like the world to me, it was quite a bargain.

I called Bill Elmer, he gave the go-ahead, and suddenly I was the proud owner of a beautiful, race-ready 1969 Mercury. I still have the car today, and I love looking out in my shop and seeing it fully restored.

We painted "Terminal Transport" on the side. It was one of Texas Gas's companies, and they decided that it would benefit the most from a sponsorship. The company was based in Atlanta, and I'm not even sure they knew they had a race car, but it eventually became known because of all the effort on the part of the home office.

We were preparing to run the car for the first time at Daytona in February, but we heard about a race in November 1971 at the Texas World Speedway (this is not the same track as the current Texas Motor Speedway near Fort Worth). Stevie's family is from Texas, and we thought it'd be the perfect test of our car, as well as a nice excuse for a family reunion.

We headed off to College Station, Texas, with a tiny truck to pull a small, open trailer carrying the race car. Stevie and I, our only crewman, Bo Brady, and our dog, Charlie Brown, all crammed into the truck and we were ready to take Texas by storm.

It felt like forever to College Station, and to top things off, once we got into town we got lost trying to find our way to the racetrack. At that time I was becoming a pretty recognizable name. Racing fans in Tennessee, Kentucky, and Indiana knew who I was, but imagine my surprise when this four-door Ford with a couple of big ol' boys with ten-gallon hats came rolling up beside the truck, waving and gesturing at me.

"Honey, look!" I beamed. "They recognize me! All the way in Texas!" I got all puffed up and full of myself. Whooo-hoooo! I was even bigger than I thought.

Then the car pulled in front of us, the blue lights came on, and they told me to pull over. It was a Texas Ranger car, and the officers were going to write me a ticket for running someone off the road. I guess we were paying more attention to trying to find the track than to what lane we were in. They turned out to be pretty good guys, and thankfully I got away with only a warning.

■ ■

We qualified on the pole. I beat Bobby Allison for the pole in a car I had never raced, at a track I'd never seen. I was pretty proud. After qualifying, it dawned on me that with our small crew we had no way to make pit stops during the race. We were used to the shorter races at the local tracks, where making pit stops was not a part of the strategy. Luckily I knew Harry Hyde from racing against him in Louisville. Harry was the crew chief for the K&K Dodge team, a Winston Cup team that raced the number 71 car. I made a deal for Harry and his crew to pit my car during Saturday's race.

When I said we were ready to take Texas by storm, I really didn't mean it literally. The night before the race, it looked like it might rain, so we put the race car on jack stands just in case the dirt area around the car got a little damp. It rained. And rained. Then harder and harder. All night long. When we arrived in the morning, we found that the Sportsman garage area was the lowest point in the infield, and the jack stands had sunk into the mud. The water was inside the car up to the floorboards, and we had to wade over to the car until we got a wrecker to pull it out of the bog.

Somehow, we got it dry enough to make it to the grid. I sailed off and led the first fifty or so laps at the start of the race. Then the engine blew. Harry and his guys didn't even get to do a pit stop. We blew an engine and lost a lot of money on the trip. But in the end, we knew we had a fast car to take to Daytona.

As February 1972 arrived, we huddled again into the ol' pickup and sputtered to Daytona. I was focused on running the Sportsman Series Permatex 300, the race held the day before the Daytona 500. The 300 was like the opening act at a big concert, and I felt it was a very big stepping-stone for me. I was excited about going to Daytona, but it wasn't my first time there.

■ ■

The first time was in 1967. I had been beating everyone on the short tracks. I was the man. I was the "Wild Child" and "Mr. Owensboro," but those tracks were only one-quarter mile in length, a half-mile at the most. Now, I'm taking my short-track car, a 1958 Ford, to Daytona, which is 2.5 miles in length with 31-degree banking in the turns. If you stand at the bottom of the banks and look up, it's unbelievable—they tower above you like a four-story building. We used to joke that a "superspeedway" was a track with flush toilets, but Daytona was a superspeedway in the truest sense.

I drove into the infield for the first time through the tunnel that runs under turn four. You can see only a small section of the track from there, so I didn't even see the entire track. I had no concept of how big it was.

It was Ray Skillman and me. He was one of my Owensboro buddies who's now a very successful car dealer in Indianapolis. We brought the car to Daytona on an old farm truck. We got there and didn't have any way to get it off of the flatbed, so we went to the Pure Oil gas station outside of the track and convinced them to let us back up to one of their lifts, and then we rolled the car onto the lift. We might have been the first guys to tow our car into the garage at Daytona International Speedway with a rope.

We didn't have any money. It was an Owensboro

community effort, as a lot of people pitched in a few bucks to help us get there. The main investor was Paul Freels, who probably gave up his retirement fund to help us. But he loved racing, so he was happy to help. We were so poor, we had to stay at someone's house while we were there. Luckily, Freels had made friends who lived in Daytona, and they let us sleep there.

We couldn't pass technical inspection, because our car didn't have any of the things needed to run at such a big track. We didn't have a fuel cell, and we didn't have a driver's-side window that rolled up. That was one of the rules back then. It seemed like we were regular visitors at the junkyard just down the road from the speedway on Highway 92. That junkyard is still there today, and we wore 'em out looking for parts for the 1958 Ford.

I don't remember how many days we were there before I was even allowed on the track, but I learned so much without even turning a lap. This was before the invention of Nomex, the fire-resistant material that the drivers' suits eventually were made of. The drivers would take normal coveralls and dip them in some sort of fire-retardant goop. Then they'd hang the coveralls on the fence until the stuff dried. You'd see coveralls lining the whole fence line alongside the garage. I was like one of the jumpsuits: I was soaking up all the knowledge I could, except I didn't need to be hung out to dry each night.

When we finally were allowed to get the car on the track, I got into my dipped coveralls and off I went, down the pit lane of the famous Daytona International Speedway. I had never been around the track, and I had no earthly idea it was that big. I was cruising along the apron into turn one when I realized that a giant, banked turn was looming over me. It was like a huge wave in the ocean, rising into the sky.

"What the . . . How do I . . . Wait a minute . . . How in the world do I get up there?!"

I drove around on the apron for a full lap, in awe of the 2.5-mile-long track. It was five times longer than any other track I'd ever driven. And it was the first time I'd seen more than just the view from the garage or the turn-four tunnel. I pulled that baby right back in the pits and asked: "How do I get up on the banking?!"

Once I figured it out, I was OK. I could get up there and make it around the banked turns, because we had a giant 427-cubic-inch engine we had bought from Holman-Moody.

On the local tracks, we would use slick tires made for drag racing called M&H Racemasters. They were HUGE. We had the wheel wells cut out so the enormous tires wouldn't rub. But at Daytona, the car looked hilarious because we used smaller speedway tires.

When I got out to practice with the other cars, I noticed that the revs on the engine would go up. The engine would cruise along, *grrrrrrrrrr* . . . then cars would pass by and it would wind up, *GGGGRRRRRRR-RRRRR!* I thought we were having clutch problems. I was OK by myself, but when we were in traffic, the engine would rev. We never found a problem with the clutch, but we figured out that when the other cars were around me at such a high speed, the aerodynamic turbulence would get inside those wheel wells and lift the rear wheels into the air.

We did pretty well in the race, but I spun out on somebody's oil and slid into the grass in turn four. I was bouncing along, trying to get to pit road. There were no in-car radios back then, so I had no idea what was happening when I came around and saw a huge fire near our pit area. (One of the other teams tried using an electric wrench to take off the tires, and it set their fuel can on fire.) A few laps later, we had some alternator problems and the battery went dead. But we had fun and learned a great deal.

After that low-key debut at Daytona, I was looking forward to going back with a real car (the Mercury) and a real sponsor (Terminal Transfer). As I looked over the schedule for the 1972 Daytona Speedweeks, I realized I could also run the Automobile Racing Club of America (ARCA) race there the week before the 300. The rules were close enough where you could enter the same car and compete in both races. It was an easy decision. I'd get to run my car, get some experience, and make a little money. And this time, I wouldn't have to stop and ask how to get up on the banking.

I qualified, but Stevie realized we hadn't told her dad we were going to enter the ARCA race. We sure didn't want him to see it first in the morning newspaper, so she called him.

"Whatever happens," he insisted, "tell Darrell that he can't wreck the car, because the sponsorship money is for *next* weekend. We're bringing everyone to the track!"

Stevie reassured him I'd be very careful with the company car. I started the ARCA race confident and ready to win. But on the second lap, Ramo Stott blew an engine in front of me. I spun in his oil and hit the wall. *SMASH!* This was not a glancing blow; this was a "what in the world are we gonna do now?" kind of crash. I was OK, but the car was junk.

It was certainly not the result I had in mind, and it was a sign of what was to come in my entire career at Daytona. I would bet money I've crashed at that place more than I have crashed at all the other tracks combined in my entire career. Oh man, I hated Daytona, because even though I eventually won a lot of races there, my results were awful most of the time.

I started off wrecking, and after that, it seemed like I

always wrecked at Daytona. It was the opposite at the other tracks: I went to Charlotte later that year and I finished seventh. I had never seen the joint before, but I loved Charlotte right away. It was the same at Atlanta, Darlington, Bristol . . . man, I fell in love with them. But Daytona, she was a different animal for me. It never did feel right. I loved Talladega, and I could drive my butt off at Talladega, but when I got to Daytona, I'd be holding my breath. Daytona was never wide enough, and it always felt like I was going way too fast and the track was way too narrow.

I needed someone, anyone, to help me get the car fixed. Honestly, it was beyond repair and it should have been sent home in a box or sent somewhere to be rebuilt, but that wasn't an option. I *had* to get it fixed, because my father-in-law and the people from Texas Gas were coming down next week to watch me race in the 300 and see how their investment was holding up.

I worked on that thing all week with anyone I could get to help me get it pieced together so I could make a qualifying attempt for the race. If I didn't start that race on Saturday, I was in big trouble. To make it worse, the car had been, well . . . let's just say "customized" by Holman-Moody, which meant the baby was narrowed, altered, and "cheated up" so bad that none of the standard replacement parts would fit! It was a mini-Mercury, and that's one of the reasons it was so fast. If I had bought any stock parts, they would have dwarfed the thing—and it would have tipped off the inspectors!

I called Holman-Moody to tell them of my predicament, and they recommended a couple of guys who had just started a new race car parts business. So I found Dick Hutcherson and Eddie Pagan. When I see the Hutcherson-Pagan parts truck at every Winston Cup race these days, I think about how they saved me in 1972.

When I spoke to Hutcherson, he suggested I should talk to Jake Elder. "Crazy Jake" they called him, or "Suitcase Jake," because he was always switching from one team to another. He was working for Hutcherson-Pagan and he had been a crew chief for many years. Even better, he had worked on this very car when David Pearson drove it. If nothing else, maybe this legendary crew chief would have the dimensions or measurements that could help me.

I found Jake and somehow talked him into stopping by. He only needed one look. "Boy, there ain't no way," he grumbled. "You better just go on home."

"My sponsors are coming," I pleaded, "and I have to be in that race!"

He sighed and offered to get his notes out of his toolbox. At least we could have the dimensions to fix what we could.

Somehow we got it fixed, at least enough to make a qualifying attempt. Wobbling and shimmying, I qualified 18th or something in a car that might as well been held together with chewing gum, fishing line, and Band-Aids. But I was in the show.

We were parked in the garage area next to Tom Pistone, a guy who had won a Winston Cup race at Nashville in 1965. Tom tried to reason with me. He came over, took me aside, and wrapped his arm around me.

"I see what you're doing," he said. "And I appreciate it, I really do. You've worked hard, but you need to park that thing. You've already crashed once, and in the state that car is in, you are probably going to crash it again on Saturday. If you do, you are in real danger of being called a 'crash artist.' That's a guy who may be fast but crashes all the time. Nobody wants to hire a crash artist, so you'd better think about that."

I did think about it. For about two seconds. I *had* to be in the race.

Once the race started, Pistone was right, I couldn't drive it. Not even someone named Andretti or Pearson could have driven the thing. It was too torn up. The frame was crooked, and everything else on the car was out of alignment in one way or another. I was in a car that should not have been allowed on the track. It was darting and dipping and weaving all over the place like James Brown on four wheels. It must have looked exciting from the stands, but it finally bit me and I crashed again.

Oh, by the way . . .

■ □ ■ □

Ray Skillman, Owensboro native,
Indianapolis-area auto dealer.
Still active as a driver in the All-Pro Series

From day one, anyone who saw Darrell in a race car knew there was really something there. We just weren't sure what it was. It was like he had a pure talent bottled up, waiting to be unleashed.

I have great memories of our trip to Daytona in 1967, including when Darrell thought he was going blind. You had to have a physical to be certified as a NASCAR driver, and Darrell passed it easily. But when he took the vision test, he couldn't see a thing! Well, the lens on the machine had become greasy, and made it impossible to see anything. When he went back for a second test, he passed.

CONTINUED

After he spun out in the race, there was mud every-where. He rolled into the pits, and we had to jack it up just to get fuel to flow into the car. I was able to get the fuel in, and off he went.

That night at dinner, Darrell said, "The car wasn't very good until you put the new tires on."

"We didn't put any tires on," I told him.

"Why did you jack it up during the pit stop?" he asked.

"It was the only way to get the fuel in." I laughed.

His slide through the infield bent something on the car, and suddenly, it handled much better even on the old tires.

7

Winston Cup Beginnings

I don't know what you plan to do with this heap of junk, but it won't cost you any more to rebuild it as a 1971-model Mercury than it would take to rebuild it as the 1969 model," Dick Hutcherson told me after the debacle at Daytona. "The 1971 body style is eligible for Winston Cup. You oughta think about it, because you could run it a lot more often and for more money."

I loved the idea, but my father-in-law wasn't so sure. He thought I might need a little more 'sperience before I went out and started running with the big guys. He didn't want me to be the latest, greatest crash artist or, even worse, the late, great crash artist. I'd already blown up or crashed it in every race so far. But since it would cost the same to rebuild it as a '69 or a '71 model, he agreed.

The 1971 model was what Pearson and the Wood Brothers team were running, so I thought it was cool. I could own a Winston Cup car. Crazy Jake Elder and his guys rebuilt that sucker until it was ready to race. It was May before it was ready, but it was a beauty once again.

The next Winston Cup race was at Talladega, Alabama. Think Daytona is big and fast? Talladega is even bigger and even faster. It's 2.66 miles long. When it was built in 1970, the top drivers got together and refused to race because of problems with the tires at those incredible speeds. Big Bill France went out and put a bunch of drivers and cars in the starting field from lower categories of racing and ran the race anyway. (Richard Brickhouse got his only Winston Cup win that day.) That was the last time anyone has ever heard of a drivers' union, and it was a perfect example of NASCAR's belief that the show is bigger than anyone. The fans have paid their money to see a race, and they saw a race regardless of who was in the starting lineup.

NASCAR has always had a very old-school view, doing what they could to prevent a drivers' union. It's because they control everything. They own most of the tracks, they get nearly all of the TV money. It's their ball, and if you don't like it, you can take your stuff and go back home. The drivers have never been paid what they should be paid. I mean, we all have nice houses and motor homes and airplanes, but our share of the pie has always been too small. The drivers are the ones risking their lives each week, and the drivers are who people buy a ticket or turn on their TV to see.

I borrowed a trailer from P. B. Crowell and drove to Talladega alongside Stevie and Charlie Brown. What a sight we must have been that day! The three of us rolled into the garage in an old Maxwell House coffee truck. These days, the huge transporters show up at the track with their sponsor logos everywhere, but I hadn't been paid a cent by Maxwell House.

After Daytona I went to the Oldsmobile dealer in Owensboro. My father-in-law bought all of his cars there, and a lot of his company cars as well, so they knew they'd better take care of me. Or maybe they just took pity on me. A local business had traded in an old truck with Maxwell House logos on the sides. It was a two-ton truck and had a big box body on the back, which was perfect to carry equipment and tow a race car. I tried to paint over the logos, but you could still see them underneath the paint.

Hutch's place had done a good job of rebuilding the race car with a big, 427-cubic-inch engine in it. It was a first-class car, but I didn't have anything else to go with it. Even so, Hutch agreed to "rent" Crazy Jake to me for the weekend as my crew chief.

Jake was there as the car was rolled off the trailer, and he opened the back of the coffee truck and stared inside. "Where's the rest?" he asked.

He couldn't believe it, but I had gone to the local Western Auto store and bought four jack stands. The smallest and cheapest ones I could find. I also had a standard jack, one that you put under the car and ratchet up. I also bought a Craftsman toolbox, but it had only a few tools inside. That's all I could afford, or at least all I could sign my name for.

We made it through inspection the first morning with Jake raisin' heck the whole time, saying, "We don't have anything . . . we have junk tires . . ." and on and on.

I had arranged for a group of Tennessee friends to be my pit crew. Harry Hyde and his bunch, who we had borrowed at Texas, were running their own Winston Cup team, so they couldn't help me. My guys were inexperienced, but they were enthusiastic, and they were *free*. Jake was livid, but he didn't see any other solution.

I didn't care. I was at a Winston Cup race, ready to wear out these ol' boys. I had tires that were no good, a little, empty toolbox, four jack stands, and a little old jack. No pit equipment . . . nothing. Jake finally said, "I'm goin' home. You've got no business being here."

"No, don't go!" I fired back. "Tell me what we need.

Whatever I need to do or whatever I need to buy, I'll get it."

I went over to the Ingersoll-Rand trailer, where they were selling pit equipment. I bought two air wrenches and the other gear we needed: hoses, regulators, and a real racing jack. I was signing for everything. I didn't have a cent to my name, so it meant I had to make the race or I was in big trouble. I kept saying, "I'll pay ya next week."

The first time we went out for practice, a cross member on the chassis, one that supported the engine, was hitting the ground. In those days, we were running about 200 mph at Talladega, and it hit so hard it lifted the tires off the track. Somehow, we qualified while this cross member was smacking the ground, bouncing and slamming. It would rattle the fillings out of your teeth, but I was hanging on and pushing my right foot down as far as it could go.

I told Jake, "I could go much faster if this thing wasn't hitting the ground."

"Well," Jake mumbled, "we'll just cut that cross member out."

"What!?" I yelled. "I might not be very smart, and I may not have been to too many races, but I know you can't do that!"

"We'll just cut it out and it'll be fine," he said.

"No way!" I yelled, since I was the car owner, but especially because I was the poor guy who was going to be out there driving it. "What's gonna keep the frame from collapsing?"

We got into an argument that grew louder and louder, featuring some very choice adult language right there in the garage. Finally, Jake threw up his hands and said, "That's it! I'm outta here. You don't know what you're doing, and you won't let me do what I need to do. I'm leaving. I'm going home! You're not gonna embarrass me!"

"Go on!" I yelled in the heat of the battle. "Go ahead! Go home! I don't need you anyway!"

So he left.

Having no other choice, I went over to some of Bobby Allison's crew guys I knew, and asked if they'd come over and help me out.

"C'mon, boys. Look at this crossbar," I pointed out. "It's hitting the ground, and Jake wanted to cut the whole thing out!"

"You can't do that," one of the guys laughed, "but we can 'skinny it up.' We'll make it thinner and then weld it back in place. It won't hang so far below the car, and then it won't hit the ground."

"Good. Let's do it," I said. "That'll show ol' Jake!"

We worked on that thing all afternoon, fixing and welding and getting the cross member fixed. I felt really good, because I didn't need him around. I could do this.

The whole episode became even more bizarre when I learned that Crazy Jake had had the same "bottoming" problem a few years before at Talladega with the same car and a German driver, Rolf Stommelen. The official results show that the team dropped out of the race because of "engine problems," but the real problem was Jake had cut the cross member and the chassis eventually collapsed! The nickname was right. He *was* crazy!

The long day in the garage ended, and as Stevie and I pulled up to our hotel in Anniston, Alabama, I saw someone sittin' at the pool, laid back, relaxing and sipping a cold beer.

"Is that Jake?!" I asked Stevie. I can't believe my eyes. "Is it that darn Jake sittin' there?!"

I hopped out, mad as a hornet. "You scoundrel!" I screamed. "I thought you said you were goin' home!"

"Nah," he said between another sip and a few glances

at some of the finer swimsuits around the pool. "You didn't think I'd just leave ya, did ya?"

"Yeah!" I spat back. "I thought you were crazy enough to leave!"

"D'ja get that car fixed?" he asked.

"Darn right I got it fixed! And I didn't need you, either!"

"I knew you would," he said. "So I figured I'd just come back here to the pool and have some beer while y'all worked on that race car. I'll be there tomorrow for the race."

My first Winston Cup start, and I have all this craziness around me. But lemme tell ya, I was so excited I could hardly sleep. It seemed like an entire week passed by that morning before the green flag finally flew.

I was coming around to start the race, and I'm thinking, "I've made it, made it to the big time." Right away my car felt good. The thinner cross member worked beautifully; it didn't bottom out and seemed solid and stable. I was no match on pure speed for Pearson, Petty, or Allison, but as far as I knew, the car was good. At least it was good until the engine blew. David Pearson won, and I finished 38th. Even with the big-money purses today, 38th place at a Winston Cup race isn't going to pay many bills, so it meant I was a little further in debt. But by then I was used to it.

◼◻

That was my first Talladega race, but for pure entertainment it was nothing compared to our return later that year. The Talladega 500 was held in August, so we thought we'd try again.

I still had the Maxwell House truck, and not much more. The only thing of value I had—even though I had no idea at the time—were 16 tires and wheels that had old Talladega tires on them. I couldn't afford new ones, so I had old tires. Four were on the car and twelve were in the truck. As usual, Jake didn't like the look of any of it, but he especially didn't like those tires.

Goodyear had produced a new tire for the event. Previously, they used treaded tires everywhere except at Talladega, where they ran slick tires because of the high speeds. Goodyear came up with a new design with treads they believed would work well. But the old slicks were all I could afford.

I had my buddies—my volunteer crew—back down there for the race. We had been there before, so we felt like Winston Cup veterans. As the race began, my fear was that if the last race was any indication, we'd be one of the cars the fast guys would be lapping several times during the event.

The green flag flew, and the Mercury was pretty decent.

Then, all of a sudden . . . What the . . . I can't believe it . . . I am passing cars! A LOT of cars.

"Man! That was Buddy Baker!" I sang to myself. "I just passed Buddy Baker!"

Another lap. "I just passed Cale Yarborough!" I chuckled. "Oh man! I can't believe this."

Then I passed David Pearson and Richard Petty.

"Hey! This is easier than I thought," I said as I passed not just one or two cars, but bunches at a time.

This was before we used two-way radios in the cars, so I had no idea that nearly the entire field was having terrible problems with the new Goodyear tires. The treaded tires were flying apart. The fast guys were tearing them up about every 10 laps, and the only way they could keep from blowing out or damaging the tires was to slow down. Slow waaaay down.

Here I come, with these two-year-old tires that aren't worth a nickel, a skinnied-up cross member, and a 1969-

turned-into-a-1971 Mercury, and I'm passing Richard . . . Cale . . . Buddy . . . Bobby . . . and the whole pack. I'm leading the race.

I was battling it out with James Hylton for the front spot. Turns out Hylton's team had the old tires as well, but he was no match for the Mercury with the kid driving and the crew guys in T-shirts and Jake Elder as crew chief, and we're leading and . . . wait just a minute . . . Jake Elder?! Aww man, it finally dawned on me. Crazy Jake! The notorious cheater.

"What has he done to this car?" I wondered, imagining the things he could have cheated up to make it so fast. I had no idea it was only because everyone else had to slow down. I couldn't stop thinking about ol' Jake in the pits. We were gonna get busted for cheating. I just know it. The new kid shows up and leads the race? How does that happen? Who would have figured that?

As I pondered the possibilities and newspaper headlines and the fact that I could pay my bills if I won, it was time to make another pit stop. I'm barreling into the pits, leader of the pack. I'm pounding on the wheel and yelled, "We're leading! We're leading!" But, of course, they already knew that.

I had my buddies there, and God knows they were trying their best, but the pit stop took forever. It could have been timed with a sun dial, so when I finally got my tires changed and a tank of fuel, I slammed it into gear and out of the pit stall, tires squealing. This was before there was a speed limit on pit lane, so I'm haulin' through the gears as fast as I can. As I was going down pit road, everybody pointed at me: The other teams, the officials, everybody was pointing. My heart sank, and I thought, "Oh no. We've been caught." I suspected it before, but now I'm sure we must be cheating. Something had tipped 'em all off.

I got to the end of pit lane, and all of a sudden there's

this big *THUD*. I had run over something with the rear tires. I have no idea what it was, wondering what had fallen off my car, thinking maybe it was some secret cheater part or maybe it was the "skinnied-up" cross member from the previous race. Either way, I'm in T-R-O-U-B-L-E.

In the confusion of the pit stop, the guy working the jack hadn't let it down all the way, so when I took off at full throttle, the jack wound up being pulled and dragged along under the car, and that's what everybody was pointing at. All these sparks flying behind me, and I was in my own world, wondering why they were pointing out.

My $150 jack was junk, but we were back in the race—that is, until the engine blew. It was pure dejection, because we had 'em beat. James Hylton, the guy we had passed earlier in the day, won the race with his old tires, and it turned out to be the only Winston Cup victory of Hylton's career.

Oh, by the way, here's the best part. Here I am, my engine is broken, my heart is broken. Out of the race, smashed jack . . . it's all over. Woe is me. How am I gonna pay for all this?

But, as soon as we dropped out, crewmembers from all of the teams along pit lane were running down to our pit stall, yelling, "We wanna buy your tires! We wanna buy your tires!" They had figured out how we had been so fast, and a bidding war commenced.

I won $680 from my 27th-place finish, but I made $1,500 from selling the rest of my tires to the other teams. I was able to pay for all the gear I had signed for. I made a whole lot more money selling old tires than I ever imagined making in the race itself. Welcome to the big time!

Oh, by the way . . .

■□■□■□

David Pearson

I tried to be honest with anyone who asked for my help. I told Darrell the truth if he wanted to know something. He was a good young driver, and you could tell he knew he was good. You have to think you're better than the other guy. If you think somebody else is better than you are, they're gonna beat you. When Darrell came up, he bragged a bit, and it upset some people. There are a lot of good drivers out there, but you gotta really want to win. I always believed, if you want to do something bad enough, you can do it. Darrell wanted to win, and I did too. I always felt like the race car doesn't know who's drivin', so it was important to believe you were the driver that was going to win.

8

![decorative bar]

Small Fish, Big Pond

I came into Winston Cup from the short tracks that ran on Saturday nights, where you'd race a little and fight a little and the promoter would hand you a plastic trophy and then skip out with the purse. Almost all of the guys in Winston Cup, then and now, got their start in a similar fashion. I was a big winner at a lot of those tracks, the king of my own small world.

My biggest payday in the summer of 1972 was at the Nashville Fairgrounds, where they held the Tennessee 200, a big United States Auto Club (USAC) race. I had yet to make my name in NASCAR, and the USAC boys included the big names from Indy: Gordon Johncock, Bobby Unser, Al Unser, Roger McCluskey, and their stock car champion, Butch Hartman.

The race was held during the state fair, and there was a big luncheon the day before the race. I was at the head table with all of the hot dogs, sitting at the end of the table minding my own business.

"How do you feel about this rookie?" a reporter asked, pointing at me. "He's the local hotshot that's going to be in this race with you guys."

"Awww, that's really nice," Bobby Unser said. "A

local hero. We're glad to have that kid in the race. That's really a *neat* thing."

Jake and I had the Mercury ready to go when it came time to qualify. We had what you could call a home-field advantage, and I won the pole by a huge margin. Very quickly, the USAC boys were no longer so happy about this local hero. They didn't think it was so *neat* that this kid was kickin' their butts. USAC officials were telling their own drivers and teams: Do whatever you gotta do to your car, take out all the extra weight. Whatever you have to do to keep up with the number 95 car, do it!

They're all in there working on the cars, doing everything they could. But it wasn't as simple as removing weight. You had to know how to set up your car to run high on the banking so it wouldn't bottom out. These boys were tearing oil pans off the bottom of the engine, tearing up everything they had. They couldn't raise their cars high enough to keep them from bottoming out.

I won the race and lapped the field. I probably lapped some of them five times in the 200 laps. Not only had they lost to the local kid, I embarrassed them.

The race was over by two o'clock in the afternoon, and they protested our car. By eight o'clock that night, we were still taking the car apart, tearing down the motor, tearing down this, tearing down that.

They finally said, "We want to check your fuel cell. It better be twenty-two gallons."

Jake and I looked at each other. We knew darn good and well that the fuel cell wasn't 22 gallons; it was probably more like 30 gallons.

Back in those days, the way they built fuel cells was each corner of the cell had a place to insert the fuel line. Jake had rigged copper tubes that would come out of whatever corner we wanted to use. The inspectors told us to jack up the car and let all of the fuel drain out, then they would roll the car to the gas pump and refill the tank to check the capacity.

Jake jacked it up on the right side and got underneath the car. While he was under there, before he unhooked the fuel line, he slid his vice-grip pliers onto the line that comes out of the cell. He clamped the copper tube until it was about half closed. This thing drained fuel for what seemed like an hour, just barely trickling out. Finally, it quit.

"All right," they told us. "Put the line back on it and let's take it to the pump."

Jake slid under the car, connected the line, and we rolled it down to the gas pump. We were holding our breath as the pump rolled along, gallon by gallon. . . . It was like slow motion: 13 gallons . . . 14 . . . 15 . . . 16 gallons. Then it stopped. Sixteen gallons!

By this time, the USAC officials had seen enough. They all threw up their hands and said, "You won the race. Get the money and get the trophy. It's time to go home."

This was one of the biggest days of my career. I took home more than $5,000. It was the biggest payday of my life to that point. And, no matter if it was 30 gallons or 16 gallons, it proved that when you came to Nashville, you had to beat me.

■ ▫ ■

I was a very small fish in a big pond when I arrived in Winston Cup. Nobody knew who I was. They didn't care who I was. They didn't know my name, and they didn't wanna know my name. It didn't take very long for this attitude to get under my skin. Everybody thought the only drivers who lived were Richard Petty, Cale Yarborough, David Pearson, and Buddy Baker. The only way I could get somebody to pay any attention to me was to be a little bizarre. Or controversial.

That's who I was and that's how it was. It was obvious to me that, if anyone was going to notice me, the media was my best friend! Petty was really good with the fans and media; Benny Parsons and Buddy Baker too; most of these other drivers couldn't do an interview on TV or talk to the media. I decided I was gonna be the man who would talk to anybody. Just like my days in Nashville, when I was on TV most Saturday mornings, I knew I could get attention by talking about my fellow competitors. So I did.

They called Petty "King Richard," and he was like the biggest bully on the block, so he was my first target. As a small fish, I needed to shoot for the biggest fish.

"Hi, I'm Darrell Waltrip. I'm here to retire Richard Petty." I'd say things like that, and I'd get my name in the paper in the same paragraph as Petty's name.

"Some people are lucky," I'd say, "to be born with a certain name. I mean, he wouldn't be the king if his name wasn't 'Richard.' They wouldn't call him 'King Joe' or 'King Larry,' would they?"

Suddenly, people were talking about me. I mean, it was a mixture of shock and anger, like I had kicked their dog. *Nobody* had ever said anything bad about Richard Petty! He was the KING! People thought I was out of my mind.

I thought it was funny, although it didn't always come across that way on the printed page. But whatever message I wanted to send to someone, I just talked to the media. The old writers, they loved me. I could almost write entire stories for them.

Quickly I realized that everyone was reluctant to speak up about NASCAR as well. When I did, I became, in the minds of the people who ran NASCAR, a troublemaker. *Nobody* bad-mouths NASCAR! Not in public! Not in the media.

My first top-10 finish in a Winston Cup car came at Atlanta when I finished eighth, but it was also the track where I got my first taste of what it was like to lock horns with NASCAR.

The worst thing you could do in this sport, and this is very true even today, is ask "Why?" The first time I asked "Why?" was 1973. It was the first year when I ran most of the races, and I was aiming for Rookie of the Year.

These days, the competitors in the garage talk about NASCAR's "big red truck," an 18-wheel transporter that serves as office space for the officials at the racetrack. It also works like a principal's office. If they want to see you, they tell you that you're wanted in the NASCAR hauler. Bad boy! Go to the principal's office!

In 1973 there was no big red truck. NASCAR was a much smaller operation. The only red thing they had was an old oily shop rag. What they did have was a wacky points system. I think Benny Parsons won the championship that year based on how many miles he completed, or something really goofy like that. At the start of the 1973 season I didn't go to Riverside, the first race of the year, but I did go to Daytona and then Richmond.

One of the next races on the calendar was at Atlanta. I was there, and Jake had a great setup. We were third fastest in practice. We had been telling anyone who would listen, "Wait until we get to Atlanta, we'll really show you guys something." And now we were backing it up on the racetrack.

It started to rain when it came time to qualify, and qualifying was washed out. So NASCAR came up with a bizarre system of setting the field. I don't even remember the formula. I think they took something like the first 17 cars based on points. Whatever the number was, if they took the top 17, then I was 18th. I could understand if they chose to take the top 10, the top 20, even the top 15, but *17*? How do you pick that number? Did they pull that out of a hat?! Did they throw at a dartboard?

"What's going on?" I asked, getting pretty steamed up. I thought it was a personal thing against me. "They don't like me?"

They lined up the front of the field by points, but only up to the 17th position, then everyone else had to draw their starting position out of a bingo wheel. I didn't like this at all, and I liked it even less when I drew the 40th position: dead last. Now, not only was I not starting 18th, but I was starting last. The crowning moment for me was when some young kid in his first speedway race drew 18th. Here I am, a guy with good finishes in 1972, 18th in points, starting dead last while a real rookie is starting in MY spot. I went ballistic.

I asked, "Where is the guy who made this up? Who is it?"

Somebody tells me, "Lin Kuchler."

So I went looking for Lin Kuchler. He was the NASCAR competition director. I didn't know him at all, didn't know what he looked like, but I was determined to hunt down the man who made this decision.

"Where is Lin Kuchler?" I asked everyone.

"You can find him there inside the media center," I was told. "It's right over there. If you want to talk to him, you have to go there."

"You got that right!" I spat, as I stormed off to the media center. I yanked open the door and blasted my way in there.

Kuchler was at the front of the room talking about how they were lining up the field. "Does anyone have any more questions?" he asked.

"Yeah! I got one!" I yelled.

I marched into the middle of the crowd, right among all the guys sitting there.

"I want you to explain to me how you can do this!" I complained. "This isn't fair. You can't do this!"

It didn't dawn on me it was a media function; all I knew was I was really worked up.

He was visibly angry, but somehow Kuchler finished with the media. Then he said, "You come with me."

This was the equivalent of going to the big red truck. At Atlanta, it was in the scoring tower. And I mean, he told me right quick, he put me in my place right away. Made it very clear who was running the show.

"*You* are *not* going to make it in this sport with *that* attitude. *We* run the show. *We* make the decisions. Not you."

The next day, because of where I had spoken up, it was the big story in the major papers in and around Atlanta. Now, not only had I asked "Why?" but I had embarrassed NASCAR. So, with pressure from the media, NASCAR decided it wasn't safe if drivers who had never raced at Atlanta started in the middle of the field. Somehow, it was worked out with this poor guy to switch positions with me. I can't even remember his name, but I started 18th.

Man, I ran really well that day. Richard Petty and Buddy Baker and I had a great race going, a whale of a race, and I was so happy. That's when racing is really fun, ya know? Going all out against the best there is. But someone crashed in front of me, and I went down onto the apron of the track to miss the wreck, and it broke a left-front spindle when the car bottomed out.

From that day on, in the eyes of NASCAR, I was a bad guy. I was perceived as a smart aleck, a big-mouth, and I wasn't going to fit into the sport as a troublemaker. And this really cost me down the line.

At the time, I didn't feel I had done anything wrong; I felt like I had been done wrong. But that was the beginning of asking "Why?"—and from that point, I was a thorn in NASCAR's side. Why are you doing this? Why are you doing that? What's that for? That was me, and they didn't like it at all.

I finished highest in the points and won more money than any rookie in 1973. I had a best finish of second place at Texas, the same track where my car had been flooded, but they gave the Rookie of the Year to Lennie Pond. There was no rookie point system, no criteria other than NASCAR picked who they liked, and who should be rewarded. They decided I had asked "Why?" a few too many times.

It was a decent year for me. I was very competitive, and had some good finishes with my own team on a shoe-string budget. When Mr. Elmer said, "We'll give you $25,000 sponsorship for the year," I thought I was set for life. But, by the third or fourth race, I spent all of that money on the team. We continued racing, and no matter what anyone thought of me, loud mouth or not, it was obvious I was going to be a contender with the right team.

Bud Moore was one of the elite car owners for many years, and Bobby Isaac drove for him that season. At the second Talladega race, Isaac pulled into the pits and got out of the car. He was spooked. He said he heard a voice telling him to get out of the car.

Bud called and wanted me to drive the car in place of Isaac for the rest of the season. I thought it was a big break for me, but it turned into a disaster. I got out of my own car, what you would call an independent team, and I got into Bud's car. But it wasn't as simple as it seemed. At the time, NASCAR was making a transition from big motors, like 427 cubic inches, to smaller ones of 351 cubic inches. Even though Bud owned one of the big-name teams, he used the smaller engines. So it was a David and Goliath thing. George Follmer saved me because he brought RC Cola as a sponsor, so I was out and he was in as the new driver. I was relieved to get out of there. I drove seven races for Moore, and blew up or crashed out of almost all of them. I finished only two races, and it was a disastrous way to end my rookie season.

When I first got into the car, I had to wear Isaac's helmet, because they were one of the first teams to use two-way radios, and they had only one helmet wired for the system. Oh man! The helmet didn't fit, but I got a bigger headache from hearing Bud Moore telling me, "Do this . . . do that . . . go here . . . go there . . ." My own dad never yelled at me that much!

After driving for Moore, I knew what voice Bobby Isaac was hearing. I knew where that voice came from: Bud Moore's mouth!

Moore has a historical record of all the top drivers who drove for him, and it's a very impressive list. But you'll never see my name on there. I had seven awful races, and it's like he never acknowledged I ever drove for him. If you ask him, I don't think he'll admit to it. He'll deny it to this day.

"He didn't drive my car. He wrecked it," he'd say.

I must have made a deal with Moore. "If you never mention I drove your car, I'll keep quiet too."

He sure kept up his end of the deal.

Oh, by the way . . .

■■■■□

Bobby Allison

I was good friends with P. B. Crowell, and P. B. bought three cars from me for Darrell to drive [in and around Nashville]. Darrell and I started off with a good friendship because I could see he had talent. Most of all, Darrell had a great desire to succeed. He worked hard and he had good people around him to help. But it did get pretty bad between us when he got to Winston Cup. We were so competitive about everything, and I thought he took advantage of the privilege of being a Winston Cup driver. He took advantage of his standing in the sport.

9

Crazy Jake and
the Number 95

Auto racing is a game of numbers. I've already explained the significance of the numbers on that stopwatch, but car numbers also have great importance. You almost never see the number 13 on a race car, because it means bad luck. Racers don't wanna mess with that number.

After the disaster with Bud Moore at the end of 1973, I went back to my own team for 1974. I had Crazy Jake and Robert Gee with me that year. Gee was one the best fabricators in NASCAR history, and he worked on my cars for many years. (Oh, by the way, Gee is the grandfather of Dale Earnhardt Jr. and Tony Eury Jr. Their fathers married Gee's daughters.)

My Mercury was number 95. NASCAR gave me that number for no reason other than it was available. NASCAR allocates all of the car numbers to the team owners, and they are obligated to use the car number to keep it active. As long as a team continues to utilize that number, they can keep it forever if they choose, or they can sell the rights to another team.

I thought the number 95 looked beautiful on the Mercury. That was the number pictured on the Wheaties box along with my smilin' face. But, according to Jake Elder, that number was awful.

"You will NEVER win with that number," Jake would yell. "Nobody wins races with high numbers. Ninety-five! Ninety-five! No way! If you have a low number, it means you've been here awhile. These numbers are important."

If I was going to keep Jake around, we were gonna need another number. Whatever it took, I promised I'd try to get a lower number (other than 13, of course).

I bought the car from Holman-Moody, and I found out the number 17 belonged to them. That's a lot lower than 95, so I went to John Holman. He was really gracious, and wrote a letter to NASCAR to release the number to me as a car owner. I think the only reason they ever let me have it was that the car had used that number before. Jake had been the crew chief when David Pearson drove it, and he kept saying, "Seventeen, that's the number we need. That'd be good, because we're never gonna win races with that high number."

Once I had the number 17, it simply became my number. It felt right, I liked it, and people identified me with that number. From that point forward, whenever I had my own car, it was 17. When I had my own Busch team, all of those cars were number 17. When I drove a Craftsman Truck series race, I was 17.

Yeah, I did drive the number 88 and the number 11 for other teams in Winston Cup, but once I hooked up with Rick Hendrick for the 1986 season, I got back to 17. NASCAR had assigned it to someone else because I hadn't used the number in Winston Cup for some time. Eddie Bierschwale had an orange and white car that even looked like my old car, and he had the 17. We paid the guy $10,000 for the number in 1986. Rick paid $5,000 and I paid $5,000, but we got the number 17. MY number. But I'm getting ahead of myself.

When I told Jake we had the right to use number 17, he was thrilled. I was, too, because it had been Pearson's number. I loved David Pearson. I had a lot of heroes, but he was at the top of that list.

He is the coolest driver ever to wheel a stock car. Just look at his 105 career wins. I know Richard Petty has 200 wins, but Richard ran every race for a lot of years as part of a factory team. Pearson made less than half of the career starts that Petty did, and he almost matched Petty for career pole positions. I know Earnhardt and Petty each have seven championships, while Pearson has only three. But, race by race, pound for pound, I think Pearson's the best ever. He usually ran a limited schedule, picking and choosing his races. A large number of David's wins were significant because of that. When it came to the big races, no one was better than Pearson. In 1973, driving for the Wood Brothers team, he entered 18 races, and won 11 of them. That's a 61 percent winning record, and it's like a driver winning 22 races in one season with the current schedule!

Richard Petty and I had our differences. I was open about not being a Petty fan when I raced against him. My stance has softened since we are no longer on the track fighting every Sunday, and because I respect and admire what he accomplished. How can you argue with 200 wins? But I saw a side of him only a fellow competitor would see.

Pearson was a huge help to me when I was starting out in Winston Cup. He and Bobby Isaac were the guys I talked to most. Buddy Baker, too. I went to those guys when I needed someone to tell me the truth. It was tough as a rookie. If you needed someone to talk to, to ask about setups or particular tracks, where do you go? You needed somebody you trusted, and I trusted Pearson. Most of the guys I was competing against would give me whatever answer came easy, whether it was the truth or not. I could trust Pearson to give me info that wasn't gonna get me in trouble. I always felt confident he was giving me the best advice he could.

I tried to emulate that graciousness during my career, but I learned something very funny that always amazes me: If you tell people in this sport the truth, they don't believe you. If you wrote it down, they'd tear the paper into a thousand pieces. Everyone is so skeptical, so why bother asking?

Guys would ask me about the springs or the gears I was using. I liked soft springs and low gears. That was my preference. I liked the feeling of soft springs: getting the nose of the car to dig down into a corner. I also liked low gears because of the acceleration off the corners. I'd back off early and kind of float it into the corners, and it was the fast way around most tracks. That was my style and my preference. But a guy would come over and ask, "What are you runnin'?" I'd tell him, and he'd say, "Awwww, man! No way!"

I'd have a 620 gear at a place like Martinsville and somebody else would be running a 543 gear, so when I'd tell them what I was using they'd say, "No way! You can't run a 620 gear here!" I'd even offer to show them our setup books, our notes, just to prove it. They'd say, "You must be keeping two sets of books."

I always laughed at that. I never was worried about telling the truth, because I figured it didn't matter. If they had the same thing, the exact same setup I had, I'd still beat 'em.

Until the mid-1980s, a lot of teams didn't run a full schedule of events. Before all of the big non-automotive sponsors like Tide discovered how much NASCAR could help promote their business, the "factory teams" were supported by major manufacturers like General Motors, Ford, or Chrysler. That meant there were only four or five teams equipped or financed to run every race. The championship didn't pay worth a darn. As a team owner, you didn't look at the championship as a source of cash; you looked for the big-money races.

Money makes this sport go. How many zeroes at the end of that check? That's the important question. There is that word again: *numbers*. It keeps coming back to numbers, doesn't it? The numbers on those sponsor checks and prize money are the key to winning in racing. It's an expensive game, and if you can't afford to spend it, you can't hope to win.

Some drivers will try to tell you the trophy means more than the money, but I do *not* fall for that line. I'd have to see that lived out before I ever believe it. The guys who say that . . . I'd like to see the money taken away and give 'em a cheap ol' trophy one time and then we'll see who's left. The Winston Cup guys, like my brother Michael, who do double duty by running in the Busch Series races on Saturdays, say it's "for fun" or "for more experience" or "extra track time." No way. It's the money. Me, Dale Earnhardt, all those guys, we ran on Saturday because it was supplemental income.

When I started in Winston Cup, I'd race at least two or three additional nights a week, just to help pay for my Cup deal. When I was racing at Talladega, I'd go somewhere Thursday night—maybe Huntsville, Alabama—and then race somewhere else Friday night. I'd hurry home to race Saturday night at Nashville and then go back to Talladega on Sunday morning. I was always looking for a deal. If you are a recognizable name, the promoters would offer you money to come to their track. They'd pay you to come and race. Even if I didn't win, I'd make money. I did it through almost my entire career. Always looking for the deal. You want me to come out and run at your track so you can sell some tickets? Then let's talk about what you're going to pay me to help you sell those tickets.

I started with no money, no backing. But Jake and I were a good pair, and when the Winston Cup series went to Nashville in 1974, we entered the race and I ran third.

The next season, with the number 17 instead of number 95 on the car, I grabbed my first Winston Cup victory at Nashville on May 10. I don't remember a lot of that race, other than Cale Yarborough being the fastest, but he slid into the wall trying to make it onto pit lane. We went past, leading the last 79 laps to win. It sounds strange to say I don't remember much of the actual race, but we expected to win.

We expected to win because we had finished in the top 10 in six straight races that season, and we were coming home. We had already won a big USAC race there in 1972. I grabbed my first Busch Series race victory there in 1970, the same year I won my first season championship. If we couldn't win at Nashville, we might as well give up and go home. There were plenty of people in the garage who knew we had what it took. We had no money but plenty of talent, and talent prevailed that Saturday night.

What made it special was winning with my entire family there. It was Mother's Day weekend, and everyone was with me in Victory Lane, including Granny. Having Granny and Paps there made it unforgettable. Mom and Dad were there, and Stevie too, of course. There are photos from Victory Lane that night, and we're all on the hood of the car, celebrating. I was hugging everyone and holding the trophy like I was never gonna let go. The feeling of happiness and satisfaction stays with me to this day. Having my family there makes it even more vivid, because I was able to share my joy with all of the people who had sacrificed to help me get there.

Oh, by the way . . .

■□■□■

David Pearson

I won the championship three times, and I had three boys, so I thought, "OK, that's a ring for every boy," but I suppose I should have tried to win one more for myself. I felt like I won it every time I really ran the whole season. When I ran for the Wood Brothers, we only had two cars, and we didn't run the short tracks. It was good enough for me. I was happy and I made a living without doing all of the races. Darrell's one of my favorite people. I appreciate him, and consider him a true friend. I appreciate his kindness toward me, and all the nice things he says about me on TV.

10

■■■■■■

Attitude

You need attitude to win at Bristol.

The Winston Cup races at the track in Bristol, Tennessee, get more popular every year. Bruton Smith, the track owner, can't build grandstands fast enough to keep up with the demand. When the track was constructed in 1961, it had 18,000 seats. Now Bristol has 160,000 seats, and each of them is filled for every Winston Cup event. It's the hardest ticket in American racing. The track had a waiting list almost as long as the distance around the half-mile track. Lemme tell ya, they stopped keeping the list because most of the people would change addresses or pass away before they became eligible for tickets. You can't build any more seats, and you can't squeeze one more skinny NASCAR fan into the Bristol track on race night.

I am asked a lot about what has changed in Winston Cup since the bad old days. The simplest thing would be to show someone a photo of the track at Bristol with only 18,000 seats, or maybe Charlotte (now Lowe's Motor Speedway) back in the early 1960s, or even the early 1990s. Then I would show them a photo of those places today. The explosion of our sport is very evident in these giant stadiums, where the grandstands climb into the sky and enclose the entire track. They are modern palaces, and they dwarf any football or basketball arena in the world.

Bristol is all about the mood, the atmosphere, the excitement, the attitude. It's a half-mile concrete bowl with 36-degree banking and grandstands that start at the edge of the track and angle upward like they're on a trajectory to the moon. The Rose Bowl on steroids. It's super-fast and it produces the most action-packed, let-the-rough-side-drag, fender-crunching races of the year. It's like a world championship heavyweight boxing match. The fans love every minute of it. So do I.

There are a lot of tough tracks on the circuit, but there's something special about Bristol. For almost a decade, man, I could do no wrong there. I won for the first time in 1978, and from March 1981 until August 1984, no one else won a Winston Cup race there. I won seven straight races. *Seven.* That's 3,500 laps around that tight little track. Even I have a hard time comprehending that: 3,500 laps without one crash, without one part failure, without anyone finishing ahead of me. Nobody could beat me. In 1992, it was one of the last big races I won. It seemed like I never finished out of the top five. I have the track record for victories, and I pulled into the Winner's Circle 12 times. If you go there today, I recommend you walk around to check out the stands in turns three and four—that's the Darrell Waltrip Grandstand!

It was not just because I had fast cars and good luck, it was because I had the right attitude. The right swagger. And I chose to take that attitude before I ever saw the place or drove a single lap.

I was driving toward Bristol for the first time in 1973, cruising down the road, working my way up and down the radio dial as the stations would fade in and out through the Tennessee mountains. As I dialed across a station, I heard Cale Yarborough's voice. I knew that voice, and as usual, he was complaining.

"Oh man, this track?! Bristol? Awww, I hate this place!" Cale griped. "It's a hard place. Five hundred laps? That's just too many laps here . . . They should shorten this race . . . Blah blah blah . . ."

Even for Cale, that was a lot of whining. He was worked up about it.

I could hold the signal only a few minutes until it faded out, and I start turning the dial again. The next station to blast through the static was broadcasting another voice I knew right away. It's Richard Petty, and he's saying, "I'll probably have a relief driver . . ." I mean, this is the King saying this! "The track's too fast . . . there's too many laps and the banks are too high . . . it's too tough."

I haven't even seen the place yet and I'm listening to this moanin' and groanin'. The answer came to me in a flash, like I had hit the wall. *Attitude.*

"Waltrip," I said to myself, "this is a great opportunity. This is your chance! These guys hate this place, they don't wanna run here, they hate racing here. They're whipped. I'm going to pull in there, and my attitude will be as if I've never been in a more beautiful place. I'm gonna look at it like it's the greatest racetrack I've ever seen! I love *everything* about this place. I can't wait. Five hundred laps? Only 500?! I wish it was *5,000* laps!"

Race car drivers are like that. If you say one thing, they'll say the other. If you said, "I think red makes the prettiest race car," I'd say, "No, I think black makes the prettiest race car." Drivers don't agree on anything, but this made all the sense in the world for me to be different.

I was young, I was in good shape, and I told the world

I was ready to go all day and all night if I had to. But it really was a tough, tough track. (I actually finished last in my first race there, but it was much better from there.)

I'd run 500 laps, and win or lose, I was absolutely exhausted. I had to be carried home. I was in bad shape. I was taken out of that place too many times in the backseat of a car with my legs hanging out the window because I had cramps. The way the track is configured means the air doesn't circulate very well inside the car, so the fumes were unbearable. There were times when I threw up for a couple of days, but it never bothered me, because I thought it was just part of being a race driver.

I would get as sick as a dog after the race when I drove the Mercury, and I just assumed that was how it was supposed to be. Then we discovered that the old water jug in the car was full of awful crud. It looked like the bottom of the ocean, but nobody had even thought to clean it out since I bought the car!

I had terrible headaches for several days after each race. Sometimes I'd climb out after a long, grueling race and I'd wobble around like a rag doll from exhaustion and the fumes. I don't know if it was a high tolerance for pain, or an ability I had to block that kind of thing out of my mind, but I never let things bother me when I was in the race car. In 1981 the floorboard of the car became so hot, I burned the back of my heel so bad, it charred the bone. Talk about bad to the bone! I didn't know it until after I got out of the car. It took so much concentration driving that car, it was like my brain said, "Whatcha don't know can't hurt ya."

My philosophy is simple. At the end of any race, the driver is supposed to be worn out, the crew worn out, and the car certainly used up. If you have anything left, you haven't done your job. You need to lay it all out there to win, because if you don't, someone else will.

But if you push past that limit, the consequences are very high for man and machine.

I told myself I was going to like Bristol, and I did. I fell in love with it. Not everyone likes seafood; some people prefer steak. That's the way it is with drivers and certain tracks. Me? I love ice cream. So Bristol was like a big double scoop of chocolate almond crunch. I think it makes a huge difference when a driver says, "This is my favorite track," and it has the opposite effect when he says, "This is my least favorite track."

I talk like attitude was all it took, but I was prepared in many ways to do well at Bristol. It took attitude and aptitude. I had grown up racing at places like Salem and Winchester, both in Indiana, which were similar, high-banked, half-mile ovals. Even more important, it was like Nashville. So when I came to Bristol, I didn't have to learn anything. I walked in and felt like I knew the track. I knew what to do. I loved the banked turns. I loved to feel the car sink into those banks. But you also had to know how to make the car last, because it could hurt you in a big hurry.

My record in the long, grueling races, at places like Bristol or Pocono or especially the Coca-Cola 600 at Charlotte, was awesome. I had a knack for knowing how hard to go, especially early on and into the prime of my career. That knack was important, because the cars could not last 600 miles if you drove them hard every lap. Physically, you had to save a little bit too, because the cars were hard to drive. It took effort, so you man-handled them.

Bristol was a place where, until the later stages of my career, you had to know when to *ride* and know when to *race*. The cars weren't built as well, and the drivers surely weren't in as good shape as they are now. That many laps is torture on man and machine. If you went out there in the early laps and slung the car around like a madman, you'd use up your equipment before the end of the race.

I always had some kind of sixth sense when it came to knowing when to *go*. People say I snuck up on victories or I backed into wins, but most of the time it was because I held a little something back, saving my equipment until the last 50 laps or whenever the right moment might be. They pay you to lead the last lap, so that was the goal. Go as hard as you can but not harder.

It's hard to explain what it feels like when you dive into a turn at Bristol with such steep banking. It's a combination of extreme sensations, and it feels like the forces of gravity are trying to throw you out of the seat, right out the passenger window, headfirst. But you have forces pushing you down as well, planting your butt deep into the seat. It's like you have two guys pushing down on you and three guys pulling sideways, trying to pull you out of the car. I don't know the exact numbers of the G-forces, but it feels as if your body is going to rip apart in several different directions at once.

Your head, supporting a helmet, feels like a giant bowling ball, so your neck needs to be in superb condition, as well as your arms, legs, and torso. You go into the corner so fast that it flips the car down into the banking so hard it blurs your vision. In 1992, I won the night race, but the track surface was so rough when I'd come out of turns two and four, looking into those bright lights, it looked like the entire earth was shaking. And that's for 500 laps, 1,000 times out of the corners like a 7.0 earthquake on the Richter scale beating you around like a punching bag.

It wasn't a concern to me, not even a second thought, because what makes a driver click on such a short, fast track is pure instinct. You instinctively do things. That's what distinguishes a great driver anywhere, but especially on short tracks. You just respond. You don't think. You react. I believed I was able to make my way around Bristol blindfolded.

I don't know any feeling that can match it. Maybe you can feel a small version of it if you water-ski, when you pull hard across the wake of the boat and swing out as wide and as fast as you can. It takes your breath away for a split second, hangin' on for dear life like a rock on the end of a string.

Maybe if you're in an airplane and it takes off really fast, it pushes you down in the seat. Shakin', rattlin', and rollin'. That kind of thing. It sounds like you're in the front row at a heavy-metal concert. You can feel the noise rumble in your chest. Maybe you're driving down the highway a little too fast, or, if you're like me, a lot too fast. You know you're going too fast, and your palms are sweating and your hands are shaking and your heart is pounding. You're late! You need to get somewhere now, and you're driving faster than you should be. You've got all of that anxiety building up. Your heart is pounding. What if a cop is on the other side of this hill? If anything happens, if you make a mistake driving that fast . . . in the back of your mind, Woe be unto me.

Take all of those feelings, all of those sensations, put them in a blender, and turn it on high. That's the feeling every time you make a turn at Bristol.

I always believed if you are cornering at the highest possible speed, the slightest touch, a paper-light touch, on the back or the side of the car would send it sliding into the wall. You want those four small patches of tire that touch the surface to be at their absolute limit. If you don't run on the absolute edge of adhesion, someone else will, and that someone else will be faster.

That's on the edge, baby. If you are right there, you hope the rope don't break. That's the difference between being fast and being *really* fast. It's an art, driving on that edge. You don't drive so hard the rope breaks, but you drive hard enough so there is no slack in the rope. Within a hair of being in control and a hair from snapping the car in two. That's the art of not just being good, but being great.

Almost anyone can get in a well-prepared race car and go around a track like Bristol or Daytona. Really. I could easily teach almost anyone to do it. You would get a rush of adrenaline, because it's really noisy and drives nothing like a street car, and you'd be going faster than you have ever driven, but what's hardest to conceive, unless you have done it, is driving with 42 other people doing the exact same thing and fighting to get to the exact same spot.

I struggle to describe the absolute focus and the level of concentration needed not to let anything bother you or distract you. To be so focused and concentrating so hard, you are aware of your own limits and your car's limits, even if there's a guy on your left and a guy on your right, and a guy behind you ready to knock you out of the way, and a guy two inches in front of you who you are trying to pass—that's what makes a professional. The track gets very narrow, very quickly.

Then the crew chief gets on the radio and asks, "How's the car?" or "How do the gauges look?" or the spotter is telling you, "Inside, inside . . . outside, outside . . . three-wide, three-wide, you're in the middle, hold your line . . ." To be able to process all of that at one time and not lose your focus, that is the key.

I won so many races by taking care of my equipment that it actually caused problems for me in my latter years. As the equipment improved, the cars were able to last longer and they were easier to drive. The young guys coming into the sport in the mid-1990s were in better physical condition, so it took a much different approach to win the long races. It changed the way teams and drivers approached races, because a well-built, well-prepared car and a well-conditioned driver could charge hard for the entire 500 laps at Bristol or 600 miles at Charlotte. There was no more riding; it was *only* racing.

I wasn't used to going hard all the time. It wasn't that I wasn't able to do it, but it took time for me to reprogram my brain, like reprogramming a computer, to believe it could be done. I didn't think it was the best strategy to push hard all the time. My experience was you had to save something; you had to hold back a little bit. You had to be sure you didn't take it to the limit until it was necessary. Now you go out there and you drive it as hard as it'll go and hope nothing happens to it. That's the difference at Bristol between then and now.

Even Jeff Gordon, who's still a young guy despite his career numbers, says that's the hardest thing for him to get used to. He told me, "Man, these kids will wear you out. They don't quit. You can't rest. You drop the green flag, and these young guys are just going crazy."

The computer analogy can also explain the differences between young drivers and old drivers. It's why every car owner out there today is looking for the newest, youngest star, the next Jeff Gordon, the Next Big Thing.

If I'm an older driver, I'm an early model of computer: almost out of date the moment they hit the shelf. There's always a newer, quicker model coming out next week. I might have just as much memory, but I can't get to the information fast enough. My old computer believed it was impossible to run hard for 500 laps, until a newer, faster computer came along and discovered something new.

It takes a little longer for the old brain to process everything I need when I'm driving down into that corner. These young guys are processing all of that information and they're able to act on it as fast as possible. I may be smarter, or have more information in my memory bank, but if it comes out slower, it does me no good.

All of that information gets in the way of instincts. I still have the instincts to go fast, but they are hampered by all of my 'sperience. Instead of driving each lap as pure and as fast as possible, my brain is telling me, "Uh-oh . . . whoops . . . whoops . . . whoops . . . you're too high, go lower, go lower, no, no, you're too wide, too wide. You drove in too deep . . . too deep." Then you make it through, and you say, "Phew . . . OK, reset!" But before your brain processes it, it's, "Whoa—look out! Here comes another corner!"

When I was young, nothing affected me inside the car. Strap it on and let's go! I'll carry this thing if I have to! But as I got older, things became more complicated, and I no longer had that attitude. This seat doesn't fit me right. The car isn't perfect. . . . I hated everything that wasn't perfect, and small things became an annoyance.

I was bogged down with all of this info, while the young kids were running purely on raw instinct, saying, "Too cool!" My brain knows if you go too high in turn four at Charlotte at 190 mph, you're gonna bust yer butt, because I have done it several times. But these young kids don't know that. They may get in there too high, and somehow, someway, they don't bust their butt. All you have to do is back it into the fence or slam it into the wall a few times and you'll get a little less carefree. Big red flags flashing on the computer screen! *Don't do that!*

I was the only "young gun" when I first broke into Winston Cup, but that theme is getting more and more attention today. There are some great young drivers out there now, and unlike when I started, they have an opportunity to come in and do well right away. Kurt Busch. Kevin Harvick. Ryan Newman. Jimmie Johnson. Dale Jr. Matt Kenseth. Tony Stewart. The list goes on and on. They all had the talent to take advantage of their opportunities right away.

It used to be a sport where young drivers would come in with inferior equipment. Even if they got an opportunity to drive for a good team, the car would blow up or maybe they would wreck and a great opportunity would pass. They may never get another chance, or they would hang around year after year, just hoping to get one good chance. It was so easy to get discouraged and say the heck with it. There are so many things that happen to you that you don't have any control over. Dale Earnhardt was in the right place at the right time when Ron Osterlund called and gave him his start, but he still struggled for many years. These young drivers: They're all in the right place at the right time, because the sport's looking for young drivers. Thirty years ago, or even ten years ago, nobody was going to put young, inexperienced drivers like Jimmie Johnson, Kurt Busch, or Ryan Newman in first-class equipment.

The kids today, they get an opportunity and BAM!, they seize it. Like Kevin Harvick winning in only his third race in Dale Earnhardt's car. Or Jamie McMurray winning in his second start in place of an injured Sterling Marlin. There are a lot of examples out there like Dale Earnhardt Jr. He hadn't won a thing on the local tracks when his dad put him in a Busch Series car in 1998. Everyone thought the kid had been handed the golden spoon because of who his father was. But, because he had struggled for years with his own cars and none of his dad's money, Dale Jr. was prepared when the call came. He kicked everybody's butt and won two Busch Series championships before he moved to Winston Cup.

Or take Kurt Busch, who was an unknown when he

won a Jack Roush tryout/audition among a bunch of drivers. It seems as if he was born to be in a Winston Cup car. In 2003, Kurt's younger brother, Kyle, became the latest, greatest thing. He had to wait more than a year to be allowed to drive in the top categories of NASCAR because he was only 16 years old when he entered his first Craftsman Truck series race. He was 17 years old when he signed a deal with Rick Hendrick, who signed him away from Jack Roush. Kurt is a star with Roush, and I think a lot of people assumed that Kyle would follow his footsteps. But Kyle wanted to step out of his older brother's shadow, so he signed with Hendrick. He's a kid everyone is watching, and the truly talented ones don't blow it.

In a perfect world, someone would come along and say, "Here it is, here's the golden platter. It has everything you need. All you have to do is not drop it." But the kids who really have the drive and the talent, they take it and run with it. That's cool for me to see, and I think this sport has the potential to continue to grow and create a long list of new, young superstars for many years to come. But they better keep working hard if they think they can win seven races in a row at Bristol like ol' DW!

Oh, by the way . . .

Dale Earnhardt Jr.

I remember being a kid, playing on the hill at Bristol before they had all of the grandstands. You could look down on the cars as they went by. You could look right in and watch the drivers working the wheel. I'd love to be able to go back to those days. Man, it'd be great to be out there racing against Pearson, Allison, and especially Darrell in that green Mountain Dew car. . . .

11

Rule Maker, Not Rule Breaker

I was a rule *maker,* not a rule *breaker.* That's a very important distinction. Guys like me (and all my crew chiefs through the years) weren't breaking the rules; we were being smart and creative about the gray areas, innovating in areas where there were no rules. Sometimes NASCAR would find things they didn't like or agree with, and they'd have to make a rule to prevent it. I promise you, NASCAR added a lot of pages to the rulebook to keep up with us.

I enjoyed thinking of creative ways to improve the car. New ways to go faster or win more races. That was always a fun part of the game. There were things we did that went virtually unnoticed. If you did the same things today, you'd end up in NASCAR jail. The entire approach now is much tougher, much more regulated. They have measurements, gauges, and templates for everything. Now teams call the inspection area the "room of doom." It wasn't always that way.

Jake Elder, my first Winston Cup crew chief, was known to come up with creative sidesteps to the rules. Almost all of my crew chiefs were very creative. I had guys like Buddy Parrott, David Ifft, and Jeff Hammond. Gary

Nelson was a crewmember with me at DiGard, and he was eventually considered to be such a good cheater— uh, I mean *innovator*—NASCAR hired him away as the director of competition, essentially becoming their top cop. We all spent hours and hours thinking about how to get something past NASCAR. That was always our goal, and it was always exciting. Most of the time, NASCAR never had a clue.

It was like robbing a bank and then riding around wondering if you were gonna get caught. After a few days went by, you'd breathe a sigh of relief. Even if you did get caught, it was a small smack on the hand. The beauty of it was you'd sit at the bar the next week and brag about it to your buddies, and sometimes even your competitors.

Even if NASCAR did catch on or stumble across a violation, they wouldn't penalize a driver or team by taking away points or handing out expensive fines. It has only been in the last three or four years that NASCAR has started taking away championship points for violations. They used to say, "Take that away, and don't ever do it again." Sometimes they'd confiscate a part or two, and that was the last you'd hear about it. The benefits outweighed the punishment by so much, you'd always be thinking of the next innovation. It was perpetual, and I'm sure, as tough as NASCAR inspections have become, there are still a lot of brilliant innovations in the garage now.

Sometimes it was something really simple, like a headrest. I mean, NASCAR would not allow you to have a headrest. How crazy is that? I would go to Bristol with no power steering, and race for 500 laps, and no matter how physically fit I was, the first thing that gave out was my neck. I'd tell the team, "If I could have something to rest my head against during the race, I know I'd win a whole lot more."

Jeff Hammond came up with an ingenious device that he'd quickly bolt onto the back of my seat right before the race, and I could go lap after lap, resting my head on the brace. Nothing like today's custom seats built for safety and comfort; it was a little piece of aluminum with padding. Did we worry about getting caught? No way. Nobody looked at anything after the race. We'd just bend it out of the way.

The rulebook said the fuel cell capacity was limited to 22 gallons, so we'd go through tech inspection at the legal size. But, before the race, a lot of teams would take an air hose and pump more than 250 pounds of air pressure into the tank, and it would stretch to hold more fuel. You'd see cars rolling onto the grid with the fuel tank all bowed out and distorted. Or we'd use long, long fuel lines that would hold an extra half-gallon or so between the tank and the engine. Junior Johnson was brilliant at devising things like a spacer below the carburetor that held a small reservoir of fuel. Or maybe he'd have a huge fuel filter on the engine. If you could gain a quarter gallon here and a quarter gallon there, it might add up to a victory by the end of the race. And it wasn't illegal, because the rulebook said only that the *tank* had to be 22 gallons when they measured it before the race.

Another old ploy was the "shop rag" trick. You'd cover something with a towel or shop rag as if you were hiding some new magical, speed-producing part. Then everyone would try so hard to find out what was beneath the rag, they'd never notice the *real* trick pieces on the other side of the car.

All the teams, sooner or later, would discover and utilize the tricks. The key was to always be first and ahead of the curve. Be around the curve and halfway down the backstretch, so to speak. Once all the teams had something, NASCAR would somehow stumble upon it, and write a rule to ban or regulate it. Or they'd pull out the famous catchall phrase that still remains in the rulebook: "actions detrimental to stock car racing." That meant they could basically make up anything they wanted on the spot and call it "detrimental to stock car racing."

Even though I was looking for an edge, I always had a thing about the engine. Never cheat on the size of the engine. You couldn't cheat on the size of the motor. Because when they tear down that engine, it is what it is. There ain't no smoke and mirrors there. You can't lie about how big the engine is, so it is one thing I never considered. But I might have *known* some people who did things like that. . . .

When I started with the DiGard team, I learned why they were known for qualifying really well but had reliability problems in the races. Mario Rossi was building the engines for them, and those things would blow up regularly. But they always seemed to be great for a lap or two. It turns out they had a bottle of nitrous oxide in the car. If you know anything about nitrous, you know it's like pouring instant horsepower into the engine. It was also illegal. In 1976, there was an additional $5,000 for winning the pole at the Daytona 500, so the team was really shooting for it, and we felt pressure to perform well for our new sponsor, Gatorade. They had used nitrous when Donnie Allison drove for them, and even once or twice when I stepped in. NASCAR had warned them to never bring it back.

When I said they had a bottle of nitrous in the car, I meant they literally had it *in* the car. Rossi had built an ingenious contraption that placed the bottle inside what we called the Petty bar. The Petty bar is the roll bar that runs through the cockpit of the car, along the right side of the driver, toward the right-front corner of the frame. It was usually covered in padding. They had rigged the bottle inside the bar, then welded it shut. The nitrous ran to the engine in a fake fuel pressure line, and all the driver had to do was open a valve and the nitrous would inject right into the air cleaner. Magic! Speed in an instant. It was ingenious, but it was the most blatant cheating I was ever involved with.

We went to Daytona to begin the '76 season, and the car wasn't too good in practice, but no one seemed too worried about it. During qualifying, we improved on our practice speed by 10 mph! Yeah, 10 mph. A. J. Foyt, who was driving a car for Hoss Ellington, improved just as much, and he and I qualified for the front row of the Daytona 500. Dave Marcis was third quickest. Those huge improvements really tipped off NASCAR, and to make it worse, the other big teams figured the only way we'd get caught was if they held back in qualifying. To the inspectors, the dramatic difference in speed was like waving a red flag at a big, mean ol' bull.

What a scene it was in the garage! Marcis was disqualified for some illegal aerodynamic improvements, but NASCAR said they were gonna get out their blowtorches and start taking apart our car and Ellington's car until they found the nitrous.

A. J. Foyt is a man as fast to throw a punch as he was fast on the track. He was snorting and stomping. I thought he was gonna get into a fistfight with Bill France Jr. We were raisin' a cloud of dust of our own as we debated and argued with NASCAR for several hours. Finally, Hoss broke down and told NASCAR that he had *forgotten* that the bottle of nitrous was in his car.

Rossi and Bill Gardner weren't quite so quick to admit what they had in the car, but they somehow negotiated an agreement with NASCAR. If our car was allowed to requalify later in the week and then run in the 500, the team would tell NASCAR where the bottle was located the day after the race. Our qualifying laps were disqualified, along with Foyt and Marcis. Ramo Stott ended up being handed his one and only career Winston Cup pole position.

"I'll let you run that car in the 500," France scolded us. "But, after the race, that car is *ours*. We'll find out what you're doing if it means we have to cut it into a million pieces."

We didn't even make it to the halfway point of the race before the engine blew a rocker arm. The finish of that race was one of the most amazing in the history of the Daytona 500. David Pearson and Richard Petty crashed in turn four on the last lap, spinning into the infield grass. Pearson was the first to get his car refired, and he limped across the finish line to win the race.

We hoped our little agreement with NASCAR would be forgotten by race day, but as soon as I rolled into the garage, the inspectors were waiting for us. They impounded our car until the next morning. I guess Rossi couldn't stand the thought of having his engine and his car cut apart by NASCAR, so he pulled off the padding from the bar, took a torch, and cut out that piece of the roll bar, revealing the bottle. The inspectors had been looking for that thing for more than a week, hanging all over that bar, crawling inside the car, never having a clue until that moment.

Bill France turned to me, red-faced and angry. "What if you had crashed?!"

I had never considered that part of it.

"Yeah," I said, "but I coulda been on the pole!"

■□

We also used something called propylene oxide from my early days when I raced karts. You'd mix it with the fuel and it was like liquid oxygen. It was instant horsepower, and because it was odorless and clear, it was almost undetectable in the fuel. When you put it in, it was like magic. You could pick up a few tenths of a second no matter what track you were at.

Neil Bonnett and I both ran Budweiser cars when we were teammates with Junior Johnson. But really, we operated as if we were separate teams. One race at Pocono I qualified on the pole alongside Bill Elliott, but Neil hit a deer on his first qualifying lap and had to go back out in second-round qualifying the next day. His crew chief, Tim Brewer, must have poured a gallon of propylene oxide in the fuel, because Neil went out and set a track record.

NASCAR couldn't believe the speed, so they took a fuel sample from Neil's car. I didn't know they also took samples from my car as well. We always assumed it was undetectable in the fuel. The race was long over, and everyone had gone home without a second thought, until, a few days later, my phone rang.

"Darrell, lemme ask you something." It was Bill France Jr. I always felt honored when he'd call to confide in me or to ask for input on a subject. "What would you do if you found out someone was putting something in their gas? An additive of some kind . . ."

"I'd throw them out!" I said immediately. "Make an example of them!"

"So you wouldn't have a problem if I threw out Neil's track record?" he asked.

"I can't imagine Neil would do such a thing!" I said. Sure, he was my teammate on paper, but I didn't mind at all. "But if you have to make an example of him, fine."

"Darn it, DW!" France barked. "Yours was *worse* than his! DON'T DO IT NO MORE! We'll be watching!"

In 1985, Bill Elliott became known as "Million Dollar Bill" when he won a million dollars from R. J. Reynolds for winning the Daytona 500, the Winston 500 at Talladega, and then the Southern 500 at Darlington. He won 11 races, and understandably people forget that I beat him for the championship that season.

After he won so many races, the grumblings in the garage were mostly about the engines he was using. He and his brother, Ernie Elliott, built some great engines in their shop in Dawsonville, Georgia. But the real secret to their success wasn't the engine. That may or may not have been legal, but it was the car that was unique. It was a "mini"-Thunderbird. It fit the few templates NASCAR had then, but it was a tiny, tiny car that just sliced through the wind at the big tracks.

The finish I still hear about is The Winston in 1985. When Winston announced they were creating a big-money nonpoints race, Junior Johnson and I set our sights on winning that thing. Junior was always a genius with engines, but for that race, since it was a shorter distance than usual, he created a special engine that was lighter and had components built for the sprint-race format. The engine blew up crossing the finish line, and people still talk about that. It passed postrace inspection. The motor didn't disappear; it just had oil all over it.

When they blow up, contrary to what we tell the Internal Revenue Service, there are still some parts left, and you can salvage the parts that aren't damaged. When I owned my own team, I was audited by the IRS. This little guy showed up in his suit and tie, with his briefcase and his notebook, checking all kinds of things. He wanted to see what a wrecked car looked like, so we showed him a wrecked car. He jotted some notes in his book.

"When a motor blows up," he asked, "what happens to it?"

"Oh, it's junk," I told him. "A write-off . . ."

"You mean you can't use it? There's nothing left?"

It was just my luck; we had an old engine that had been lying out behind the shop forever. It had a big hole knocked in the side of it, and it was all rusty and nasty.

"See that thing lying right there?" I pointed. "That's a motor that blew up."

He kind of stared for a second. "Ahhh ... Yeah ... Hmmm ... I see what you mean," he said.

◼▭◼

Sometimes it's the least obvious things that make the difference. NASCAR had rules for the minimum total weight of the car, as well as the percentage of weight on the right and left side. If you follow Formula One, you know they have a constant debate about the strategy of cars qualifying or starting the race with a light load of fuel, and what an advantage it can be. It's simple physics: The lighter the car, the faster it will go. On an oval, because you are making only left-hand turns, you want a large percentage of the weight on the left side of the car to help it turn better.

In the 1970s, NASCAR would only weigh the cars before the race, never afterward. There were thousands of ways to get the car through the inspection at the legal weight of 3,700 pounds. It was very low tech. NASCAR weighed the cars on an old grain scale. Once you were through that inspection, it was anything goes to try and shed as much weight as possible.

I'd sit and watch every week. It was all part of an elaborate game. Don't tell on me, I won't tell on you. Everybody was trying something, so you were afraid to be a whistle-blower. You were stupid if you didn't do all you could to keep up.

It seemed like there were only two ways you would get caught. One, if one of your employees moved to another team and told all of your secrets, or two, if one of your competitors discovered what you were doing and ratted you out to NASCAR. "Psssssst . . . hey, over here," they'd whisper, pointing at one thing or another. "Look at this over here . . ." The best inspectors are the other competitors, not the guys in the "NASCAR OFFICIAL" shirts. To this day, that's why NASCAR still has such open garage areas, with the teams bunched together. It's hard to hide things when your toughest opponents are only three feet away in the next garage.

But the tattletale scenario didn't happen as often as you might think. Crazy Jake, he was great about that. He'd see something suspicious on someone's car, but he wouldn't go to NASCAR and complain. He'd go back home and do the same thing to our car for the next race. Whatever it was, one guy would do it, then another guy, then four or five guys would do it. It was important to be ahead of the curve before it was all over the garage.

It became pretty ridiculous, and even hilarious sometimes. Stevie and I would always travel with our dog, Charlie Brown. He was an awesome little dachshund, and he was friendly with everybody. Sometimes, at the end of a day of practice, we'd let him roam around the garage area, just checkin' everything out. After a while, some teams would get quiet when Charlie came by. They thought his collar had a microphone on it and we were using him to spy!

Junior's team had a set of gray wheels. God only knows how much those things weighed, but they were massive, at least 50 pounds each. We'd roll through tech with those, then we'd make our first pit stop in the race and put on the lighter, standard wheels. The trick wheels were too wide as well, and the inspectors finally caught on. I'm not sure how they discovered it—something about the weight balance of the car was wrong, or the wheels were offset incorrectly.

They called us over to the car.

"You can't run those wheels. They're too wide," the inspector explained.

"All right," I said. "We have some more wheels back in the truck."

We rolled the car back to the truck, took the wheels off, and carried them inside. We grabbed black spray paint and painted all four wheels. We brought them back out and bolted them right back on the car. We pushed the car back to the tech line and watched as they checked the car again.

"OK! You're good to go! We sure appreciate you boys working with us," they said.

As we were pushing the car away, one of the inspectors hollered out, "Oh, by the way, guys, the paint is still wet on them new wheels."

One week Junior let Bonnett use the wheels on the other Budweiser car. In the first segment of the race, I almost lapped him, but once they took off those monster wheels, Neil came back and won the race. I was so mad. I mean, it was OK if *I* got to use 'em, but I sure didn't want my teammate beating me that way!

That was a big part of the fun, ya know? It was a "top this!" kind of thing, like having bragging rights. All of the teams and drivers stayed at the same hotels each week. We'd all ride back to the hotel after practice or qualifying, whatever it was. Somebody would stop at the liquor store and get a fifth of whiskey or a few cases of Budweiser. "What are ya'll doing tomorrow?" we'd tease each other. "What are you trying to get away with?" Sometimes you'd mutter to somebody as you were rolling the car into tech.

"Watch this," you'd say with a chuckle.

One of the things that has changed for the better is the focus on safety. It's no longer about fun, it's about making sure the cars are as safe as they can be. In those days, I never imagined getting hurt, let alone killed, in one of those cars. I know it happened around me, but I had blinders on. I didn't know any better, and no one else did either. It was ignorance. Early in my career, I never thought about getting hurt, especially once I was strapped in the car. Once that engine roared, it never entered my mind. I could've been at the Bonneville Salt Flats going 645 mph. I did not think about getting hurt until I got hurt. I realized after my 1990 Daytona crash that I could've been killed in that thing. Until then, I had been in every wreck and I had hit everything as hard as it could be hit. I got beat up in a few crashes, but nothing serious. Nothing bad was ever gonna happen to me. That only happened to other drivers, lesser drivers. Earnhardt was the same way. People will argue forever that he didn't have the latest, safest stuff in his car on the day he died. In his mind, I'm sure he believed what he had was safe and was the best option for him.

I can't believe how dangerous some of the tricks were. People would build cars with the roll bars made out of exhaust-pipe tubing. It was thinner and lighter, and much more fragile. Bo Brady, who was with me from the early days of my career, built a Busch Series car for me to race on the short tracks. It was the lightest car I had ever seen. I couldn't see anything tricky about it; it looked like everybody else's car.

"Bo, how did you build a car this light?" I'd ask.

He never did tell me, until I got hit on the right side during a race and the whole passenger-side door came off. I sat there in rubble, with nothing remaining on the right side of the car.

"I didn't do that to the driver's-side door!" he promised me.

The issue of weight finally bothered me enough that, as usual, I spoke up and asked "Why?" I stood up after the drivers' meeting at Martinsville one year.

Bill Gazaway was the NASCAR director holding the meeting.

"Why don't you weigh all these cars after the race is over?" I asked. "It's ridiculous what people are doing!"

"No need to," he said.

"What do you mean, no need to?!" I asked.

"When those cars go on the line," he answered, "they weigh 3,700 pounds, and when we put them on the line, we know they're right."

"Let me just ask you," I continued, smart aleck that I was. "Let me hypothetically ask you a question. What if my car doesn't weigh 3,700 pounds after the race?"

"Oh well, then we'd deal with you after the race," he said.

But they would not weigh the cars after the race. In the course of a three-and-a-half-hour event, if you could get rid of 300 pounds, nobody cared. It was a huge loophole that we could drive through at top speed.

All of the teams used lead to distribute weight throughout the car. Crazy Jake would always tell me, "The best place for lead is back on the truck," but Harry Hyde devised a way to use bags of lead shot. You could buy the bags at any sporting goods store: 10-pound bags, 50-pound bags, whatever size you needed. Once you had the car on the grid, you would slip the bags out of the car and onto a pit cart. I remember those bags hidden everywhere, even under my seat, and we were always coming up with ways to sneak them out of the car. Some teams would weigh down the cover that slid over the car. It looked like an ordinary cloth car cover, but once it was on the grid, it would take two big, strong guys to take it off the car, and a cart to roll the cover back to the pit area. It would have tools and wrenches stuffed in it—a whole toolbox hidden. Crew guys would be stuffing weights in their pockets and walking away from the car with their pants about to fall off their hips.

The deception became more inventive when NASCAR finally caught on.

We had a radio that was made out of Mallory, a metal alloy that is extremely dense, and it weighed 50 pounds. It had an antenna, knobs, everything on it. If you placed it beside another radio, without picking it up, you probably wouldn't have known the difference, it was that realistic. We'd put it in the car to go through tech, and then, when we were ready to qualify or race, we'd take it out and put in a real radio. One morning at Charlotte, Earnhardt, Rusty Wallace, Bill Elliott, and I were standing in the garage as the cars were coming through tech. Dick Beatty, NASCAR's director of competition, walked up holding a radio on his shoulder.

"What's wrong with your radio, Dick?" I laughed.

He took that thing and threw it at my foot. If I hadn't jumped, I might have been out of action for a while. "It ain't my radio," he said, staring at me, "and I don't have to tell you where we found it."

I had a helmet made to look like the real thing, but it was made of lead. It was basic, but it worked. It would rest inside the car until I'd get in, then I'd put on my real helmet. The water bottle too. Before the race started, we'd just swap the heavy hunk of metal for the real thing. The cars were more fragile than they are now, so a few hundred pounds meant not only faster laps but a smaller chance of parts failure.

In 1987, I won the All-American 400 at Nashville. It was one of the biggest short-track races in the country every year, and I had Tide sponsorship on a little Camaro. This was a sweet hot rod I drove at short-track races on off-weekends from Winston Cup. We went through practice and qualifying on Saturday and had everything ready for Sunday's race. The officials came to look at my car again on Sunday morning. The rules allowed straight frame rails on the right side of the car, which my car had, but the rules said a car with straight frame rails had to weigh 50 pounds more than the other style of frame.

"It's SUNDAY MORNING!" I yelled. "You can't do that!"

They said, "It was our mistake, but it's your bad luck. Sorry, you have to add 50 pounds."

My crew chief, Eddie Jones, looked at me, not knowing what we were gonna do.

"Get me two 25-pound bars of lead," I told him. "We'll slide 'em up inside the tailpipes, then, before the race, you can reach in there and pull 'em out." Easy, right? Except we hadn't figured that during pre-race inspection, they would ask us to jack up the car on the right side. When we did, the lead slid way down inside the tailpipes. As we are ready to start the race, I'm strapped in, and poor Eddie Jones is bent down, reaching as far as he can inside the tailpipes—and he's panicking. "I can't get 'em out!"

I was confident as usual. "Aww . . . it'll come out!" I said.

The field rolls off, and as we're scrubbing our tires on the pace laps, I hear a scraping sound: grrrrr-skkkkkk . . . BOOM! A big crunch under the rear wheels. I thought we would be all right, but the guy behind me saw it come out. So he's calling his crew: "Lead came out of Darrell's car!" The official runs out on the track, picks up the chunks of lead, and holds it up to show it to me as I roll past. "What am I gonna do?" I say with a shrug.

The officials came to our pit area, and they told Eddie, "We know you dropped it out, so when this race ends, we're throwing you out if you're one pound below weight!"

It didn't look like we would have anything to worry about early on, as we dropped one lap down. But 400 laps at Nashville is a long way, and there was a lot of attrition. We got back on the lead lap, and then, with 10 laps to go, we got a break when there was a caution. There were only a few cars left on the lead lap, and we were the only ones with fresh tires in our pits, so we came in and got two new right-side tires. I came flying through the pack like Jack the Bear when the race restarted! Mark Martin was leading, and he held me off for a few laps, but he had worn out his brakes, so, going into the third turn on the last lap, I got past him and won the All-American 400.

"Oh geez, now what am I gonna do?" I climbed out and looked at the team and said quietly, "Go on about your business like we won this race."

We went through the whole thing: the pictures, interviews, the guitar. (Nashville is famous for presenting the winning driver with a guitar rather than a trophy.) I trudged off to the media center to do more interviews, but I was dreading the signal to get in the car for the weigh-in. The driver and car were weighed together for a total weight.

One of the officials caught a kid on my crew trying to get the "special" heavy radio in the car. We had more than one of those radios, and the kid got caught. They knew they had us as I slid into the car and we rolled it forward. And it weighed . . . EXACTLY the right amount! We were just as shocked, lemme tell ya! So they made us roll it off so they could readjust the scales, and then we rolled it forward again. EXACT weight.

The next day we were sitting in the shop, wondering how in the world . . . ?

We rolled the car out of the trailer and started to inspect it. We discovered that inside each wheel well was a pile of debris, pellets of rubber with piles of junk stuck to the rubber in each corner of the car. Fifty pounds of junk! There are still people who were there that day wondering, "How did they do that?" Just amazing.

◼◻◼

Now, I don't want to make the NASCAR guys seem like they were idiots, because things were much different then—less stringent and more easygoing. Sure, we were usually a few steps, a few BIG steps, ahead of them, but sometimes they'd have some fun at our expense as well.

The team was doing a radio check on a Sunday morning before a race at Martinsville, so I had my helmet on, getting wired up, checking to make sure the system was ready to go. All of a sudden, a big voice comes on our channel and says, "This is Kingsport, Tennessee. WHO is on my channel?! Please get off this frequency immediately!"

I got all excited. "Hey! Junior! Someone's on our channel all the way from Kingsport, Tennessee! What are we gonna do?!"

Harold Kinder, the NASCAR flagman, had somehow grabbed one of our radios, and he decided he was going to have some fun with me. Harold just laughed and laughed.

◼◻◼

The best deception of all was what we called "Bombs Away." NASCAR learned about the bags of lead shot, so they made a rule that all lead weights must be bolted down. This was while I was with DiGard. Buddy Parrott, Gary Nelson, and I were brainstorming, wondering what we could do.

What if we put the lead pellets inside the frame rails, and then rig a hole in the rail so it would run out of the car?

It turned out to be simple, but effective. We would start the race at the legal weight, with the frame rails full of pellets. We knew we couldn't just drain them out before the race right on pit lane, so we devised a solution. During the first yellow flag or even the pace laps, I would take a small wrench, reach down to the left side of my seat and loosen a bolt that ran down into the jack stop. The jack stop is the small post below the body on both sides of the car where the jack lifts the car. As I would turn the bolt, it would release the lead shot out of the car like a drain. Suddenly I was driving a much lighter car. Then I'd take the wrench and close the drain.

What made this trick so much fun was that NASCAR knew we were doing something. They *knew* it, but whenever they would jack up the car to look, the jack itself would hide the evidence. The harder they looked, the more frustrated they became—and the more we enjoyed it. The frame was welded solid at both ends, so they thought we must be OK. And we'd chuckle under our breath.

Dick Beatty used to walk around the track each weekend. It was something he liked to do, just take a look at everything on the track up close. One day, he came to me carrying a small Styrofoam cup filled with rusted pellets.

"I have been noticing something new, Darrell," he said as he dropped the cup in front of me. "I have been finding small, rusty pellets on the inside of each track. Do you have any idea what that could be from?"

"Wow," I said, full of wonder and sincerity. "I have never seen anything like that before. I have no idea what that would be from."

There was only one time when we came close to getting caught. Before each race weekend the guys would load the pellets into the frame rails—they called it "loading the cannon"—and one week before a race at

Bristol, they poured it full of lead, and then, for whatever reason, washed the car. Moisture got into the rails and caused the pellets to clog up and stick together. I had no way of knowing they were rusty, so when they said "bombs away," I opened the cannon door and assumed all of the shot ran out like usual.

When the green flag came out again, I was racing along into turns three and four, and all of a sudden it felt like I hit ice. I spun around, but I got lucky, because I didn't hit anything. I ended up facing down the pit lane, so I shoved it back in gear and took off. As I went through the pits, that buckshot was hitting people in the pits! Junior Johnson was raisin' Cain! He was peppered with BBs! There were several cars that came down the pit lane to avoid my spinning car, including Dave Marcis, and NASCAR couldn't tell which car was throwing the shot. After the race, NASCAR had handfuls of the stuff they had picked up in the pits, and they came over to jack up our car. Of course, as always, this covered the evidence. "It can't be this car! It's sealed tight!" Poor ol' Marcis, I think they tried to point the finger at him on that one.

Finally, NASCAR got smart enough to weigh the cars after the race, but only the total weight. They still didn't look at the percentages between left and right or front to back. And after the race, they weren't very thorough, because everybody's anxious to get the heck out of there.

Why is it different now? Safety is the main motivating factor, and it should be, but there are other reasons as well. One, there are corporate sponsors that do not want to be associated with a team that has a reputation as a bunch of cheaters. And because the penalties are more severe, and because each race and the overall championship are so important, teams cannot afford to have points taken away.

And third, millions of people are paying attention. NASCAR has become a major sport, with a giant audience watching on TV every week, plus hundreds of thousands in the grandstands. The media coverage is huge. We saw only a few reporters each week when I came into Winston Cup. We had no TV coverage, and we raced at tracks that held crowds one-tenth the size of what you see now. To hear my races on the radio, my brother Michael and the rest of the family had to drive to a hilltop more than an hour from home just to get a fuzzy, faraway radio station with race coverage. You might see a few seconds of the races on *Wide World of Sports,* between Ping-Pong, sumo wrestling, and ski jumping, but that was it.

We had only the print media, and they were in on the conspiracy. I mean, they drank beer with us, they played cards with us, and they stayed in the same hotels. Each of them was just one of the guys. To use the bank robbery example again, you can rob a bank and get away with it if there aren't too many accomplices, but if you get a big crowd in on it, you're eventually going to get caught.

Oh, by the way . . .

■■■□

*Jeff Hammond,
crew chief*

Darrell was genius at coming up with a story or an explanation for everything, no matter what. Most of the time NASCAR bought his story. He could be pretty convincing. The day they discovered our special "heavy radio" and Dick Beatty threw it at Darrell's foot, we were called to the NASCAR trailer. It was so funny, because Beatty said to Darrell and me, "You guys can either pay the fine, or you can wear this radio around your neck for the rest of the weekend."

12

Brittle

The cars were fragile in the '70s and '80s, and you never knew when they were going to snap. At least that was the case when I was with the DiGard team. The engines were so brittle, I usually drove with one foot on the gas and one foot on the clutch. I never knew when something was going to go off like a grenade. Everything about DiGard was brittle—especially my relationships within the team.

The funniest example of how frequently we suffered mechanical woes took place soon after I started. In 1976, two-way radios were a relatively new thing in the sport. The radios we had were no good. They didn't work worth a darn. We realized what a difference it could make during a race to have better communications and kept lobbying for better equipment.

Bill Gardner, one of the owners, got sick of hearing that, so he decided we were going to have the latest and the greatest radios. He spent a small fortune on them. Everybody had brand-new radios—the best ones on the market! Not just the crew chief and the driver, but everyone on the crew had radios. The first race with the new radios, we ran only 30 or 40 laps, when I came on the radio. "We're out! It blew up!"

"You know," Gardner came back to me on the radio, "I've spent $30,000 for these darn radios and that's the same thing I could have heard on the track's PA system." He was so angry! "I didn't need to spend all that money just to hear that," he yelled.

■□

With Crazy Jake, Robert Gee, and my own little team, we had proven we could win. We were the underdogs, the guys with no money. No matter how well we did, it became a real drain on me, on Stevie, on everyone because we were building a mountain of debt. Or, as I called it, the Grand Canyon of Debt.

No matter how much you want to win, or how hard you work, if the money runs out, there's very little you can do. Even though we were showing promise, we knew our banker couldn't hold on to the overdue notices much longer. We still had Terminal Transport on the car as a sponsor, but the money they paid barely got us started. Something had to change, and it did after the Firecracker 400 at Daytona in July 1975.

DiGard was based in Daytona Beach, which was unique. Even now, almost all of the teams are centered around Charlotte because of the proximity to most of the races. The NASCAR schedule is slowly spreading to new tracks across the country, but in the mid '70s, we ran most of the races in and around the Carolinas. The Daytona Beach location gave the team a sense of home-field advantage at Daytona, but it also meant travel to most of the other races was significantly longer than it was for the other teams. The distance from Charlotte made it tough for the team to hire the best people. Most of the topflight crewmembers were hesitant to move because of the additional travel demands.

Donnie Allison was key in the formation of the team. He was the driver from the start, bringing together the team's owners: Mike DiProspero and the Gardner brothers, Jim and Bill. During the week, Donnie also acted as the team manager, so he was integral to their effort. Even though they were a fast team that qualified well, they never found success in the races. My team had already grabbed our first win at Nashville, but DiGard had never found the way to Victory Lane. That was the scene in July when the teams rolled into Daytona for the Firecracker 400. DiGard was the hometown bunch, so there were a lot of expectations inside of the team that they should be the team to beat. Those expectations only increased when they won the pole.

I had shown up with my ragtag bunch, and had a pretty good weekend. We qualified fourth and ended up finishing fourth, one lap behind the winner, Richard Petty. Donnie finished fifth, a full lap behind us.

The discord inside the team came to a boiling point after the race. Bill Gardner wanted to know how in the world he was spending so much money and that SOB Waltrip was still beating them every week without two pennies to rub together! They fired Donnie that night.

After the race, Stevie and I went to Vero Beach to relax and spend some time with her mom and dad. When we got into the car to head back to Charlotte, we stopped at NASCAR's headquarters in Daytona to pick up our winnings from the race. We needed every cent of the $6,210 to keep the bank away for another week at least.

"Did you hear Donnie Allison was fired?" someone asked me. I hadn't heard—we had been relaxing on the beach. I thought it was a bad deal, because Donnie had done a lot with the cars, a lot more than most of the other drivers could have, for sure. We got our check and turned north to Charlotte. At our first stop for gas, we're sitting there at the station and along comes Jim Gardner. He walked over to the car, laughing.

"Funny that I should run into you here," he said. "We've been trying to find you. We want you to drive for our team."

I told him I appreciated the thought but I was committed to my team and my sponsors for the rest of this year.

"I would be glad to talk about doing something next year," I told him.

"Here's my number," he said, handing me his card. "If you change your mind, call me immediately."

I got back in the car and told Stevie what had happened. We talked about the possibility of me driving for another team—it represented a light at the end of the tunnel of debt we had accumulated. Mile by mile, the offer seemed harder to turn down.

The best sponsor I had was my banker. The problem was, his bank didn't know it. Wayne King was vice president of Winston County Bank in an era when you had a little hometown bank and did business on a very personal level. Wayne was a huge fan, and he helped all he could, but one day he called and said, "Do you know I'm holding ten checks?"

"Gee, Wayne, I didn't realize I had written ten checks."

"What am I supposed to do?" he asked. "You're fifty grand in the hole."

"Don't worry, I'll get it," I told him. I had no idea how or where.

This was the pressure I was under when we stopped a few hours later for more fuel and dinner. Wouldn't you know who showed up at the same restaurant? Jim Gardner. He acted like it was a coincidence, but I'm sure he had been following us. We laughed about how odd it was that we had run into him again. I told him his offer was more appealing now than it had been a few hundred miles back. "Can I call you tomorrow?" I asked.

Stevie and I talked about it all the way to Charlotte, and, as usual, we called her dad for input. He was thrilled at the idea of Texas Gas no longer paying to sponsor my little team, so that cleared the way for me to accept the offer. DiGard didn't have a sponsor, so we were able to work out a deal to have Terminal Transport on the side of the car for the rest of the 1975 season. We wrangled with all of the contractual details, and even arranged to use some of my team's cars on the short tracks where we had excelled.

For the remainder of the season, it was one mechanical failure after another, with an occasional top-five finish thrown in. When we reached Richmond in October, we were still looking for the right combination, and it didn't look good when we fell three laps behind early in the race. Then all of the heavy hitters started falling out, and the race was in the hands of Lennie Pond, who had never won a Cup race. Lennie was leading by a large margin, but I managed to get one lap back with some hard racing, then gained another on a well-timed yellow flag. Pond ended up being penalized for an infraction on pit lane, and suddenly we were in the lead, and went on to win the race. (Pond got his only Cup win at Talladega a few years later.)

It was the first win for DiGard as a team, and it stands out as the only highlight of the last half of the 1975 season. Even though I didn't start two races, I ended up seventh in the final point standings. This was the season NASCAR started using the modern point system, and I started a streak of 15 consecutive years of finishing in the top 10. (As of the end of the 2003 season, I have scored more total points than any driver since the current point system was instituted, even though I retired from driving in 2000.)

The pieces were almost in place. We were a fast team that could win if our engine didn't expire, but we still didn't have a sponsor for the 1976 season.

In the category of "it's who you know," this one certainly fits. Dennis Hendrick, a guy who worked with Frank at Texas Gas, had gone to school with Bill Stokely, who was a key player with Stokely–Van Camp. One of Stokely–Van Camp's brands was Gatorade.

Gatorade had dipped a toe into the sponsorship pool in 1975 with Johnny Rutherford, a three-time Indy 500 winner. But, in a story typical of the Indianapolis Motor Speedway and the United States Auto Club, there were difficulties trying to get credentials for the executives to attend events and they were treated very poorly. The decision was made within the company to discontinue their motorsports involvement.

Stokely knew of me but believed my little operation wasn't the image they wanted to project. But, once I was with DiGard, a state-of-the-art operation based in Florida, they decided to take a second look. (Gatorade was originally developed to help the Florida Gators football team stay hydrated, so that's why the Florida connection made sense.)

Stokely agreed to travel south to take a look at the team, and instantly he and Bill Gardner hit it off like they'd been friends forever. In a very short time, we were painting green stripes on white cars and placing large Gatorade decals on everything for the 1976 season.

◼◻◼

The year started with the drama at Daytona and the nitrous oxide debacle, but another subplot at Speedweeks was the response to the green color on the car. Racers are superstitious about numbers, but they are also superstitious about the color green. I don't know why, and I'd love to learn how that superstition got started, but when we showed up in our green uniforms with the orange flash of lightning down the front, a lot of people were uneasy. David Pearson was the worst. He wouldn't even park next to the Gatorade car. He didn't want to be anywhere near it. "How can you show up here with green on your car?" he'd say.

It made 'em nervous, but not me. I was so far in debt, I didn't care about superstitions. The color green meant one thing to me: money. I needed it, they had it, and I'd drive a car painted any color the sponsor wanted.

The 1976 season was much like '75: Go fast, break down. We won only one race, at Martinsville, and finished eighth in points. For me, it was a step back from the results of the year before. I was dissatisfied, and I made my feelings quite clear to the Gardners. The engines were junk, and I believed we needed to move to Charlotte to have any chance to hire the best crewmembers.

I recommended we hire Robert Yates, a young guy who was working for Junior Johnson at the time to improve the engines. I became friends with Robert when I started my team, because I bought a lot of parts from him out of Junior's used motors in an effort to save money. He was hesitant to leave, but we made an offer of more money than he was making at Junior's, so he agreed to join the DiGard team. Whoo—I'll tell ya, Junior was NOT happy!

Part two of the equation fell into place as well: The owners decided they would move the headquarters from Daytona to Charlotte. I was really happy with the decision, but these things don't happen overnight, so we started the 1977 season in a strange way: building a new shop in Charlotte while working out of the shop in

Florida. Robert and I tried to make the best of the arrangement by staying in a Days Inn in Daytona between traveling to the races and Charlotte.

Once the new shop was in place, we were ready to go. We had a good engine builder, and we were able to establish a better overall team by hiring topflight guys like Buddy Parrott and David Ifft.

We started the season slowly, but once we gained momentum things really began to take off. I won my first superspeedway race at Darlington with a wild pass through the debris, and then we won five more races while I waged a verbal war with Cale Yarborough. We grabbed fourth place in the final standings, so finally the momentum was pointing in the right direction.

But from the start the whole team fought six days a week. That's what made the deal strange and unique. Six days a week, everybody argued, fought, disagreed, and couldn't get along. When Sunday came, we all did our job. I always said winning can cure anything, and for the most part it did. We'd go out and win a race, and I'd look at the good things instead of the bad. But if we dropped out or lost the race the next week, I'd look at the bad things again. It was like a roller-coaster ride, working with people you didn't want to work with. We won races, because every week we knew we had a chance to win, but the more we won, the worse the problems got.

That was the saga of DiGard. During the season, I wanted a raise. I was driving for a 40 percent share of the prize money, plus my expenses. Those expenses were very limited, but I could get a rental car, a hotel room, and per diem. I wanted to move it to 50 percent of the winnings. That was not uncommon for a proven driver. Bill Gardner was incensed that I would even ask. Every time I'd try to renegotiate, they'd add another year to my contract. It felt like my contract was being extended for so many years, my grandchildren would be under contract to DiGard.

"As much money as I'm spending and as much money as I am losing?" he told me. "I can't believe you have the audacity and the nerve to ask for a raise."

He was really put out by it, and it got worse because he was vindictive. When he got mad at someone, he would figure out a way to get even. I was near the end of my contract, and I wanted 50 percent and my expenses.

The final race of the year, I was ready to get in the car at Riverside, when Jim Gardner walked out to the car and said, "Here's your contract, and we'd like you to sign it today."

I had a race to run and I didn't have time to sign a contract as I climbed into the car.

"It's everything you asked for, in lieu of your expenses," he told me.

"Well, OK," I said. "I don't have a problem with that."

I was dumb enough to sign it on the grid. I didn't read it.

A week or two went by, and I'm at the shop when the accountant walked over and asked, "Where's your American Express card?"

"In my pocket," I laughed. "Why?"

"I need it. I'd like to have it."

"What do you mean you want it?" I asked. "Are you gonna give me another one?"

"No," he said. "You don't have an expense account anymore."

I laughed at the guy. "Don't tell me that. I just signed a new deal. I know what I got."

"You must not," he said. "You will receive 50 percent of the winnings, but you'll pay all of your expenses."

So *that's* what "in lieu of" meant. . . .

It was in the contract, and I had signed for three more years. I was really stupid to sign it without having gone through everything, but that's how they worked.

By the time the accounting and the service charges and every other element was subtracted from the deal, it was like I owed them money. It was a hard bunch to do business with.

The worst was when the paychecks stopped coming entirely. I waited more than three months at one point, and every time I'd call, it was every excuse under the sun. Every cliché: "Did you not get that yet? I thought we sent that to you. . . ." Or: "Yeah, Darrell, that check is in the mail." I got so frustrated and upset, I booked a seat on a plane from Nashville to Charlotte and showed up at the office. Surprise! I'm here, and I want my check.

"Wellllll . . . look at what we found here! It's your check! How did that get lost in there?! Wow, sorry. But, here ya go, buddy!"

Then, somehow, no surprise, the check wasn't good.

"Oh, yeah . . . we're transferring the money from another account, and if you could just hang on a few more days, the money will be there."

■□■

After doing so well in 1977, we were one of the favorites in '78. But, with all of the turmoil, we started the season very poorly. Morale was awful. Buddy Parrott and I, along with almost everyone else, were at each other's throats pretty good. It never helped that I wasn't shy to say what I felt in the media. Then they'd do the same.

We won at Bristol, my first win of what would become a long list of successes at that place. Things seemed to be turning around—at least on the track. We won a few more and then captured the World 600 at Charlotte on Memorial Day weekend. It was another first for me, and again, it started a trend of success in that particular race.

It was no secret about the bickering and unhappiness, so a few other car owners approached me. Would I be interested in driving for them? The Gardners were livid. They'd sue me, and any new owner, in any way they could. I wasn't gonna drive for another team, because my contract with them now extended well into the future. Despite it all, we finished the season in third place in the standings—an improvement—and we won six races for the second consecutive season.

We won the opening race of 1979 at Riverside, my first road-course win. Then we went to Daytona and were behind the melee that became one of the most famous finishes in racing history, as Cale Yarborough and Donnie Allison crashed each other going for the victory on the last lap. When Bobby Allison stopped to help his brother, the fisticuffs broke out! The entire nation was watching the Daytona 500 live for the first time ever on CBS, and they got to see the brothers and Cale duking it out! Most of the Northeast was snowed in by a huge blizzard that day, so the ratings were bigger than expected. Almost forgotten in all of the fury on the backstretch is that Richard Petty beat me to the finish line by barely a car length, and I just missed getting a win in the Daytona 500. (Bobby had the best line: "Cale's face kept hitting my fist.")

We became the team to beat every weekend. We went to Bristol and finished third behind a first-time winner by the name of Earnhardt. When April rolled around, we went to Darlington with the lead in the point standings. That day has to rank right up there among my favorite wins of all time, because Petty and I battled all day. Every lap it seemed we would pass each other, and then we traded the lead *four times* on the last lap and I ended up winning by half of a car length!

The race marked the end of the longtime association between David Pearson and the Wood Brothers. The pace we were setting was so fast, Pearson left his pits in a hurry to catch up. He left before the lug nuts were tight, and the left-side tires fell off his car. He was so mad, he climbed out and walked off. Pearson had been the undisputed best at Darlington, and it was symbolic that he walked away. He was fired from the Wood Brothers team the following week. The Pearson era was ending as the DW era was beginning to pick up momentum.

We struggled with mechanical gremlins for a few weeks after that, but we were back in the Winner's Circle at Charlotte for the second year in a row in the World 600. As the summer wore on, we continued to be aggressive, going out and pushing hard to win every week. Our points lead increased, and most of the team—Yates, Buddy Parrott, and the Gardners—believed we should start running a more conservative pace to preserve the lead. I disagreed completely, but despite the different views, we went out and won the race at Bristol in August before we went back to Darlington for the Southern 500.

If my earlier victory at "The Track Too Tough to Tame" was one of my career highlights, the return to Darlington would rank at or near the bottom. We had a 160-point lead over Richard Petty after we won at Bristol, and the championship was down to a battle between the King and I. Cale was third, but more than 300 points behind.

We were great that day, leading easily and stretching our lead to more than a lap on the entire field. With less than 100 laps to go, I was flying. I had everyone beaten—until I hit the wall! I was pushing too hard, and I flat out lost it. I ended the race 12 laps behind, in 11th place. Ironically, David Pearson won in a Chevrolet—his new ride after being let go by the Wood Brothers. I had led 167 laps, and I completely blew it. Petty didn't finish much better, but it was like the air had gone out of my sails.

Driving is about confidence. You have confidence in yourself, but the team really helps feed it, particularly when things don't go well. If the team believes in you, it makes everything easier for the driver. But everybody was mad at me after the crash, and I never felt any support from that day forward. I lost my rhythm. I started to drive differently. I was trying to get everybody back on my side. But the hole got deeper and deeper. Ultimately, we blew apart and lost the title.

At North Wilkesboro I had another great car and led more than 100 laps until I let my temper get the best of me. I forgot about the championship as Bobby Allison and I ended up beatin' and bangin' on each other until he put me into the wall. I was so mad, I retaliated, and NASCAR put me in the "penalty box" for two laps. I finished 13th, and our lead over Petty had shrunk to 17 points.

The season came down to the finale at Ontario, California. I had a two-point lead. We had struggled while Petty clicked off strong, consistent finishes, closing a few points each week. All I had to do to become champion was keep Petty behind me, but I spun out trying to avoid another car that was spinning in front of me. We lost a lap, and we were never able to regain it. I finished eighth, one lap behind Benny Parsons. Petty finished fifth, on the lead lap, and won the title by 11 points.

We won seven races and led the points almost the entire season, but the failure to win the championship was a crushing blow to me and the team. Buddy Parrott was fired, even though he was right in arguing that we should have taken a more conservative approach in the latter part of the season. Bill Gardner announced that he had lost money during the season, mostly because his driver had made such a high percentage of the winnings.

(Believe me, my tax returns that year sure didn't match what he was claiming.) Gardner told the team, "I spent all of this money, and we finished second? I'm never gonna do that again."

Losing the title was a terrible thing, but it was a lesson that would help me in the future. We beat ourselves. There is no question in my mind: Petty didn't win it—I lost that championship. It was a lesson that was seared in my brain: Never beat yourself.

The mood carried over into 1980. The entire organization was still bummed out because we hadn't won the championship the previous year. Everybody was reeling, because we knew we'd given it away.

Before the season started, Bill Gardner announced that DiGard was becoming a two-car team. I was being joined by Don Whittington. Along with his two brothers, Whittington was known primarily for making an occasional run at the Indy 500. He had a ton of cash to spend, and Gardner was ready to accept it.

I was distraught. I never liked the idea of having a teammate. I believed it was going to hurt our focus on winning the title and erode morale even further. It seemed like our car broke down or blew up in the first few laps of most of the races in 1980. The worst was at Michigan, where the car blew up during both qualifying sessions and we never completed a qualifying lap. This was before the days of provisional starting positions, so we weren't even in the field. We bought our way in by paying team owner Joel Halpern to let our team race his car, which had been qualified by Chuck Bown. Ironically, I almost won in that car. I led 67 laps, more than any other driver, and finished fourth.

Somehow, we still won five races in 1980 and finished fifth in the championship. Earnhardt won the title in only his second year. My teammate Whittington finished 46th in points, running only seven races.

I was 33 years old, and I had won 27 Winston Cup races but had not won the championship. We were a bunch of renegades, and we didn't know how to win a title. If I had been driving for Junior Johnson, I would have won easily. It would have been a no-brainer, because I was on top of my game.

Cale Yarborough decided he was going to leave Junior's team at the end of 1980 to work for M. C. Anderson. Cale wanted to cut back on his schedule, running a limited number of races. One day in May, he pulled me aside in the garage at Charlotte.

"Now, look," he whispered to me. "I'm going to give you a little inside tip. I'm goin' to tell you something. I don't even like you, but I'm getting ready to tell Junior I'm quittin'. Junior likes you. He's had his eye on you. You need to get yourself in a position where you can take that job. You'll make more money driving that car than you've ever made in your life."

Johnson's choice to replace Cale came down to two drivers: It was between Earnhardt and me. I was a little older, and even though he won the championship in 1980, Dale was tearing up a lot of equipment (his own and a lot of others) in those days. Junior said Earnhardt wrecked too much and he didn't need those headaches. He knew I could take care of equipment. Johnson sent Henry Benfield to tell me that if I could get out of my deal, he wanted me to drive for him. He had Pepsi coming aboard as a sponsor (with the Mountain Dew brand), and my heart jumped. I was perfect for that deal. I remembered back to the days of riding with my dad delivering soft drinks around Owensboro.

I had to do whatever it took to get out of my deal. I also heard from some other car owners, like Harry Ranier and even Roger Penske, who was looking to start a NASCAR team to go along with his successful Indy car team. But Junior had the best team in the business, and his interest in me made my confidence soar. If he was willing to pick me, I knew I had the chance to be the best driver with the best team.

The DiGard situation was a fiasco, and I began negotiating to get out of my contract. It was very public: me wanting to leave and them not willing to let me drive for someone else, particularly after we lost the championship. My contract had three years remaining, and it made me sick to my stomach to think of driving for this team another season, let alone three. I felt like I was in prison without parole. They were going to get an injunction so I couldn't drive for another team. Bill Gardner said, "You'll sit in the grandstand before you'll sit in anyone else's car, and trust me, I can make that happen."

I went to see several attorneys about my contract, and it looked grim. I chose Ed Silva, who has been my attorney ever since, and told him we had to figure a way to get out of that contract. Ed's father-in-law was a very prominent attorney in Franklin, but he had another important case taking all of his time. He suggested I talk with Ed, a recent graduate of Boston College and new with the firm. I wasn't so sure at first: Ed had a New England accent, and he didn't talk like I did. But I realized he spoke the same language as the Gardners, so he and I went back and forth to New Haven, Connecticut, where Bill Gardner lived.

My contract was complicated, and it involved a stipulation that there wasn't a value or dollar amount placed on my services. It sounds strange, but it was considered in the same way as a piece of art or a historical object that has no price tag. The worth is merely what someone is willing to pay. There was no tangible way to place a dollar value on the services I offered to the team. That's the way the contract was written, and they used it against me when I wanted to buy my way out. They wouldn't give me an amount for a buyout because the contract didn't stipulate my value or worth.

We finally came to terms when the Gardners decided they were going to let me buy my way out of the contract. We ended up agreeing on a figure of $300,000.

It was an off weekend from racing, and I was relieved the deal had been agreed upon. I had a 1978 Indy 500 pace car replica, a Corvette I had owned for a while but hadn't driven. Stevie and I decided we were going to take that Corvette and get away, go see a show in Louisville, but Silva tracked me down before the play started.

"There's been a change," he said. "The Gardners say we have to be in Charlotte Monday at 8 A.M. with the full $300,000."

"What?!"

I couldn't believe it. It was Friday night, and the banks were closed. We hadn't made any arrangements to get the money that quick, but Ed said if we weren't there at eight o'clock Monday morning with the money, the deal's off. They had another driver they wanted to sign that morning, and it was another chance for them to stick it to me.

"Ed, where are we going to get $300,000 before then?"

"I don't know," he said.

"I don't know either," I said, "but let me call Junior."

Johnson was very generous. "I can have $200,000 waiting on you at the bank. We'll call it an advance against your salary. I can get $100,000 and Pepsi can kick in $100,000. I'll have to call my buddies. I've got a friend at the bank, and he'll meet you at 8 A.M. But you're going to have to get your own $100,000."

I had already arranged for my share, but I had no idea I'd need it so soon.

Stevie and I ran through all of the options, and I finally said, "Honey, we don't have any choice. We're going to have to ask your dad to loan us the $100,000."

"We're not going to do that," she said. "There's no way. I'm not going to do that."

Her father had helped me a lot, but this was beyond the call of duty. We spent a miserable night in Louisville, and the next morning Stevie said, "OK, I'll call Dad." She told him the situation. He wanted me to get away from the Gardners as well, because he didn't like the way they had treated Stevie and me.

"I'll get in touch with a friend at the Owensboro National Bank and get it from the bank today. You'll have to come pick it up. I'll have it here when you get to the house." So we drove to Owensboro, picked up $100,000 from Frank, then drove back to Franklin late Sunday night. The next morning, Ed and I flew to Charlotte before sunrise and met Junior's banker with the $200,000. We walked across the street to the attorney's office and were sitting in the lobby with $300,000 at 8 A.M., as they had demanded.

It couldn't end that easily, of course. In the midst of the final settlement, we had come to an agreement on the amount and were ready to sign. Then the Gardners and their attorneys had one more surprise.

"There's one more thing," they said. "You're going to be in the Busch Clash [now called the Budweiser Shootout] next year, and you got into the race because you're driving our car. You'll probably win it, so we want half of the driver's share of that money as well."

They agreed to accept an additional $25,000. After we signed the agreement and we delivered the money, I walked out of the room a free man. Released!

Ricky Rudd was sitting in the lobby. He was the one they were going to sign to drive the car. He was in the same boat I was when I started driving for these folks. He had been running his own car, spending all of his own money, and here was a chance to drive the Gatorade car for DiGard. From the outside, it appeared to be a heck of a deal.

"I want to warn you of one thing," I said to him. "You're making the biggest mistake of your life."

I had invested $325,000 in my own future, and it was the best investment I ever made. They were right about one thing: I did win the Busch Clash in 1981. Teamed with Junior Johnson, I would win a whole lot more than that in the next six years.

Oh, by the way . . .

Ed Silva, Waltrip's attorney

Darrell's contract with DiGard was the first of its kind in NASCAR. I think the Gardners were smart enough to have the contract written in a way that gave them all the benefits, all the power and leverage. Once we were able to come to an agreement, Darrell and I went to dinner with Bill Gardner the night we signed the deal. A kind of "gentleman's dinner," I guess you could say.

"You won," Gardner said matter-of-factly. "Darrell Waltrip, only one per box." Darrell opened his jacket and leaned in like he was speaking into a hidden microphone. "Testing . . . testing . . . can you hear me in the truck?"

CONTINUED

Tom Higgins, motorsports reporter, the Charlotte Observer

My favorite memory of Darrell dates to April 8, 1979, the day he outdueled Richard Petty to win the Rebel 500 at Darlington Raceway. They swapped the lead four times on the last lap! It was a sensational finish that left all who saw it limp in excitement.

After night had fallen and a bright full moon was rising over the speedway, Darrell returned to the press box, where he had conducted the winner's interview a couple hours earlier. He looked out over the moonlit old track, spread his arms, and sang: "I'll see you in my dreams . . ."

13

Anybody but Waltrip

When the drivers are introduced before each race, you get a sense of how the fans really feel. Huge cheers, indifference, or loud booing—lemme tell ya, when you're up on that stage, one guy booing sounds a lot louder than 100 guys cheering. In the past few years, Jeff Gordon seems to be the one who gets booed more than anyone else. I don't know why. I never have understood it, but a lot of people tell me they think he's a little too perfect—too politically correct. Plus, if you were an Earnhardt fan, you weren't supposed to like Jeff. But Gordon never experienced the sort of booing and hatred I received throughout the middle of my career. I remember being introduced and hearing the boos wash over me like a huge bucket of cold water. I remember seeing T-shirts and signs with big hand-painted letters: "Anybody but Waltrip!" At various stages of their career, Gordon, Rusty Wallace, Earnhardt, and now Kurt Busch—they all had a taste of it. But ain't nobody had it as bad as me.

The signs, rude T-shirts, the booing, it was everywhere. One of the best was "I hate hot beer, cold women and Darrell Waltrip." People took their dislike of me to very creative levels. At the time, I didn't believe I had done anything wrong, but factors played into me becoming the bad guy in the eyes of a lot of fans. I downplay it now by saying I deserved it. I was a smart aleck and I deserved it, but it certainly went well beyond that.

I think it was Buddy Baker who said, "They'd boo Darrell driving down Interstate 77."

I tried not to let it get me down, because it did not affect my performance once I strapped on that helmet. That was my safe haven, inside the race car. The ones it really hurt were Stevie and my family. I hated it for them, and they suffered the most. It was ugly, and I can't begin to describe how bad it became. My poor wife would weep, my mom and dad would just about cry. That's what hurt me the most: Seeing them suffer tore my heart out.

Nobody wanted to walk down pit road with me. I could have caused a riot at any racetrack I wanted to in the early 1980s. I thought about walking down pit road and giving everybody the finger and then running! Just once. Bill France Jr. would have raised the catch fences around the tracks a lot sooner if I had done that.

I always waved at the fans on the parade lap. I always loved that from sprint car racing and in the Indy cars, when the drivers would give the fans a wave on the warm-up lap. It was cool, so I made darn sure I always did that as I was rolling off of turn four. Here I come, I've got my big ol' left hand out the window, waving to everybody. Some friends of mine were sitting in the grandstands next to a woman who said, "Look at that old SOB—even his *gloves* are dirty!" Hah! I had worn those gloves three times, maybe four times at the most. I always thought that was a funny line, but it showed that they were looking for any reason to dislike me.

During my first few years in Winston Cup, man, you talk about feeling like an outsider. . . . I felt like I was an intruder, an interloper into NASCAR. The fans thought so too. I didn't grow up in the NASCAR garage like Earnhardt did, or Richard and Kyle Petty, or Dale Jarrett and all those guys, and it was ridiculous. I wanted to scream, "C'mon! I'm from KENTUCKY!"

I wanted to come into the sport without waiting for someone to open the door for me. I didn't want to slip through a crack as the door opened slightly. I wanted to kick that door down, hinges and all. And I would tell everyone. Just like my days in Nashville, I took on the giants—the guys at the top of the hill. So if you were a fan of Richard Petty, you probably didn't like it when I told people he was stuck up or he was never helpful to me or . . . Well, you get the picture, because I would talk about any of those guys. I didn't care, and I wasn't afraid to speak up.

I think a lot of people in the stands and in the garage got the impression I was a rich kid. My family never had any money, but because my father-in-law did, and his company had been one of my first sponsors, they believed I never had to work a day in my life. My reputation was that I "bought" my way into the sport, which couldn't have been further from the truth. I wish I could have taken all of those people back to Franklin and let them talk with Wayne King, the banker who kept $100,000 or more worth of bad checks in his drawer. The poor guy, he never knew he was the best sponsor I ever had.

The fact that I argued and fought in public with NASCAR, other drivers, and even my own team made it worse. I was very open about it, because I had learned that the only way you got NASCAR's attention was through the media. If I had a problem with someone, I didn't go tell them, I would tell the media. If I was unhappy about something NASCAR did, I made a big deal out of it and the writers would put it in the paper. Those reporters must have loved being around me, because I was sure to say something that would upset someone. "Ohhh . . . call the editor, we got us another Waltrip doozy!"

In early 1977, I was disillusioned with the poor reliability of the engines and my car. I knew I could win as a driver, but my equipment was letting me down more often than not. When I had a car that would last, I was always in the fight for the win. By May the season was starting to heat up, and I had already won a few races, including my first superspeedway win at Darlington, where I drove through the debris of a big crash to pass Pearson, Petty, and Donnie Allison for the victory. When the three of them slowed to avoid junk on the track, I put my right foot down, and slid past them for the lead. The race ended under the yellow flag and I had my first superspeedway win.

Following the Darlington victory, we headed to Talladega. This was before there were restrictor plates on the engines, so we were really haulin' around that place. It was the era of the slingshot pass. You wanted to be in a position behind the leader, because you could get a run in his slipstream and slingshot past into the lead. That afternoon, I managed to get out in front far enough that I broke the draft of the cars behind me. While Cale Yarborough, Benny Parsons, and Donnie Allison were battling each other, I slipped away and won the race. This did not sit well with Mr. Yarborough. He was mad because he didn't win with the fastest car.

"Waltrip was lucky," he spouted. "He probably had only the fourth-best car out there today."

The reporters were happy to tell me what Cale had said.

"If I had the fourth-best car," I said, "then I must have won because of superior driving ability." Score one for Waltrip.

Ohhh, that really made Cale mad. As the summer progressed, the war of words escalated. He and I were battling for the lead in the points, and we were battling for the attention of the media. I mean, the reporters would almost sprint, going back and forth as he and I tried to top each other.

By the time we got to Darlington on Labor Day weekend, it had become a regular duel on and off the track. At the Southern 500, Cale and I had a great race going. We were clearly the two best cars, and we traded the lead back and forth. With more than 100 laps left, I got a little too aggressive. I made a mistake and ended up running into Cale, as well as D. K. Ulrich and Terry Bivins, who were innocent bystanders in the battle between me and Cale. I should have been more patient, but I wasn't, and it cost us both a shot at the win. Yarborough ended up fifth and I was sixth, but we were both more than five laps behind the winner, David Pearson.

After the race, Ulrich wanted to know why Cale had run into him.

"I didn't hit you!" Cale said. "It was Jaws!"

"Who?" asked Ulrich.

"Jaws Waltrip!" Cale said.

The movie *Jaws* had been a huge hit, and I'm sure Cale didn't know at the time what he had created. The media was all over it, and suddenly I became "Jaws."

That nickname stuck to me for many years, and it meant I needed a response to Cale. But I had to pick the right time, and it took a few weeks to develop.

The race at Martinsville at the end of September was held on one of the hottest, muggiest days I've ever seen at the Virginia short track. Cale won the race, but he was whining afterward about how tired he was, how the length of the race needed to be changed, and on and on.

The next week, we went to North Wilkesboro, where I beat Cale for the win. We were the only two cars to finish on the lead lap. I had my chance, and I was ready with my return volley.

I rated the race as a 1.5 or a 2.0 on the "Cale Scale," a new measure I had invented to judge how difficult a particular race was and how much whining Cale was going to do. I was bold enough to suggest that the heat and humidity had nothing do with Cale's troubles, but that his advancing age was responsible. Cale used to get really red in the face when he was mad, and I thought his head was gonna explode, because it was about as red as I've ever seen it. It was like a cartoon: You could almost see the red creeping up his neck and right up his face.

The next race was at Charlotte Motor Speedway, where Humpy Wheeler was the promoter. He's still known as the best in the business at publicity stunts and inventive ways to capture the attention of the fans. Humpy knew an opportunity when he saw it, and this was a golden chance to promote his event. Humpy brought in a shark—a real shark—and put it in the back of a truck. Then he had a big chicken stuffed into the mouth of the shark! Cale's sponsor was Holly Farms, the chicken producers. He had someone drive this truck around the garage area. It was the funniest thing anyone had seen in a long time—at least the people who were upwind from that darn shark. Whew, that thing reeked something bad! I'm sure if he did that kind of thing now, all of the animal rights people would have a fit. But man, that was a stroke of genius.

After that, the season didn't go as I had hoped. I hurt my shoulder in an IROC practice crash, and then it became worse when a donkey stepped on the same shoulder. Yeah, a donkey. I was doing a promotion for Winston, some sorta goofy donkey race. I fell off, and the darn thing stepped on me. Cale loved that.

Yarborough had the last laugh that year, as he won the championship with Junior Johnson's team, while I ended up fourth in points with six victories. And the booing continued to grow every week.

I had a hard shell, and once I strapped that helmet on, I didn't care if they didn't like me. I couldn't understand how I could be as dominating as I was, doing what I was doing with a race car, and yet nobody liked it. They didn't appreciate it. That was the thing that really hurt me, the fact that I was on the racetrack kicking butt and people didn't like it. I tried to understand why people were booing me, but the lack of respect was the thing that was hardest for me to accept. It's like an entertainer with fans who loved the music but booed when they went to the concert. In order to deal with it, I'd act like it didn't bother me, or I'd make some wisecrack before my brain was in gear.

The most famous of those mouth-before-brain moments was in 1983. That was an awful year for me for many reasons. A low point was when I dropped out of the race at Charlotte and a huge roar, a great cheer, went up. The crowd was celebrating that I had blown up. I got out of the car and made a comment about "meet me in the Big K parking lot! We'll settle it there!" And I sure didn't mean meet me there for an autograph session! I was mad, frustrated with dropping out of the race. Once I cooled down, I understood how people failed to appreciate my poor attempt at humor.

■□

This is the perfect time to point out that I'm not a fighter. I've been in only a couple of fights my entire life. I'm like every race car driver I have ever known: We are bad to the bone when we are behind the wheel of that car, but outside the car, we are the fastest to turn a 180 and get out of there before a fight breaks out (except A. J. Foyt). The wimpiest guys in the world are always mouthy when they are in that race car, but they get out and they are like "Oh, golly gee, sorry 'bout that!"

To win as a driver, you have to have a certain state of mind. You become Superman when you get in that car. I am the Man of Steel. I can dodge bullets if my car is handling well. You can't be afraid to use what we called "the chrome horn" to move someone out of the way. This was when we still had chrome bumpers on the front of the car.

Earnhardt was that way, maybe the best (or the worst, whichever way you want too look at it). He said, "they wouldn't have called 'em bumpers if you weren't supposed to use 'em." But he was no fighter; he was what I call a "mouther." He'd mouth off or knock you around on the racetrack. He was such a big old grouch at the track, and you'd think sooner or later he was going to knock somebody out. But, as many times as I watched him put somebody in the fence on the racetrack (me included), I never saw him get in a fight. He was really a big ol' teddy bear when he was outside of the car.

The thing that irritated me the most, the thing that made me most angry at Earnhardt, was his knack of blatantly crashing you, then somehow making you feel like it was your fault. Like you happened to be in his way. It would make me so mad, but then I'd end up thinking, "Well, *did* I do something?" I hated that. People loved him or hated him, but I don't think the Intimidator ever got booed more than me in my bad ol' days. I don't know if I'm bragging or complaining about that fact.

Oh, by the way . . .

■ ■ □ □ ■

Humpy Wheeler, president and general manager, Lowe's (née Charlotte) Motor Speedway

Every once in a while, I try to put a little levity into this very serious business, and I thought "Hmm . . . maybe we can come up with something funny here and take a little of the seriousness out of the whole thing."

We got in touch with Captain Poo McLaughlin, who was a commercial fisherman out of Little River, South Carolina. I asked Poo to catch the biggest shark he could and bring it up to the speedway.

The shark he caught weighed about 200 pounds, and he brought it in the back of a pickup truck, iced down. When qualifying time came, I had a wrecker go get the shark, raise it up on the hook, and stick a chicken in the shark's mouth, letting half of the chicken hang out. He put the whole rig next to the qualifying board near the garage area, which was where everybody went on pole day.

CONTINUED

It turned out to be pretty funny, although I do recall Cale getting a bit upset about it. After the shark hung there for about two hours, things began to smell pretty bad. It drove everybody away from the qualifying board, but we left it there until qualifying was over and then disposed of it properly.

14

![decorative divider]

Junior Johnson

Junior Johnson is NASCAR's living folk legend. He was there in the beginning of the sport. He turned to the racetrack after being in and out of jail for running moonshine. He tore it up as a driver in the 1950s and '60s, earning his reputation as the hardest of the hard chargers. He won the Daytona 500 in 1960 because he discovered something we take for granted now: the aerodynamic draft. By running closely behind one or more cars, his car could slice through the air easier and turn faster lap times. He won that race by using the draft, then making a slingshot move at the end of the race to beat cars that were much faster than his.

Thomas Wolfe, who wrote *The Right Stuff* and *Bonfire of the Vanities,* wrote a story about Junior for *Esquire* magazine in the mid-'60s. Wolfe called him "The Last American Hero," and eventually it was turned into a movie of the same name, starring Jeff Bridges as Junior. Bruce Springsteen wrote about him in the song "Cadillac Ranch." Some people called him the Legend of Ingle Hollow, referring to his shop nestled in the mountains of Wilkes County, North Carolina.

He won 50 races as a driver, then became a team owner and won another 139 races. When NASCAR celebrated its 50th anniversary in 1997, he was named one of the 50 greatest drivers in stock car racing's history. As a businessman, Junior brought R. J. Reynolds and NASCAR together, although he had intended to sell the tobacco company a sponsorship for his team, not a package for the entire series.

I'll never forget being a kid, dreaming of race cars and listening to races on the radio. It was always Junior Johnson driving the white number 3, a '63 Chevrolet with a 427 mystery engine.

"Man, this guy's got to be the coolest in the world!" I thought. "He's got a 427 Chevrolet and there ain't no such thing!" A 409 was the biggest motor I'd ever heard of, but he had a 427 Chevrolet *mystery* engine. I thought, "Wow! What a cool guy!"

If it was a 400-mile race, he would win. If it was a 500-mile race, it seemed like the 427 would blow up every time. But he never took it easy. He didn't believe in taking it easy. If you drove for him, you'd better not do anything but hammer it. He'd say, "If it breaks, I'll fix it."

As a driver and an owner, he would rather lead a single lap and blow up than hang around in fifth place. It was "go or blow." But, despite the all-or-nothing attitude, he had developed a deep understanding of the quest for championships. His team won three consecutive Winston Cup titles in 1976–78 with Cale Yarborough. We won three more when I came aboard.

I always wanted to win every race, because if you won, you were the hero and you got your name in the paper. If I didn't win, I'd just as soon go home early. Junior taught me about taking a longer view. But his cars were so good, it was the best of both worlds: I could think championship and also win a lot of races.

Junior chose me because I was a hot shoe and I fit the mold he had for drivers. I was the right age at the right time. Junior had Leroy Yarborough when Leroy was hot. He got Cale when Cale was hot. And he had me when I was hot. It was classic Junior—he told me one time he wants a driver to be "in his late 29s or early 30s!" Figure that out? That's what he told me one time, and I laughed so hard.

I started in Winston Cup in 1972 with my own team because it was my passion. I had to do it myself because I didn't like people telling me what to do. I was more than broke when I signed with DiGard. I hated driving for them, because they controlled everything. I was surrounded by some of the greatest talent in NASCAR history, but as a team we had no leadership and no togetherness. I was just a driver, and I didn't want to be just a driver. I wanted to be THE driver, and driving for Junior gave me that opportunity.

When I heard Junior wanted me to drive for him, my confidence soared. To have him pick me to drive his car was the ultimate boost for me. A validation of what I had believed all along—that I was the best driver out there.

After all of the drama with the DiGard contract, it was refreshing to sign with Junior. It was a simple, one-page deal. When Ed Silva and I went to negotiate the final deal, if we needed to add or change something, a li'l old guy would take the contract, walk out of the room, and make changes with an antique manual typewriter. He'd hunt and peck, taking forever.

It was very simple for Junior. "I don't want no excuses," he said. "I'll give you the best car and everything you need to win. You'll drive it, and you better win!"

Silva asked, "What are you going to do for Darrell if he wins the championship?"

Junior sat and stared at Ed for a second.

"I'll tell ya what I'm going to do to him if he don't."

The first time I came to his shop as the new driver, I was eager and anxious to please. It turned into one of my daughter Sarah's favorite stories. We were getting ready to take the car to Martinsville, Virginia, for a test, and I said, "What can I do to help? Tell me what I can do!" I wanted to show the team I was willing to do whatever it took.

Junior has a thick mountain accent, and he said "Boy, ya see them thar tires over there?" He pointed at a stack of about 40 tires mounted on green wheels. (I had moved from Gatorade green to Mountain Dew green.) "Go over there and bounce them tires." Coming out of his mouth, it sounded like "tars."

The tires then were different than they are now. They didn't have an inner liner, so you'd fill them with air and bounce 'em once or twice hard on the ground, just to make sure the tire was sealed against the rim.

I was going to be the best darn tire bouncer the world has ever seen, and I bounced the daylights out of those things! One after another . . . Boing! Boing! Higher and higher. One or two got away from me, and they rolled down the hill. Another one got away and hit one of the trucks parked outside. They were all over the place. It looked like a tire truck had tipped over.

Junior walked out of the shop and yelled at me. "Boy, what in the world are you doin'?"

"Junior! I'm bouncin' these tires like you asked me!"

"Boy, have you lost your mind?" he asked. He turned and pointed at a tire-balancing machine in the corner of the shop. "See that machine over there? I said *balance* those tires!"

I loved driving for Junior, because he was a racer. He was one of the best drivers ever, and there's something different about driving for somebody like that. He had a family operation; he did things the way I would have. It was like driving for your dad or your grandfather, a part of the family, ya know? He did it the way he wanted, with his shop behind his house. You know, he'd get up in the morning, eat breakfast, walk out to the garage, and his guys were already out there working. His shop wasn't big and fancy, but it was very practical. The garage wasn't his secret to success; the key was always thinking ahead of his time, far ahead of everybody else.

Junior's cars were the best out there, and they complemented what I had already learned. His cars were good enough that I didn't have to worry about them blowing up every week. There were several times when I was more than a lap ahead of the field, and I'd decide, "OK, I'm kinda comfortable here, and there's only 10 laps to go. I'm gonna take a break and breathe a little bit here."

He'd come on the radio. "Boy, you ain't laying down on me, are ya?"

I'd snap to attention! "No! No, Junior!"

"You better not slow down," he'd say.

We had a lot of fun together. We named the cars, and the Buick we took to Daytona in 1981 was called "Kermit." I had a little Kermit the Frog plastic toy that I'd carry in the car just for fun. Every year at Daytona they take the official pictures of the car and driver for that season, and Kermit is right there in the grass beside me in all of those pictures. He's hard to see in the green grass, but he's there.

The first year I drove for Junior, I won 12 races and my first Winston Cup championship. The next year, I won the championship and 12 more races. In two years, I racked up stats that would make a great career: two championships, 24 victories, and 18 poles. This was when we were running only 30 events each year. I was winning almost half the races, and we weren't winning by just a few inches, either. We were dominating.

How dominating? If you took my results from only those two years, I would be in the top 25 in all-time Winston Cup victories and pole positions.

Those two years were as close to perfect as it gets, the most perfect years of my career. It was my time to shine, and I was able to take advantage. I won a lot of other races in my career, but I was never completely satisfied except those two seasons. It was the best feeling in the world. Whatever there was to win, I won it.

You know you're in "the zone" when nobody can beat you. It didn't make any difference where I qualified. I knew if nobody wrecked me or something didn't break, I was gonna win the race. That's when you know it's your time. Occasionally, something would break or something strange happened to stop us, but it was more of a surprise to me than winning. In fact, some of the crew guys eventually stopped coming to Victory Lane. They just wanted to load up the truck and go home. That's how much we expected to win. It wasn't that we didn't enjoy it, but we took it as the way it ought to be.

As an athlete, you are a part of teams all your life, and you may not win a thing no matter how hard you try if the team isn't right. Then you get with the right team and you're in the Super Bowl or the Final Four. You've got the ring. That's the timing thing, and I had joined the right team at the right time.

Talk about getting booed! Oooh, it got worse and worse. When I signed to drive for Junior, I was already a guy who told everybody how great I was—like stock car racing's version of Muhammad Ali. Now I was sticking it down their throat every time I won. Being in Junior's car made it worse. The fans felt like he had an unfair advantage and NASCAR played favorites for him. No matter what the fans said, once I started driving for Junior, I was thrilled to finally have a team that matched my desire to win. But Junior could still make me livid sometimes.

Cale Yarborough had driven for him for so long, Junior would call me "Cale" on the radio out of habit. He'd say things like "Ten-four, Cale." I would get all bowed up, and my lap times would improve by a tenth of a second or more. He saw that, so he began calling me Cale on purpose. He'd be standing in the pits during a race, and he'd turn to Jeff Hammond, the crew chief, and say, "Watch this . . ." He'd push the talk button on his radio: "Cale, you ain't layin' down on me, are ya?" Awww man, I'd get angry about that.

One of our most memorable radio conversations was at Pocono during the July 1986 race. I'd won Pocono several times, and we had always been good there. It was one of those days where you could see rain clouds inching closer and closer. I was going down the back straightaway, and I could see the rain coming toward the tunnel turn, which is at the opposite end of the track from the pit area, so I had a much better view than Junior did. Around and around we go, and I watched that big cloud get closer every lap.

"Durrll, pit next time by," Junior said.

"Junior," I said. "Man, I don't think that's a good idea. I don't know if you can see it or not, but it's getting ready to rain over here on the back straightaway." I thought we should stay on the track, then grab the victory when the rain came in and ended the race early.

"Durrrll, PIT next time by," he said.

"Junior, you ain't listening to me!" I said. "I'm telling ya, you need to look over at the tunnel turn. It's getting ready to rain back here!"

"Boy, I ain't gonna tell you again," he said. "I want you to pit that car next time by."

"Well, you fat son-of-a-bitch!" I yelled. "You oughta look over here, 'cuz it's going to rain!"

"What did I just say?" I thought. "Ooohhh . . . I should not have said that!" It wasn't even out of my mouth before I started to panic. I may have found the fastest way to get fired from the greatest ride I ever had.

"What did you say, boy?" he said.

I never said another word. The next time by, I brought that baby down the pit lane. The race was called for rain after 150 of a scheduled 200 laps. Tim Richmond was the winner, and we finished fourth.

The next morning, Junior called Hammond into his office.

"Jeff, let me ask you something. Did you hear him call me a fat SOB yesterday?"

"No. I never heard anything like that," Jeff replied. "I don't think that was us. I would have remembered if it was."

"I swear I heard him call me a fat SOB," Junior said.

"Naw," Jeff said. "That must have been some interference from somebody else's radio."

Phew! Hammond saved me. That was the moment I knew I had to take care of him the rest of his life. He couldn't wait to call me and say, "I saved your butt! You would be looking for a job today if it wasn't for me. You're lucky you were right about the rain, or I never woulda spoken up for ya."

◼◻◼

You know about David Wells, the baseball player, who admitted in his book that he pitched a perfect game while he was drunk? Well, I never raced when I was drunk, but I can tell you that when I drove for Junior and Budweiser sponsored us, there were a few Saturday nights when we were their best customers. We used to joke that we had 'em working nights at the brewery just to keep up with us. I might have started a few races with a hangover, but never, ever drunk. Tim Brewer, Hammond, and I, with Junior right in the middle of all of us—we were a bunch of characters, and add a few cold ones, well, it could get crazy.

We partied hard, but we worked harder. Junior was always two or three moves ahead of everyone else. He was like a chess master who knew his opponent's moves before they made them. Junior knew this sport is "monkey see, monkey do." And lemme tell ya, he was always the lead monkey.

He would think of things nobody else could. Some of the things he created drove NASCAR crazy. He would do things nobody had ever seen, like putting a rev kit inside the engine. A rev limiter is part of the engine's ignition system, and when the engine revved to a dangerous level, the limiter would adjust the ignition. The engines would last longer, and you could push it to the edge because you knew you had a system that stopped you from over-revving it. It wasn't illegal, because no one else ever had a rev kit. He ran that forever.

He bought parts from a long list of vendors. He'd buy stacks of things from companies that made pistons, rods, any part you could imagine. Here was the catch: The bigger pieces of junk the parts were, the more he'd buy! He had a whole warehouse of stuff he never used. While he was buying stuff from other people, he would make his own pistons, he would make his own rods, he would make his own cranks.

"What the— Why is he doing that?" I'd wonder.

Turns out he knew the moment he ordered 50 sets of junk pistons, the vendor would turn right around and tell the other teams, "Junior Johnson just bought fifty sets of pistons from us!"

"He's getting his pistons from you?" the other teams

would say. "Wow, we'd better have some too. If Junior is buyin' 'em, gimme twenty sets!"

He would buy useless stuff from people so his competitors would think they were getting the good stuff, while he was making superior parts in his own shop. And whippin' the field every Sunday.

Somehow he managed to come out ahead even when his designs didn't work. He made a manifold called the Junior Johnson Box Manifold. He actually invested a lot of money. But for some reason, it just wasn't right. He paid to have them manufactured, but they were so bad that he couldn't use them on his own cars. The Edelbrock manifold was the best at that time, so he used those. But he took the Edelbrock and hid it inside the cover of the Junior Johnson model. Suddenly, everyone wanted one because they thought that's what Junior was running.

■ ■□■

I began the 1981 season, my first with Junior, as a happy cat. I left behind the turmoil of DiGard for a team whose guys actually liked each other. NASCAR had new rules for the size of the cars that year—"downsizing" was the term, I believe—so we built 11 new Buicks.

We won the pole at the first race of the year at Riverside, establishing immediately that we were the combination to beat. Mechanical problems knocked us out at Riverside and Daytona, but we won in our third race at Richmond, and backed it up immediately with a win at Rockingham.

It was a roller-coaster ride for the first half of the season: We'd win or we'd blow up. I'd seen this movie before, and it started to look familiar. After 14 races, I was behind Bobby Allison by 341 points.

Junior was different from my previous team owners. He didn't get discouraged, he dug in deeper. He always tried new things early in the year, and if they didn't work, he'd fix or improve them, so as the season went along, we'd get better and better. We were building cars as fast as we could. After each race, Junior would call me or come over to the shop and ask about the new chassis. If we won or were a top-five car, I'd say, "Yeah, that's a good one." If it didn't handle well, I'd say so, and he would be on the phone immediately with Ralph Seagraves, the sports marketing guy at Winston.

"Ralph," he'd say. "I got another show car ready for you."

Junior would just get rid of them if they weren't up to our expectations, and Winston soon had a shiny fleet of Buick show cars to take to grocery stores across the land. I'd drive 'em on Sunday, and if they weren't up to our standards, they'd be in a Kroger parking lot on Monday.

Imagine how the crew felt after they had worked so hard, building those cars by hand. They were working overtime, building an entire new car every 10 to 12 days. Then I'd say "Naw . . ." and Junior would get rid of it. I think that created a lot of tension at first, but we were all committed to winning the championship.

Allison had a huge lead in the points, but a return to Riverside gave us a chance to win on the road course. We started chipping away at the points. I was working my mouth overtime, trying to get under the skin of Bobby and his team, owned by Harry Ranier. As we got closer and closer, I could sense it—a feeling they were crumbling like I had in 1979 when I crashed at Darlington. The cracks were showing, and I was filled with the belief that I was going to win my first Winston Cup championship.

We won at Bristol, and the point margin was only 50 points. Allison could definitely hear the footsteps behind him, or, if not the footsteps, certainly my mouth. In late September, we finished second at Dover and closed to within two points. If I was a bettin' man, I would have flown to Vegas that night and placed a bet on the number 11 team. We were going to be champions.

The next month was incredible. No other car won a pole position, and no other car pulled into Victory Lane. We had a clean sweep four weeks in a row at Martinsville, North Wilkesboro, Charlotte, and Rockingham. It's still a NASCAR record, winning four straight from the pole. There were only two races left, and we were leading by 68 points. I wasn't going to blow it like I had before. Our bid for five in a row was stopped by Neil Bonnett at Atlanta, but we were second. At the last race of the season, all I had to do was keep Bobby in sight, and even though he won the race, we finished sixth and the title was ours. The comeback from 341 points behind is a Winston Cup record.

The celebration for the champion used to be held in Daytona, but this was the year NASCAR and Winston decided the proper place to honor the champion was in New York City. It was in one of the smaller banquet rooms of the Waldorf-Astoria, but it was a great week for me, as I did the tour of all the top television and radio shows in New York. All season, we had been focused on winning the championship. Junior wanted to be the first team owner to celebrate the title in New York City, and every decision, every move we made, was with that goal in mind. Since he was the one who brought Winston into the sport, in a sense giving up what was going to be his team's sponsorship so Winston could sponsor the entire series, it always meant a lot to him to win their money. It was special to me as well, because it fulfilled a dream I had been pursuing since the days I sat next to Granny at the dirt track. I knew I could be a champion, and now it had come true.

Before the 1982 season began, we lost some of the key players on the team. Other teams were stepping up and offering a lot of money to Junior's people. Crew chief Tim Brewer, fabricator Eddie Thrap, and engine builder Harold Elliott left for big cash to work with the M. C. Anderson team, where Cale was the driver. They were the latest in a series of guys Junior had trained and molded before watching them leave for the highest bidder. He said he was done training crew chiefs only to see them leave, so he named himself as crew chief. Junior was qualified for sure, but it was a disaster. When we needed a decision on a key item, we couldn't find him. He'd be off with his dogs, hunting or fishing somewhere.

It got so bad that I finally went to Junior to convince him we needed someone in charge, especially when he was gone. The best candidate was Jeff Hammond. Hammond had been with Junior for years, and he was qualified to do the job. I think some people thought he was crazy to accept the offer, especially after we stubbornly fought each other for much of 1981, but we ended up making a great combination.

Junior always said, "You don't have to be a good boss if you hire the right people," and in this case, he was right. Hammond really began to understand me, and I trusted him more and more.

Battling against Bobby Allison for the championship was special. Allison was tenacious, probably the most tenacious and persistent guy I ever raced against. When I was starting off in my career, I learned a lot from him. But he'd get really mad when someone beat him. Bobby knew how much he was cheating, so if we were faster, then he figured we must have been cheating more! Bobby's son Davey became a great driver himself before he was killed in a helicopter accident in 1993. My favorite Davey Allison story took place when he was just a skinny teenager.

We were in Riverside, California, for the final race of 1982, and I was 22 points ahead of Bobby for the championship. I was driving a brand-new road-course car Junior had built, and it drove like a dream. It was so good, we won the pole position by almost a full second. Bobby and I always had a huge rivalry, and I think he disliked Junior as much as he disliked me. Bobby was in the DiGard Gatorade car (he replaced Ricky Rudd in the car after only one season), so he was with the team I'd left behind. Add those factors together, and emotions were running high. Here I was, going for my second title against a guy I had looked up to when I was younger. Early in my career, I slept on the floor of Allison's shop in Alabama, helping out while I trying to learn everything I could. Now he was my toughest competitor.

Our car was inside the garage the night before the race, while Junior, Hammond, and I were standing outside, chatting and leaning against stacks of tires. I didn't notice at first, but Junior peeked around the garage door as Davey was walking around our car, rubbing the fenders with his hand.

Junior slipped behind the kid, took his big ol' left arm, and picked up Davey around the neck. Davey's feet were dangling, and Junior discovered he was holding a magnet. Everybody was saying our car had a trick aluminum body on it, so Bobby sent Davey with a magnet to find out if it was true. Junior never let go, and carried him right out of the garage to the NASCAR truck. He sat him down and scared Davey half to death. He was almost in tears. Bill Gazaway of NASCAR told him if he ever did anything like that again they would never let him back in the garage.

It was a memorable race, because I won the championship by finishing third behind Tim Richmond and Ricky Rudd. I loved Riverside, but it could be a tricky place if you didn't stay on the track. It wasn't like an oval where you'd smash into a wall or guardrail; it was mostly sand and gravel on the edge of the track. If you went off the track, the rocks would stick like glue to the hot tires. You didn't even have to make a big mistake, just miss a little bit and dip a tire off into the gravel. A lot of times, you'd pick up a rock and puncture a tire. It was easy to do.

Bobby knew he had to finish ahead of me to win the championship, and he was all over the place, overdriving the car. He cut something like five tires that day, and fell farther and farther behind. He finished 16th, nine laps behind me.

After the race, we're celebrating, but Bobby, woohoo, he was angry. He had an awful day and lost the championship. One of the reporters asked, "Bobby, what's up with all the flat tires?"

"About the only thing I can think of is Junior Johnson must've had one of them Wilkes County sharpshooters up there in one of those corners shooting my tires out," Bobby said.

The reporter couldn't wait to find Junior.

"Junior!" he shouted. "Allison said you had a sharpshooter in the corners shooting his tires out today."

Junior stared at him and says, "That shows how smart that SOB is. If I had anybody out there, they wouldn't have been shooting at his *tires*!" Of course, with Junior's drawl, it sounded like "tars."

Oh, by the way . . .

Jeff Hammond, crew chief

I became the crew chief in 1982 after we lost three of our key guys. They left for more money, and I might have been crazy to take the job, but I was offered a chance to be crew chief for Junior Johnson. Of course, I was going to accept the job. "Let's show 'em," I said. "We don't need those other guys." I don't think I have ever had so much fun as that season. I had never worked so hard, but it felt great to match the results from the year before.

15

Finding My Faith

I was hard to work with, because I am a perfectionist. I have a drive to be perfect. I get disappointed in people if I feel they don't share the same passion or if they aren't as enthusiastic or committed as me. Most of the time, I'm a people person and I love everybody. But if you're on my team and you're not totally with me, then you must be against me. One thing my mom and dad taught me is you had to work hard, so I gauge people on their work ethic. That's one thing I always admired about Earnhardt. He was a hard worker, and he instilled that in his kids. That is the same way my dad was. He didn't have a lot, but he taught me that if you were willing to work, you can accomplish anything.

When I started winning races in Winston Cup, I developed an attitude where I believed the car had to be perfect. Everything had to be perfect. If that's the way your mind works, you're probably going to be a miserable son of a gun, and I was miserable a lot of the time. Even when I won, it wasn't good enough. I'd climb out of the car and celebrate, but I'd think, "I shoulda won by more." When I didn't win, it was because somebody else didn't do their job. The crew chief screwed up or a motor blew up or the pit stops were junk. It was always something. It wasn't me, because it couldn't be me. I was so committed to what I was doing that it couldn't be me. It had to be somebody else. That's how I was, and it made it very difficult for people to work with me. Only a few people could ever understand the way I was.

Jeff Hammond hated me when we met. He'll tell ya, just ask him. He'll be happy to tell you. He thought I was the world's biggest smart aleck—a cocky know-it-all. Jeff worked for Junior's team when I was hired. This team won three straight championships with Cale, and I came in and said, "These cars are dog meat. I don't know how a man drove these stupid things. These are the worst cars I've ever seen."

"Who do you think you are?!" he asked me. "We won three championships with this junk. How many have you won?"

I don't blame him. He was proud of the success with Cale, and he and I knocked heads for much of the 1981 season.

"I can't believe you won with this stuff," I said. "Somebody could get hurt. Look at all this rust. I'd better get a tetanus shot before I get in one of these."

I hated it. I'd always find fault with everything.

"Yeah, that's really nice, *but* . . ." Or "That's really cool, *but* . . ."

That's how I was—and still am in some ways. I tried to be perfect, and I really had to work hard to overcome it, because it was making me, and the people around me, miserable.

The biggest thing that helped me overcome this attitude was my faith. I was spiritually bankrupt. If you have ever been bankrupt, financially or spiritually, then you know what I'm talking about. If you're bankrupt, it means you must have had whatever it was at one time. It took some time for me to find my spirituality. I thought I had to overcome a lot to get in touch with the Lord and in touch with Christian people. It was a massive struggle to take the smallest focus away from thinking about race cars. It was a struggle to consider other people. I was so afraid that if my personal life got better, my professional life would suffer. It was always a fear.

All I knew was to keep my nose to the grindstone. If I didn't do it my way, the way it had to be done, then I wouldn't be successful. If I didn't have my hand on it or couldn't keep my arms around it, then I was going to have to rely on other people. And relying on others meant I wouldn't be successful. That's how I felt, and I didn't give it up easily.

Early in our marriage, Stevie had a miscarriage. We tried in vain for seven years to get pregnant again, until finally Stevie found out she was pregnant. We told our parents, but we wanted to wait awhile to tell everyone else. I won the Busch Clash at Daytona, and I got so excited after the race, I told the media, "I don't want to talk about this race. I'm gonna be a dad!"

Before Stevie was born, her mom had taken a prescription drug that affected Stevie's reproductive tract, and it caused us to suffer miscarriages. Four months into the pregnancy, we lost the baby. That was the deepest sadness, the deepest grief, I ever felt. I had told the world, and then we lost the baby.

In 1981, Stevie began trying to get us in a church somewhere, but I was stubborn.

"Honey, I can't go to church," I'd whine. I thought of a lot of excuses. "I'm never home. I'm gone every Sunday. How am I going to go to church? I don't feel like going to church when I'm home. When I'm home, I wanna do something relaxing."

Leonard and Ann Isaacs were our good friends. Leonard was president of the bank where we did business, but, more important, he and Ann were good Christian folks. They told Stevie about a church they were attending. It was a new church started by a minister, Dr. Cortez Cooper. It was a breakaway from the big Presbyterian church in Nashville, and they were meeting at Hillsboro High School on Wednesday nights.

I was always home on Wednesday night, so my "Sunday" argument lost a lot of its impact.

Stevie and I started going to the high school each week. Dr. Cooper turned out to be an incredible friend, teacher, and man of God. He connected with me like no one had. During his sermons, he wouldn't be talking directly to me, but I thought he was. He was pushing all the right buttons. I felt accepted in that setting.

I'll never forget a hot July night in the cafeteria. They had no air-conditioning, and it was so hot, it was like being in hell. That's how I felt. As usual, every word Dr. Cooper spoke felt like it was aimed at me. He was talking about people that were good. People like me. You know, I'm a good guy. I've always been a good guy. But good guys go to hell if they don't know Jesus. If you don't know him as your Lord, then you go to hell. Just being a good guy doesn't qualify you for anything. There's no trophy or championship. There is no reward for being a good guy. Thankfully, there is a reward for anyone, good or bad, that asks for forgiveness from the Lord. Eternal life with Christ is the greatest reward, the biggest trophy.

That night in 1983, I was in the midst of a time where nothing was going right. It was a terrible year. I lost the championship and had a number of serious crashes. I almost killed Phil Parsons at Talladega when I got into him and he went flipping down the front straightaway into the first turn. I had a bad wreck of my own as I came off of turn four during the Daytona 500. There wasn't an inside wall there then, so I backed into a dirt bank, then shot across the racetrack into the outside wall in front of the oncoming traffic. I nearly got T-boned in the driver's door. It was as bad as any crash I'd had at that time, and it was the first crash that ever sent me to the hospital. I spent a night in the ICU, and to this day I don't remember anything about racing the next weekend at Richmond, even though I won the pole, led the most laps, and finished third.

It was an awful year, and I was feeling vulnerable. I didn't know where to turn—until I heard Dr. Cooper giving the message of salvation. He got me back on course. He prayed for me and helped me put the focus on something other than myself. He really helped me, and I turned around in a short period of time. He and his wife ate dinner with Stevie and me many times. He ministered to me and treated me like a son. He cared for me and loved me when I wasn't very lovable, which is how Jesus acted. I was able to ask Jesus into my heart. From that point forward, my life began to change.

My brother Michael and I weren't as close as we should have been at that time. We had 16 years between us, and when he won what is now known as the Goody's Dash series in 1983, he wanted to move to Charlotte and give NASCAR a shot. But because I was so busy, I didn't have much time or energy to offer him. He became good buddies with Kyle Petty, and ended up moving in for a time with the Petty family. For me, moving in with the Pettys was like sleeping with the enemy, but it was a sign of how singular-minded my life was and how strained my relationships had become. I had a lot of catching up to do.

Things were better for me in 1984, and I was really back on top of my game in 1985, winning the championship for the third time. But we had a third miscarriage that year, which made the championship seem much less important than the first two.

Before the start of the 1986 season, I was sitting in my

den one Saturday, drinking a Budweiser and watching a ball game. I looked out the window, and here comes Dr. Cooper and four deacons from the church.

I ran into the kitchen and dumped out the Bud, grabbed a Pepsi, then ran back to my chair.

"What are ya'll doin' here?" I asked.

"We came by for a little visit," Dr. Cooper started. "We're worried about you."

"What are you worried about me for?" I laughed. "I just won the championship. I'm feeling pretty good about myself. I'm in pretty good shape. I'm not where I need to be yet, but I'm not bad."

"We're worried about you because you have to get out of that Budweiser car," he said soberly.

"Do *what*?!" I chuckled. "Ya gotta be kiddin! That's the best ride in NASCAR. I'm driving for Junior Johnson, the best owner. I've got the best sponsor, Budweiser. They're great! Do you know what people would do to be in this situation?"

"It's not right for you," he said calmly. "All of the things you want to be and all things you say you want to do, then you can't drive a car with that sponsor."

"Well, boys, ya'll just don't understand our sport," I said. "That's not the way it works. That's Junior's car. I drive for Junior. If he says the sponsor is Budweiser, we're going to be sponsored by Budweiser. Ya'll are just gonna have to get used to that."

"We're going to pray you out of that car," he replied.

"Please don't do that!" I begged. "Whatever you do, don't start that!"

◼◻

Stevie says she's been married to two men with the same name. The transition wasn't easy for me. I was self-ish, self-centered, and self-serving—everything you want to name. But finding the Lord meant I wanted to give back instead of just taking, become a servant instead of being served. I started mending damage I had done for many years. I soothed the feelings I had hurt and mended a lot of broken relationships. That was the biggest difference for me. My life improved. My relationships improved, and my marriage improved. It took me 10 years of marriage before I really learned what it meant to be a husband.

The "two men with the same name" comment shot right to the heart of the matter. The day Jessica was born was the most life-changing experience I've had.

Stevie got pregnant in December of 1986. (If you notice, many of the drivers' wives get pregnant in the off-season.) When we found out she was pregnant, we were on a list to adopt a child. We had to decide if we were prepared to go forward with the adoption. The agency we were dealing with had very strict rules. I was 40 years old, and they wouldn't let anyone over 40 adopt.

"This feels right," we decided. "Let's wait."

We had a lot of people praying. We were praying. We felt good about this pregnancy. We had a new doctor, Dr. Vanhooydank, and he was optimistic. But I was a mess. I had morning sickness. I was nervous; I was more worried than she was. I was really worried about her having this child. Four months into the pregnancy, the doctor said she needed to stay home and rest. That meant she wasn't with me at the track like she had been since the days of sleeping on the floor in Owensboro. I was like a lost little puppy, not knowing where to go or what to do without her. Stevie said she had never felt more cherished and needed than she did when she was pregnant.

We had Jessica in September of 1987. Well, I tell ya, when we had that kid, I became a different man. If you look at my career from that day forward, I never had

That's me at age four with my first set of wheels!

Leather jacket, helmet, go-kart—life didn't get any better than that.

Believe it or not, that's baby brother, Michael, on my lap when he was only six months old.

I loved winning those go-kart trophies!

My middle brother, Bobby, helps me celebrate my sixteenth birthday and my new driver's license.

Mr. Owensboro takes yet another checkered flag in 1965.

I am one cool dude back in 1965, huh? See, I have the sunglasses to prove it!

Me and P. B. Crowell. Stevie and I moved to Franklin, Tennessee, so that I could drive for P. B. He was the Rick Hendrick of his day.

Talladega, 1972—my first Winston Cup race in my Terminal Transport car.

My first Winston Cup win—May 10, 1975, Nashville, Tennessee. It meant so much that Pappy and Granny Phillips could be there with Stevie and me in Victory Lane. And the little boy in the brown shirt and all that hair, standing next to Granny, is Michael!

Me in my first Daytona race, in my bad-to-the-bone number 88.

Zsa Zsa Gabor presents Stevie and me the trophy for my win at the 1978 World 600 at Charlotte Motor Speedway.

What a crew! Mom, Dad, Stevie, and me in Nashville in the mid-seventies.

Stevie's mom, Letitia Rader, gives me a big hug after my victory at Richmond in 1981.

Junior Johnson celebrates with Stevie and me in Talladega in 1982.

The little half-mile track of Bristol always gives the biggest trophy!

Ol' Hammond taking
care of the driver after
a long, hot day at
Martinsville.

Mom and Dad, Stevie,
and I celebrate our
second Winston Cup
Championship in New
York in 1982.

I always liked being first at everything. Winning the first Winston in 1985 was huge!

Junior Johnson and I talk strategy!

Our basset hound, Prissy, looks thrilled to be in Victory Lane with me at North Wilkesboro.

Just having a little fun with the media after winning the pole for The Winston.

The Crash! I barrel-rolled eleven times down the backstretch at Daytona in July 1991. I walked away with only bruises. Notice in the photo that I still have the presence of mind to wave to the fans!

My baby brother, Michael, wins The Winston in 1996. What a moment!

As part of NASCAR's fiftieth anniversary in 1998, I was honored to be named Driver of the Decade for the eighties. We had a big celebration in Los Angeles. Pictured here are Dale Earnhardt, me, James Garner, Cale Yarborough, and Herb Thomas.

After winning the 1989 Daytona 500, I got to go to the White House. NASCAR CEO Bill France and his wife, Betty Jane, joined Stevie, Jessica, and me in meeting President and Barbara Bush.

Presidential candidate George W. Bush came to the Drivers' Meeting in July 2000 in Daytona. Stevie and I caught up with him, and we got to spend some time together.

The centerpiece of my Silver Anniversary Celebration in 1997. My family and the Chrome Car!

Baseball legend Ted Williams came to our Loudon, New Hampshire, race.

Before my last race at Daytona in July 2000, Dale Earnhardt and Steve Park joined Jessica, Stevie, and me for this special picture.

the same results again. It was just very different. I felt different toward my wife. I felt different toward everything. We went from just the two of us to a new and great responsibility. Because we had wanted and waited for 18 years to have this child, it was an exciting change.

I drove differently. I was more cautious, because up to that point I never believed I had much of anything. It was just me and Stevie. I never thought about getting hurt, but then after we had Jessica, I thought, "Man, if I get hurt . . . what would Stevie and this little baby do? What would they do?" It changed the way I drove, and I took a lot of heat. From 1987 on, people were telling me I needed to quit driving. I would ask myself, "Why quit? I've got everything I ever wanted."

Having a strong faith changes you, but that commitment doesn't mean everything's going to be fine. It doesn't make your troubles go away. It's a rude awakening if anyone thinks being Christian isn't a challenge. To live the kind of life you're asked to live isn't easy.

I remember at my first championship dinner in 1981, I thanked Budweiser and Winston, and I said, "Smokin' and drinkin' is what got us here, and that's what's gonna keep us here."

I have had a long, long list of beer sponsors in my career: Budweiser, Pabst Blue Ribbon, Sterling Beer, Falls City Beer, and more. I used to joke that it wasn't so much for the money, it was for the product. Sometimes the team might screw up and forget the toolbox back at the shop, but we *never* left the cooler behind! But I felt like I needed my lifestyle to change because of my new faith, my wife, and especially my new daughter.

It was awful sometimes, because I loved hangin' with the guys. I think all men are like this. They love hanging out, having a few cold ones. I was that way. In many ways, having my own team was like having my own built-in group of guys. You know, *my guys.* I could say,

"Hey, we're gonna have a barbecue, or we're gonna have some beers after work." That's what we did all the time, and it's one of the things I loved most about owning my own team.

I was never an alcoholic, but I could put away a lot more beer and more wine than I thought I should as a Christian. It has been a big accomplishment for me not to drink any alcohol since 1990. It was something I needed to do alone. No crew chief was needed. It took a lot of willpower, but I'm proud of the restraint and the fortitude it took to stick by that commitment. There are times when a couple of cold beers would be great, but I've had the willpower to resist. Now, Häagen-Dazs ice cream, I'm not sure on that one. I can never resist a good scoop of ice cream.

To live a Christian lifestyle means spreading the word, but I've always tried to be subtle about my faith. I will stand up for what I believe, but I'm not going to stand on a street corner thumping a Bible. How you live and how you act tells volumes about who you are. I can talk the talk, and I've been able to walk the walk. If I have to go out of my way to tell people I've been saved, it almost dilutes the message. I want to live and to act in a way that is an example, in a way that speaks volumes without ever having to say a word. But, I've still been able to use racing as a platform to speak with many churches and youth groups I would never have been able to reach otherwise.

One of the things I am most proud of has nothing to do with championships or race wins. Stevie and I were lucky enough to help found the Motor Racing Outreach. MRO ministers to the entire American motorsports community, no matter what series. They provide Christian services at the track, and also serve the employees and families that travel the circuit week after week, year after year.

In 1987, Max Helton was a pastor with a fine family and a successful church in southern California. At the final race held at Riverside, he introduced himself to Stevie and me. "I've been praying," he said, "and I believe it is my calling to move east and start a ministry for the NASCAR community."

Stevie and I had recently resigned from the board of another ministry. We hadn't seen eye-to-eye with them on some things, so we resigned and started our own private Bible-study group. It was a core group of six: Lake Speed and his wife Ricé, Bobby and Kim Hillin, plus Stevie and me.

The next race was in Atlanta, the final race of the year, and Max promised he'd travel there and meet with whomever he needed.

"I have a church. I'm comfortable," he told us. "But I've decided I'm going to do this."

We believed Max was exactly what we needed, but we were concerned he was giving up so much for so little. He went out on a limb, moving his family to Charlotte. He sold everything, and moved with no promise of anything. No money, no church. It was solely on faith. Just like a racer.

Max began preaching Sunday services at the track, and Motor Racing Outreach was started. There were no sponsors, no financial backing. Eventually, we were able to create a structure with a board of directors and were able to begin actively raising funds. From the day he arrived, Max and MRO became a vital part of our sport. I don't believe anyone else could have done what he did. He was a visionary who saw the need, and risked everything to fill that need. I'm proud Stevie and I helped start the organization.

Max was determined that he was going to make it, and the first year he got way behind financially. But he was doing what he felt was right. It reminded me of the first few years of my racing career. One of my favorite sayings is "You don't know where you stand until you stand up." You have to stand up for what you believe in, and sometimes you're criticized for it or you can get in trouble. But, like Max, I'm proud to stand for my faith in the Lord.

Oh, by the way . . .

■ ■ □ ■

Stevie Waltrip

I'm very moved when my children and I sit in an audience and listen to Darrell talk about his early years and the choices he made apart from the Lord. It is a huge difference from who he was to who he has become. There are so many things about him to love, respect, and cherish that I value greatly. He has overcome many obstacles, accomplished many things, but nothing compares to his relationship with Christ and wanting others to share in that as well.

Michael Waltrip

I was a different kind of cat than Darrell. He was the oldest, and from the age of 12 or 13, he was always told he was the greatest at everything. I was the youngest of five—and my closest sibling in age was eight years older than me, so I learned very early on in

CONTINUED

life to kind of make my own way . . . entertain myself, I guess. It always gave me a sense that I could do things for myself, on my own. Darrell was 16 years older, and it was like having an idol that I didn't really know.

When I was 12 years old, I called Darrell and asked about buying a kart for $600. He was so focused on his own deal, he didn't encourage me. He thought it would be a waste of time for me because he knew how hard it was to make it as a race driver. But he had done it himself, so that made me more determined. It gave me more desire to make it on my own. When you hear that kind of thing at 12 years old, you decide to not go back to that well again. I decided I couldn't really rely on him to make my way. I loved him, and he was still my idol, but he had his own deal going . . . I was never angry or had a problem with that. I was just happy that he was out there dominating and making my last name mean something special.

16

■ ■ ■ ■ ■ ■ ■

Leaving Junior

After running the table in '81 and '82, and winning
12 races each season, I suppose it was inevitable
we couldn't keep up that pace forever. I started the 1983
season with a concussion-causing crash at Daytona. We
finished second in the championship to Bobby Allison,
even though we had six wins, seven poles, and 22 top-
five finishes. Allison beat us because he dropped out of
only two races and the NASCAR point system rewards
consistency. We couldn't overcome a slow start, because
he never let up his steady pace.

In 1984, Junior added a second team, after Warner
Hodgdon bought a portion of his operation. Hodgdon
was a big-time construction and real-estate developer,
and he wanted to put Neil Bonnett in the second car.
Junior signed Budweiser as a sponsor for both cars:
They called it "Bud Thunder." The new shop for Bonnett's team was across the creek in Ingle Hollow. The
creek was symbolic, because we ran the teams as if they
were separate, not like the multicar teams that dominate now.

The most bizarre finish that year, by far, was an example of how far NASCAR has progressed since the

mid-'80s, and an example of the weird dynamics between the two Bud teams. It took place in May at Nashville.

Bonnett led most of the race, but on our final pit stop, we took only two tires and got out ahead of him with only six laps left. It was the only chance we had to win. I held him off as we rounded turn four and headed toward the white flag. There was a spin in turn three, so the caution flag came out along with the white flag. I led him across the line, and I slowed down because of the yellow flag. Bonnett never lifted, and he hauled past me at top speed. I wondered what he was doing.

Instinctively, I took off after him. The wreck was in the third turn, so he went low and I went high. We got back to the finish line and they waved the checkered flag. We both drove toward Victory Circle, and the NASCAR officials waved Neil in, saying he won the race. It was like a traffic jam.

"No, he didn't!" I yelled. "You can't pass anybody on the yellow flag! We were on the last lap!"

Dick Beatty, the competition director, said, "No, we weren't. The yellow hadn't come out."

There was no electronic scoring, and since the race wasn't televised, there was apparently no replay. It was a mess, and the bizarre part is that Junior was in the NASCAR trailer arguing, even though he owned both cars. He was arguing on the principle of the call, believing NASCAR was wrong.

"It doesn't matter what you say," Beatty told us. "Bonnett won the race—now, get outta my trailer."

"Beatty, Darrell Waltrip won this race and you're making an idiot out of yourself," Junior told him as he filed an official protest.

Early Sunday morning, I was still angry when I hopped on a plane to Milwaukee for a Busch Series race that afternoon. When I landed, three guys from NASCAR met me at the airport.

"Darrell," they told me, "don't go to the media today gripin' about what happened last night. We got it straightened out. You're going to be declared the winner based on the videotape."

"The videotape?!"

Turns out my ol' buddies at Channel 5 in Nashville had been rolling tape as the cars came off of turn four to take the yellow flag. Their replay showed I had won the race, and NASCAR made it official the next morning. I believe they never would have reversed their decision if it had been another team. But they saw the replay and realized Beatty was wrong, so they reversed it. And that's why you always hear the media refer to "the unofficial results" right after the race, because NASCAR doesn't declare the race "official" until the day after the race. That gave me four wins in a row at Nashville, and eight overall, before NASCAR took the track off the schedule in 1985.

Despite the distraction of another team, we still had more wins than any other team for the fourth year in a row, but our seven victories weren't enough to pull us higher than fifth place in the final standings. Terry Labonte won the title that year with only two wins. That drove us crazy. Junior was used to winning races and championships, but the competition was becoming tougher and more consistent. We couldn't count on our competitors breaking down every other week, and our strategy had to change.

The Winston Cup championship was what Junior lived for. He started thinking about the next championship as soon as the last lap of the season was over. As the competition stiffened, he tried new innovations, but only in the first half of the year. Then, when he saw what wasn't going to work, he'd scrap it. If you look at my record with Junior—or any of his drivers, for that matter—you'll see the second half of the year was always dynamite. That was always when we made the most gains.

His "championship mode" began to change. It wasn't about winning, it was about consistency. So instead of going out and trying to win 12 races every year, our wins tapered off. We had a new mind-set: We can't run the wheels off this thing every race or every lap. The only way we can win the championship is to finish races. So we got into a "finish the race" mode rather than "win the race" mode. Junior didn't like that.

In 1985 Winston announced they were starting a new all-star race, The Winston, and a new program called the Winston Million, where a driver would get a million-dollar bonus by winning three of the four most prestigious races of the year: the richest (the Daytona 500), the fastest (the Winston 500 at Talladega), the longest (the 600 at Charlotte), and the oldest (the Southern 500 at Darlington). We vowed we would do everything we could to grab all of those events. At the same time, Junior was dissolving his relationship with Hodgdon, whose business interests had slipped considerably.

T. Wayne Robertson at Winston had come up with the idea for stock car racing's version of country music's Fan Fest or baseball's All-Star Game. It was going to be a mingling of drivers and fans, and it was going to be a short, intense race with no pressure, no points, and a $200,000 check to the winner. Second place paid $75,000, and it dropped from there. You had to be a race winner to make it into the starting lineup, and it was held on the Saturday before the World 600.

Junior loved to be the first at everything, so he vowed to do all he could to win the first Winston. He built a special engine for the race. I mean, he worked on that thing himself. He'd tweak it and try it on the dyno. If it didn't show the power he wanted, he'd take it apart and rebuild it again. I sat with him in his garage several nights, just keeping him company while he worked on that engine.

It only had to last 105 miles (70 laps), not 400 or 500 miles like usual, so he made every component lighter. He made special rods he called "sweet potato" rods. We tested everything we could think of for that race: The body was crooked for aerodynamics, the chassis was crooked, and we used several of Chevy's top engineers to help us with the setup and the attitude of the car in the wind tunnel. We tested and tested that car until we were ready.

The Winston is now run in various segments, but the first one was a straight 70-lap race. The rules said you had to make a pit stop between lap 30 and lap 40. Harry Gant and his team chose to make a stop on the first lap of the window, while we decided to stay out until the last lap of the window.

Because he had new tires for 10 laps, Gant was going into turn three with the lead while I was coming off of turn two after my stop. I didn't make up any ground the first few laps, as my tires were slowly building to the right pressure. I was driving my butt off with Junior in my ear almost every lap.

"Durrlll, lemme ask ya something," he said. "Do you wanna win $200,000 or do you wanna win $75,000?"

"I wanna win $200,000, Junior!" I said.

As my car got stronger and stronger, Gant's tires were fading, and I chased him down. Going into turn one on the last lap, the fans were going crazy as I went high and he went low. As we swept onto the back straight, I went past.

I came to the finish line with my left hand in the air, waving, but as soon as I crossed the line to win, the engine exploded. Junior's baby had lasted exactly long enough to win, but now I had a handful. I had to get both hands on that wheel as fast as I could to keep from crashing. I grabbed for the clutch and the gear lever and anything else I could do to get it straightened up.

A lot of people claimed I blew the engine on purpose, and I still get asked about it. I mean, Johnson was a genius, but he wasn't Houdini! The engine was still there, it was just covered in oil. There were a few pieces that had big holes in them, but the engine didn't disappear, and it passed postrace inspection.

This was the era when backup cars were new. We had qualified for the 600 with another car, but NASCAR said we could put a new engine in the winning car from the Winston and race it. We cleaned up the mess and switched engines Saturday night. Sunday morning, NASCAR came to Junior and informed him they had made a mistake and we'd have to run the car we qualified. Junior was livid! We had already changed the engine, and now it was too late to change back. Junior was so mad, he threatened to load us up and take us home.

Luckily, Hammond and I convinced him we could change back in time and still win this race.

And we did—although I was a little worried as I stood alone on the grid when they called, "Gentlemen, start your engines!" The boys were pushing the car out to the line as the field started.

After winning The Winston and the 600, we took home almost $300,000 for the weekend. The Winston was the biggest single payday of my career, bigger even than my Daytona 500 victory several years later.

I can't believe everyone still talks about our blown engine, especially after Richard Petty was caught two years before at the same track with an oversized motor and trick left-side tires. I had been leading until near the end of the race, when he pitted and put on the trick tires. After that, I drove as hard as I ever had, but he blew past me and took off. He used that big engine for years! He stood in Victory Circle while NASCAR talked about fining him and taking the win away.

"After all Richard Petty has done for this sport?" he said. As if that meant he could cheat all he liked whether they caught him or not? We finished second, and NASCAR ended up fining Petty the difference between first- and second-place money. But it was a victory we never got, and I don't ever hear very many people mention that.

The 1985 season was also Bill Elliott's big year. He completely dominated at the superspeedways, winning the Daytona 500 and capturing Talladega by making up two laps under green-flag conditions. It was an incredible feat.

Elliott became a millionaire when he won at Darlington on Labor Day, earning his "Million Dollar Bill" nickname. He also had a 206-point advantage over us with 10 races to go. But his short-track effort wasn't as strong, and we took advantage of it. The only prayer of a chance we had at winning the championship was not to break. We had to finish all the races and hope something happened to Bill. Well, lo and behold, that's how we ended up winning the championship. I was still traumatized about crashing at Darlington in 1979 and giving away that championship, so I knew I could keep the pressure on Elliott and make up the huge point deficit.

I won at Richmond the week after Elliott won the million, then we closed the point margin each race, a second-place finish here, a third-place there. I knew Bill and his team were young and inexperienced when it came to a battle for the title, so I ran my mouth constantly. I was quick to remind everyone how strong we were going to be for the rest of the season. When Elliott dropped out at North Wilkesboro with transmission problems, I took the points lead and we never looked back. Elliott won 11 races and a boatload of money, but the championship was ours. "Never give up" certainly applied during each of my three title runs with Junior. We came from behind each time, and all three titles rank among the top eight in all-time championship comebacks in Winston Cup history.

We expected to do the same in 1986, but we never gained the consistency we needed. I won at North Wilkesboro, Junior's home track, so it was very important to win there every time. It's like Kentucky beating Indiana in college hoops or the Dallas Cowboys beating the Washington Redskins. If you're Junior's driver, that's a race you gotta win. Regrettably, we managed to win only two more races the rest of the year.

Rick Hendrick called me early that season. Rick and I were in the car business together in Franklin. His company managed my dealerships and helped me build my business. He'd been helpful to me for no reason other than he liked me. Rick was relatively new as a NASCAR team owner, and he had Geoff Bodine and Tim Richmond driving for him. His goal was to build a strong multicar team, and his teams were starting to win races, but I didn't believe he was quite there.

Robert Gee, who was now working with Hendrick, had been telling me, "You know, you need to drive for Mr. Hendrick. He's going to have the team everyone is going to want to be with. You need to get over here!"

That was echoing in the back of my mind when Rick called me.

"What are you going to do next year?" Rick asked. "I'd really like to talk to you about coming to drive for me."

"I don't know, I'm pretty happy where I am," I told him. "I'm not sure you're ready for me."

"I wondered where you stood," he said.

I explained I was getting ready to renegotiate my deal.

"I wanted to let you know if nothing works out with Junior, then give me a call," Rick said.

"Well, I don't think that's going to happen, but thanks," I told him.

I decided the time was right to speak to Junior about my contract.

"Junior, this is my sixth season with you," I told him. "You were paying me $150,000 salary when I came here, and I'd like to talk about getting a raise."

Junior has a way of looking at you over the top of these little half-glasses he wears. He looked up, staring right through me. Silence.

"I was talking to Rick Hendrick the other day . . ." I said. I was really winging it now. I knew he resented Hendrick because Chevrolet was starting to cater to Rick and Richard Childress. Junior had been General Motors's number-one team, but they were pulling back as Hendrick grew stronger. I figured this would be a bargaining point in my favor. "Rick said he'd pay me half a million dollars to come drive for him. . . ."

Junior sat there, looking at me over the top of those glasses. "DW," I thought to myself, "this approach ain't goin' nowhere."

"Well, let me tell you some'in', boy," Junior said slowly. "It will be a cold day in hell when I pay somebody half a million dollars to drive my race car."

That was the end of our discussion, and I walked out of the room. I figured I'd drive for $150,000 again, if that's the best I was going to get. I thought Junior would think about it and get back to me. A week or so went by, and I walked into the shop, where Hammond and all of them were sittin', just looking at me.

"What's wrong with ya'll?" I asked.

"We're planning a going-away party," Hammond said.

"What? For who?" I asked.

"You! Man, I can't believe it," Hammond said. "You're not going to be with us next year?"

"What?!" I said.

"Yeah, Junior said you're going to go drive for Rick Hendrick."

"No, no, no! That's a mistake!" I said. "I didn't say I was going to go drive for Rick Hendrick. I just talked to Junior about getting a raise. But I didn't say I was going to work for Rick Hendrick, and Junior didn't say anything!"

"Well, he came down and told us this morning that you won't be with us next year," Hammond said. He knew Junior's mind-set was very old-school, and Junior was used to drivers that would have driven for him for nothing more than a tomato sandwich.

It was a very personal thing for him, but that's the way Junior was. He wouldn't tell you himself. He would tell someone else to tell you. Junior never told me. So he went out and told the guys he'd never pay anybody half a million dollars. He didn't really fire anyone, he just didn't have anything to do with you. You were fired and didn't know it.

"Uh-oh," I thought. "I might be in deep here."

Finally, Junior came into the shop.

"Junior, uhhhhh . . . have we got a deal for next year?" I asked.

"Boy, you told me you's going to go drive for Rick Hendrick."

"I didn't tell ya I was going to! I just said he would give me half a million to drive for him next year!"

Long silence.

"You better go on down there and get that half-million dollars," he said as he turned away.

It wasn't too long before word started getting around at the track.

"I heard you might not be drivin' for Junior next year," Hendrick said when he called me again. "If that's right, I've got a deal for you."

"Man, what is it?" I perked up quick.

"It's with Tide," he explained. "I've been working on this deal awhile. That's why I called to see if you'd be available. If I could put you in that car, then I could put the deal together and Tide will be the sponsor."

My brain raced a million miles an hour, and all I could think about was how amazing it is when things work out. My friends came to me and said they were going to pray me out of that car. Now I'm being offered Tide to clean up my act. Just what they had prayed for, 'cause I had stains on me that it was going to take Tide to get out. Maybe extra-strength Tide with bleach!

The people at Budweiser were really upset. They told Junior, "If it's a money thing, we'd be glad to help out." But Junior told them I quit.

He was distracted my last year there. Hodgdon went bankrupt, and the team fell farther and farther behind. I kept complaining. When you complain about Junior's stuff, that's a no-no. Two things you never talked about were his motors and his coon dogs.

Junior was having problems in his personal life as well, and he and Flossie would eventually get divorced. But Junior had made up his mind I wasn't doing the job. He blamed me. He didn't see what was goin' on.

When we parted, it was an upsetting time. Stevie was upset. Flossie was upset. I was upset. But it seemed as if the timing was right to move forward. It had been the best team and the best sponsor—Budweiser probably still is the best sponsor in the sport—but I needed to make a change in my life. The bottom line is I couldn't have stayed, there was just too much going on.

We managed to finish second in the championship, but we were nearly 300 points behind Dale Earnhardt at the end of the year. I finished the season knowing I was off to join Hendrick and the Tide team while Junior struggled to find a replacement for me. Junior would have hired Earnhardt if he hadn't wrecked me at Richmond that year. He and Dale were starting to chum up, becoming pretty good buddies, which was typical Junior. He was getting to the point where he was tired of me, and Dale had matured. Remember, Junior likes 'em "in their late 29s and early 30s," so maybe I was getting a little too old for him and he had his eye on Dale. Then Earnhardt planted me at Richmond. But the crash wasn't the worst part for Junior. It upset him most when Earnhardt lied to him.

During the races, Junior always stood in the pit area with his headset on, one foot propped up on the wall, leaning against the wall with his other knee. That was Junior Johnson. I can see him doing it with my eyes closed. This particular day, he wasn't in the pit area as usual. He climbed on top of the hauler and watched the race from there.

The final pit stop of the day, we had taken four tires, and Dale's team gave him only two fresh tires. I was a lot faster than Dale, but he got out of the pits in front of me. This was before they updated the track at Richmond to the D-shaped configuration it is now. This was when it was a little more than half a mile in length, with a double-height guardrail around the outside. With less than 10 laps to go, I was right on Earnhardt's back bumper when Junior came on the radio.

"Durrll, don't let that SOB hold ya up."

I knew how Earnhardt was, so I was trying to be cautious. I didn't wanna do anything to make him mad, because he'd always wreck you if you made him angry. Hit him once, and he'd hit you twice. Or more. So I was trying to get around him cleanly, but the laps were winding down. I nerfed him a little bit with the front bumper, not hard, just bumped him a little bit. He slid up the track, and I got inside of him. He cut me off hard, ran me right down into the grass.

"Durrll, I said pass that SOB."

I got inside of him again, and he chopped me again. Finally, we reached lap 398—two laps to go. Twice I had been beside him, and twice he ran me down into the grass. Earnhardt always sat really low in the car, kind of laid back, low in the seat. After the second bump, he raised his right hand and made a twirling motion with one finger in the air. What he meant—politely, of course—was, You hit me again and I'm going to spin you out.

Junior was watching all of this from his perch on the truck, and he got pretty angry. He came on the radio and said, "Durrll, I said pass that SOB. *NOW!*"

We were coming off of turn four while Junior was yelling at me. As we rolled into turn one, I ran in as deep as I could and rooted Earnhardt up the track. *BAM!* I got into him enough that he slid up the track and I was able to get alongside and edge ahead coming off of turn two.

"Boy, ol' Junior's going to love me," I thought as I flew down the back straight. I had the preferred inside line going toward turn three, and I was pulling ahead of Earnhardt. It was some cool stuff right there!

At that moment, Dale turned hard left, square into

me. *WHAP!* He hit me in the right rear and turned me straight into the fence—head-on, with the throttle wide open. *SMASH!* You'd need the best sound effects man in Hollywood to re-create the noise. I went right through the fence.

Joe Ruttman was in third place and he could've won the race, but he must have been watching the two of us go at it, and he spun out, so Kyle Petty won the race on the last lap. One heckuva finish. Even though we ended the day on the outside of the track, we still finished fifth.

Junior was so angry, because he had a perfect view of the crash. Dale told him it was an accident, but Junior had an overhead view of the crash and knew what Dale had blatantly done.

"I drove in too many races," Junior said, getting right in Earnhardt's face. "You can lie to everybody else if ya want to, but you can't lie to me!"

He had no use for Dale after that. From that day forward, no matter what, Junior rarely ever talked to him or about him. Junior is one of those mountain men—when he's done with you, he treats you as if you've died.

When Tim Brewer and Harold Elliot left Junior's team to work for M. C. Anderson, somebody asked if he'd seen either man lately.

"They died" was Junior's response.

That's the way he felt. It seems cold, but that was the kind of person I needed to drive for at that stage of my life.

Junior hired Terry Labonte to replace me, but that didn't go well. Then he got Geoff Bodine, and that didn't last long. He ended up paying Bill Elliott a million dollars to drive for him. (Talk about a "cold day in hell"!) He'd gotten behind the times with his motor program, and everything else kept falling farther behind. He was the same way with Chevy that he was with people. They were dead to him. He left for Ford when he wasn't the top dog any longer. He had a pretty decent year with Elliott in 1992, going into the final race with a chance to win the title, but they lost to Alan Kulwicki.

It's kind of funny how Bill Elliott played into that deal. He drove for Coors all those years, but switched to Budweiser after Junior switched from Chevy to Ford. Bill drove for Ford all those years, and now he drives for Dodge. It's another lesson I've learned: Never say never. I don't mean in the sense of "never give up" (which I believe as well), but never say, "I'll never drive for [fill in the team/sponsor/owner/manufacturer here]." You never know when that kind of thing will come back to haunt you. Who could have imagined, after that day in Richmond, I would ever drive for a team owned by Earnhardt?

Oh, by the way . . .

■ ■ ▨ ▨

Jeff Hammond, crew chief

Junior was an innovator, and he set two major trends when Darrell joined the team.

One, he developed a road-course chassis. It was the first built specifically for road courses, and Darrell and the team were awesome with that car.

The second was the car we built for The Winston. It was an obsession with Junior to win The Winston, and I have never seen anyone work harder on one car for one race. The entire team poured our guts into that car.

CONTINUED

Darrell drove lap after lap, testing that thing. It was really the most advanced aerodynamic car ever built at that time. It fit the NASCAR templates, but we worked on every gray area to mold and shape the car.

It was a car and an engine way ahead of its time, and I don't know what would have happened to Junior if Darrell didn't pass Harry Gant to win that race. Harry was driving for Travis Carter, who used to work for Junior, so it probably would have killed him to lose that race to Carter.

17

The Dream Team?

The 1980s was when I was at my best, when I had my "A" game. If you beat me, you beat a darn good driver. My prime was 1977 through 1992. Those were the years when I could really get it done. When I went to drive for Junior, I was at the peak of my career, and I was desperate to win. Junior wanted a no-holds-barred kind of driver, and I fit that mold.

I don't want to say it was easier to win when I came into Winston Cup, but the number of serious competitors, the list of guys you had to beat on a given day, increased by a large margin during my career.

In the 1970s, David Pearson was always the man to beat on the superspeedways. Pearson, in the Wood Brothers Mercury, seemed near impossible to pass when the race was on the line at superspeedways. I loved racing with Pearson, because you didn't have to worry about him running over you. You knew when it came time to race hard that Pearson and that darned Mercury usually had the stuff to beat you, so if you came out ahead, you'd really done something. Buddy Baker was awesome on the big tracks too. The faster the track was, the more he liked it and the harder he held his foot to the floor. Richard Petty was somebody you had to beat every week no matter the size or type of the track you were running on. Petty was always there.

If it was a short track, you had to contend with Cale Yarborough. They were the team you measured yourself against when he was in Junior's car. On the shorts tracks like Martinsville and Bristol, Cale was as tough as anyone I ever raced, but he was also good at places like Daytona. When Cale was driving for Waddell Wilson, you knew he was going to try to slingshot past you on the last lap, like the day he and the Allison brothers ended up in the grass wrecked and fighting each other.

The Allison brothers were at the top of the list as well. Bobby was tenacious like a bulldog. He never stopped. Donnie was good too, especially when he had equipment that would last. Benny Parsons was also one of the guys who was a constant threat to win.

So count those up. Seven guys? Eight guys? Those were the elite teams and drivers you had to beat if you expected to win. The equipment wasn't as good as it is now, so three or four of them would fall out, one or two might crash, and it would come down to two or three guys at the end of the day shooting for victory.

As the sport evolved and continued to grow, it was almost as if someone was dragging more and more teams and drivers onto that list of weekly contenders each year. Earnhardt was a few years younger and a few notches wilder than me, and I thought it would take more time before he forced his way onto that list, but he won the championship in only his second season. Once he hooked up with Richard Childress, they got better and better. Childress was never high on the list as a driver, but he turned out to be a heckuva team owner.

Ricky Rudd became a contender. Bill Elliott blasted out of Georgia like he had been shot from a rocket. Neil

Bonnett started winning. It seemed like it took Harry Gant a long time to finally win, then he won a lot of races in the Skoal Bandit car. The late Tim Richmond won a lot as well.

It became more and more interesting with these new guys coming in challenging the older, more consistent drivers who refused to give up any ground. The influx of younger drivers added to the intrigue of each week's race. It wasn't always the same two or three guys battling it out at the finish. Now 10 or more drivers had a shot to win.

Throughout the 1980s, more and more teams grew and prospered. Hendrick started his multicar deal, running a race team with the same economic principles by which he ran his auto dealerships. More cars and more sponsors meant his entire team improved. Jack Roush came into the sport with Mark Martin, Robert Yates had Davey Allison, and it looked like they were going to be a dominant combination. Not all of the guys were from the South. We were joined by Terry Labonte from Texas, Rusty Wallace from Missouri (they would both win Winston Cup championships), and Ernie Irvan from California, who drove like Earnhardt. He crashed a lot but won a lot.

Until the mid-1990s, the equipment was the weak link in the equation. You couldn't always rely on it to hold up. You weren't able to go out and run hard all day, the way they do now. You had to be an aggressive driver, but you had to be a smart driver and know the limitations of your equipment. Now the cars don't have any limitations as far as reliability is concerned.

The cost of Winston Cup racing has always been high, but until the mid-1990s it was still relatively affordable for a single-car operation. I admired a guy like Alan Kulwicki, who could hock everything he had, put the money into a race car, and win a championship in

1992. The cost was manageable, especially if you won races. You could take the prize money, parlay it with a reasonable-sized sponsorship, and keep your head above water. When Alan died in a plane crash in 1993, the era of the successful independent, single-car team died with him.

I became a part of the explosion of multicar teams when I left Junior's team to sign with Rick Hendrick and the Tide sponsorship. I had intended to do my own thing when I first began thinking of leaving Junior. I had already built a shop on Hudspeth Road near the Charlotte Motor Speedway in 1985, where I had my own Busch Series team. We ran the team out of my shop, and in the back of my mind I thought I was going to do my own thing. Owning your own team is not right for every driver—most don't want the headaches and responsibilities—but it would have been right for me at that time, just like it was right for Bill Elliott and Ricky Rudd at the time. Kulwicki proved you could win the title as an owner/driver, but times change.

When I accepted Rick's offer I had won three championships, but I was in Junior's shadow. No matter how many races I won or how many championships I took home, there were a lot of people who believed the sole reason I won was that I drove for Junior Johnson. Junior deserves a ton of the credit, but he became less and less involved in the day-to-day operations in the last few years I drove for him. Hammond and I ran the team. We did what we wanted. We built the car and set it up the way we wanted. Junior had very little to do with it. Initially, he had been very hands-on, but he backed off, and he sold half of the team to Warner Hodgdon. Junior had become an administrator more than anything.

When Hendrick made the offer, I assumed it would be structured as if it were my own race team. We had every piece of the puzzle: a champion driver, a big-time sponsor (Tide), and a great engine builder in Waddell Wilson. Wilson had been building Cale Yarborough's Ford engines with the Hardee's team, but the chance to work with Hendrick meant Wilson would be moving to a Chevy engine program.

Rick already had two cars in his lineup when I joined: Geoff Bodine was sponsored by Levi Garrett, and Folgers sponsored Tim Richmond in the second team. When Tim got sick, Benny Parsons and then Kenny Schrader took over that ride. We were going to be the third team, and some growing pains and adjustments should have been expected.

We called it the Dream Team, which was probably the kiss of death, because we didn't get the results everyone expected. I didn't even feel like I was driving for Hendrick. He was the owner, but Wilson was the team manager and engine builder. Waddell hired all the people, so I was basically driving for him. I was excited at first, because I thought it was going to be great. Waddell and I were good friends, and his wife Barbara and Stevie were good friends. For years I had wanted to drive for Wilson. When I was at DiGard, Waddell worked for Harry Ranier at the number 28 team (Robert Yates eventually bought the team from Ranier), and he tried to help me get out of my contract. I was trying to get a deal with them before Junior's offer came along.

But we clashed almost from the start. Waddell was, for lack of a better term, a control freak. He wanted everything done his way. You name it and he wanted to control it. He hired most of his own family. His daughter, Lisa, worked for the team, as well as three of his sons. All of them were good people, but ultimately I felt like I was driving for the Wilson family. So what happened was, the guy in charge of the team was watching out for his family more than the Tide ride. And that became an issue pretty quickly.

Waddell had been building Fords for so long that the Chevrolet engines were different for him. He was really being conservative with the engines. He was insecure about the change and began building conservative engines, so we started our first season with a handicap on horsepower.

At the same time, Stevie became pregnant. By midseason, she could no longer go to the track, because the doctor had ordered her to stay home and rest. I felt lost without Stevie there, but the bed rest paid off when Stevie gave birth to Jessica Leigh. It was one of the greatest moments of my life, and it made the struggles at the shop and on the track seem a lot less important.

When Jessica was born, we hadn't won a race, but we were fifth in points thanks to the team's consistency. It's hard to blow up anything when you're going so slow, so we finished every race and wore 'em down with consistency.

In our 24th start the Tide Ride—aka the Dream Team—finally reached Victory Lane. It was 10 days after Jessica was born, and we won at Martinsville. I have 11 Winston Cup wins at Martinsville, 27 top-fives, and 31 top-10 finishes. I had eight poles: four each in the spring and fall races. All were track records, but none was sweeter than this victory. When I got in the car Sunday morning, there was a rose with a note on the seat of the car. "Win this one for me, Daddy," it said. "Love, Jessica."

We had been a lap down for much of the day, but as the race came toward the finish, Earnhardt had to pit for fuel and we got back on the lead lap. Then, with seven laps to go, a yellow flag came out and I was able to restart behind Earnhardt and Terry Labonte, who was in Junior Johnson's car. Terry tried to get around

Earnhardt, and Dale nearly bounced him into the fence. Terry was mad because Dale cut him off, and he's not looking in his mirror at me. He's focused on nailing Dale. He was going to give him a bump-'n'-run. I was closing at a high speed, and I cut under Terry in turn three. He didn't know I was there, and I hit him. That shot his car into the back of Earnhardt. They both spun out, and I drove by to win. I led from the fourth turn to the finish line that day, all of a few hundred feet. It looked like a deck of cards being shuffled as we all slid and crunched our way to the finish. Earnhardt was livid, but he had done the same thing to so many guys already that season that he didn't get much sympathy, and Junior was really angry because I knocked his car out of the way. The official lap-leader chart shows Earnhardt leading laps 381–499, then it says: Waltrip, 500. That's the lap that pays the bills.

That day was a perfect example of what was going on within the team, because Waddell had already left the track. He had parked his car by the highway outside the racetrack so he wouldn't have to fight the traffic. He and Barbara were in their car getting ready to go home when somebody told him we had won the race.

He turned around and tried to fight against the traffic, but he couldn't get back in. He had believed we were going to finish third, so he had just left.

By the end of the year, the number of victories remained the same. One win was not at all what we had in mind for the Dream Team. We finished fourth in the point standings, and for a first-year team this should have been a great accomplishment. But we were never really in the hunt for many victories, so none of us was very happy. Our fourth-place finish was more a matter of us creeping to the finish line week after week rather than threatening for the checkered flag.

We won an award that year for completing the most

miles. It was only because we didn't crash, break down, or blow up. At the banquet, I said, "Yeah, we did a great job at logging miles this year, but that's about all we did."

That didn't sit well with Waddell, who was used to being a speed demon. Sometimes friends shouldn't work together. You're better off competing against each other as friends than working together as enemies.

I'll never forget an incident with Gary DeHart and Eddie Dickerson. DeHart is a great car builder, and Dickerson is a great fabricator. They were trying to build cars, but me and Waddell and everyone else were clashing. We had the pieces of the puzzle, but none of them fit.

The guys felt Waddell was playing favorites, letting his family do whatever they wanted to, but at the same time holding everyone else to a different standard. If you weren't a Wilson, it felt like you were being picked on or discriminated against. It got so bad, DeHart and Dickerson pulled me aside one afternoon at the shop and told me they were leaving if something wasn't done.

These guys were really good, and I didn't want to lose them. I was pretty frustrated myself, so I saw an opportunity to make things better for everyone if we called a meeting. I knew Waddell wasn't going to take too kindly to our suggestions, but we had a chance as a united group. "All of y'all back me up now," I said before we went to Waddell's office. "This is going to be a little edgy, a little dicey here."

So the four of us sat down in the office: me, Eddie, Gary, and Waddell. I started off by telling Waddell it was time to look at the employees. At that time his father-in-law was sweeping floors, his daughter was his secretary, and his three boys were working in the engine room. It seemed like everybody in the shop was named Wilson.

"Look, Waddell, the rest of the guys are tired," I continued. "They say you let your boys get away with whatever they want, and you show them special favors."

Ohhhh boy, Waddell, he turned red as a beet, getting really steamed, and I turned around to the other guys.

"Uh, Eddie, Gary . . . guys . . . tell him what you were telling me."

Their faces turned red as well. "Oh really, we don't have that big of a problem with all that," one of them said.

I'm standing there and I've got egg all over my face. Waddell was getting so angry, and it scared 'em. Waddell is a big man and a strong guy. I mean, he probably could have knocked us all out with one lick.

The three of us left Waddell's office, and now I was the angry one, ready to kill those two guys. They left me hanging out there on a limb by myself. Waddell was mad at me, so he called Jimmy Johnson (not the driver), who worked for Rick Hendrick, and told Johnson he couldn't work with me anymore. Either I had to go or he had to go.

So the great restructuring began. Waddell was teamed with Geoff Bodine, and DeHart and Dickerson came along with me. I had forgiven them. We moved the Tide team into my building on Hudspeth Road. A deal was made where Rick leased the space from me and we ran the team from there.

But we needed a final piece of the puzzle, and I believed Jeff Hammond was that piece. Jeff had remained with Junior after I left, but he was becoming very unhappy with the situation. Junior had a wild idea that he would have two crew chiefs. Tim Brewer would be the crew chief at the speedways, and Jeff would be the crew chief at the short tracks. It didn't work, so Jeff grew very frustrated. I called him and said, "Man, you've got to come down here and help me. I've got myself in a mess." Soon after, we were reunited for the rest of the 1988 season.

Oh, by the way . . .

■□□□

Rick Hendrick,
team owner and business partner

My goal was to win championships. We won nine races in 1986 with our two teams, and I saw Darrell as the next step up, a big leap toward making the operation a championship contender. He taught us about winning championships.

We are great friends, and I love the guy, but I wanted to hire him as a driver because he was the guy who changed the whole sport. Until he came along, it was like all of the drivers were out of one mold, and he broke the mold. Broke it wide open. He was outspoken, but he could back it up on the track. He was great with people, and he opened the sport to new sponsors who saw the potential for drivers to be spokesmen. He was great with a crowd, quick on his feet, and that was a huge leap for our sport.

18

■ ■ ■ ■ ■ ■

The Most Popular Driver

A subtle change began to take place in 1987. The booing started to grow quieter. It wasn't that the volume decreased drastically, but rather that the taunts became less vicious. I was driving for Rick Hendrick, who was liked, so that helped. Most of all, though, I wasn't winning as much. It's not that people feel sorry for you when you don't win, but for whatever reason, they like you better. I was no longer seen as the villain who won every week. Fans started to see me more as a person. And it didn't hurt that I was seen everywhere with Stevie and an adorable little curly-haired baby. I changed a lot, too, and finding my faith in God helped immensely.

I was a better person in many ways, and I owe some of that credit in a strange way to Richard Petty. When I was driving the Gatorade car, Petty said, "I don't know how he keeps a sponsor with an attitude like his." He also said, "He'll never win the Most Popular Driver Award."

The National Motorsports Press Association (NMPA) awards the Most Popular Driver Award every year to the NASCAR driver who gains the most votes from the fans. It's one of the most prestigious awards a driver can win. I always struggled with the fact that people loved Richard Petty but despised me. I mean, he won 27 races in a season in the '60s, and people still loved him. I won 12 races in a season, and people hated me. What's up with that? It made me resent Petty that much more.

The situation showed how powerful public perception can be, and how image can get blown beyond proportion. A person's image doesn't reflect who that person really is. When you get to know someone, you might be surprised they aren't who you thought they were. That can be good or bad. The 1989 season was great for me. And not just because of how well I did on the track, but because I was happy as a husband and father. I finally had a chance to show the fans that I wasn't a bad guy.

The Daytona 500 had always been my nemesis. I'd find a new way to lose that sucker every year. For some reason, though, we felt confident going into the race in 1989. Racing is all about numbers, and this was my 17th attempt, and I was in car number 17, and most important . . . my crew added up the numbers on our fuel mileage exactly right.

My teammate, Kenny Schrader, won the pole and we were on the outside of the front row. From the start, Kenny was a rocket and led more than half the laps. We were good but not great, and when we made a pit stop on lap 147 I felt like we had a top-10 car, maybe top-five if we were lucky.

There was a yellow flag with less than 40 laps to go, and Jeff Hammond told me to stay out.

"Can we go all the way?" I asked.

There was a long pause before he answered. "It's going to be close."

We knew we could run 50 laps on one tank, because that's the length of the 125-mile qualifying races, but 53 laps? That's more than 132 miles.

I started doing all I could to save fuel. I feathered the gas pedal. which is like pretending there is an egg between your foot and the pedal and you just ease on and ease off the thing. At Daytona you can also save fuel by drafting with other cars, and I drafted behind any moving object. One by one, the other contenders went to the pits for fuel. Schrader and Earnhardt stopped for a splash of fuel on lap 189, but I was still trailing Alan Kulwicki until he had a flat tire on lap 196. I took the lead on lap 197, then I held my breath the last three laps.

You feel and hear everything in the car at moments like that. You start imagining things, listening to every noise for a hint that the engine is going to sputter or flutter or stop altogether. Would we have enough fuel? I didn't know the answer.

I rounded turn four with a six-second lead on Schrader, and now I knew I could coast home. I had won the Daytona 500! I finally ran out of fuel on the lap back around to Victory Lane. A lot of experts didn't think we could go that far on a tank of fuel, but we did it by conserving, using just about every last drop. Someone asked an inspector how much fuel was left in the tank, and he said, "For five dollars, I'd drink all that was left!" I liked that one.

It was a joyous and emotional scene. There were tears all around Victory Lane, and I even ran around the car and did my own version of the "Ickey Shuffle," a dance that had been made famous by Cincinnati Bengals running back Ickey Woods. I did a few hops back and forth, and then spiked my orange helmet like it was a football.

Rick Hendrick was so happy to be there as car owner, but it was even more special because we were good friends. A lot of people felt good about me winning that race. It was my 17th year running the Great American Race, and I had already won 16 races at Daytona, including qualifying races, but the 500 had always proved elusive. For some, the Daytona 500 has no more significance than any other race. To others, it is *the* race. It took me 17 years to win it, so I appreciated the depth of what it meant to win that much more. For those who consider themselves a part of the inner circle and those who have a relationship with the France family, you understand the importance of NASCAR, and the importance of Daytona to the family and the history of the sport. All of those things added up, and that pressure, even though it was self-imposed, resulted in victory being much harder to come by. In my case, it seemed the harder I tried, the worse my results at the Daytona 500.

To show how much things had changed, when I ran my first Daytona 500 in 1975, women weren't allowed in the pits. I wanted Stevie there with me, so I listed her as the team owner, allowing her to be in the pits with an owner's license. She kept track of the laps, fuel mileage, and anything else she could do to help out. But I must admit, Crazy Jake Elder wasn't so thrilled that I had my wife in the pit area.

I had been running mostly short-track races until then, and Stevie was concerned the 500 took almost four hours to run. She knew I loved to eat, and four hours was a long time to go without food. She made me a ham-and-cheese sandwich. In those days a normal pit stop took 30 seconds, so Stevie figured she had plenty of time to go over the wall and hand me the sandwich during one of the stops.

You can just imagine Jake's reaction. I mean, women weren't even allowed in the pits, and now she was stepping over the wall. That meant we had too many men . . . uh, I mean too many crewmembers over the wall. I waved at her to get back as she handed the sandwich to me in the car. I tore off, shifting with one hand and holding the sandwich in the other. I got a few pit stalls away and I threw the sandwich out the window. Jake had a fit, and Stevie was upset. She was almost in tears. "I don't know why he threw it out. He loves ham-and-cheese sandwiches," she said. "They're his favorite. . . ."

So things had certainly changed in the 17 years from my first 500 to my first victory.

■ ▢ ▮

After winning at Daytona, the Tide team got better and better. We won at all of my favorite places: Atlanta, North Wilkesboro, Martinsville, Charlotte, and Bristol. We scored the last win for the old-style Monte Carlo body for Chevrolet, and then the first victory for the new Chevy Lumina.

It was The Winston that proved to be a key turning point for me with the fans. The Winston race has a unique setup. The race is 70 laps that are broken into three segments: two 30-lap segments, and then a 10-lap shoot-out for the big bucks. I dueled with Rusty Wallace through the first two segments of the race. He won the first and I won the second. During the final segment, everyone fought each lap like it was the last. I led, and I could almost count the money, but our car would get loose the longer it ran. I would pull away from Rusty on the backstretch, but his car was handling better, so he'd close up in turns three and four.

With two laps to go, he hadn't made a serious run on me, and I wrongly assumed he was content with second place. With all that money on the line, I should have known better. I was protecting the inside line as we went into turn three, so I eased off the throttle a little early and floated it into the turn. He kept his foot on it and nudged me in the left rear. I spun around and through the grass.

The Winston rules say the yellow-flag laps don't count, so I stopped for four fresh tires and started at the back. In two laps, I passed seven cars because I was doing all I could to catch Rusty. But I ran out of laps and Rusty won. If only there were more time left . . .

Rusty knew how mad I was because he never slowed down on the cool-down lap. He kept going as fast as he could. His crew and my guys collided, and the pushing, shoving, yelling, and punching began as he drove down Victory Lane. I was kicking and spitting mad, but as I got out of the car Hammond made sure we all went into the team hauler to cool down— at least a little bit. I think that was one of the keys to our success: When I needed to be calmed down, he'd be cool, and when he was ready to go off, I'd calm him down. I was still mad, so when the media asked me for a reaction, I said, "I hope Rusty chokes on that $200,000!"

I don't think he did, but the incident really fired up the fans. When I was introduced the next Sunday for the Coca-Cola 600, the boos died down and I got a huge cheer. Wow! This is the same place where I'd made my infamous "Big K" comment, and now they cheered me. Rusty was no longer the young lion: He had become the bad guy. I won the 600 that day, and it felt great. I was so fast, Dale Earnhardt was ready to bite through the steering wheel because he knew he couldn't catch me. He always wore those bubble goggles, and I remember looking in the mirror and all I could see were these two big eyeballs.

We went into the race at Darlington with a chance to duplicate Elliott's million-dollar bonus because of the wins at Daytona and Charlotte. I pushed too hard, and I ended up hitting the wall twice and didn't even come close to winning the race. Other than that disappointment, it was about as good a year as I could have ever imagined.

But then, at the end of the season, things got even better. The NMPA announced their Most Popular Driver Award.

The envelope, please . . . And the 1989 winner is . . . Darrell Waltrip!

Can you imagine my reaction? I can't even begin to describe the emotion of going from the most despised man in the sport for so many years to being voted most popular. So many elements came together to make it possible, and in some ways it was almost like winning another championship. It felt that good.

Oh, by the way . . .

*Rick Hendrick,
team owner and business partner*

My favorite memory is the day we won the Daytona 500 . . . seeing him do that Ickey Shuffle and seeing Stevie crying on top of the pit box near the end of the

CONTINUED

race because she knew how much that race meant to Darrell. She's one of the finest human beings I've ever known. She won't compromise her family or her faith for anything. To be there with them on that day was the highlight. He did great things for my race team, but I value his friendship much more than that.

I do tease him about the time he left me holding the bag in front of a lot of fans. We planned a big grand-opening celebration at his car dealership in Franklin. We had a concert, and he and I were scheduled to sign autographs. People came from all over to meet Darrell. From Canada and all over the country. Qualifying had been rained out on Friday, so he had to stay at the track and qualify on Saturday, which meant I was stuck there at the dealership by myself. But no one was there to get my autograph.

"Where's Darrell?" they all asked. One after another. "Where's Darrell?" I mean, there was a line a mile long, including a woman who pulled up in a van, hauling a washing machine painted like the Tide car. I sat there signing autographs for six hours, waiting on him to show up. He finally made it late in the day, and the fans were finally happy.

19

You're Gonna Win a Lot More Races

I won seven races in 1989, including the Daytona 500 and the 600 at Charlotte for the fifth time. I also had a shot at winning the Winston Million, and the Tide team won the Pit Crew championship at Rockingham. With Hammond as my crew chief, the glory days were back and we were the team to beat.

I was selected "NASCAR Driver of the '80s" in 1999 when NASCAR celebrated its 50th anniversary. If you look at my record from 1980 to 1990, I won three championships and 56 races—more than any other driver. Undoubtedly it was my decade, my era.

I wanted the 1990s to start off well. We had built a fleet of new cars and had been to the wind tunnel to test them. We thought we had the world by the tail and started the season expecting to dominate, but it didn't go at all like we had anticipated. We finished 14th at the Daytona 500, but we weren't overly concerned. Unfortunately, we began to fall farther and farther behind the pack as the season progressed.

Before the season, Rick said, "I've built this engine program and I'd like to see it continue to grow. Somebody has to run 'em. We'll never get any better if we don't have a Hendrick engine in a car every week."

In 1989, the three Hendrick teams used Hendrick engines occasionally, but we primarily ran B&R engines that were very strong. Playing off the name, we called them "Be Ready" engines, because when you pushed the pedal, you'd better be ready. B&R wanted a car to use their engines exclusively, so they were paired with Kenny Schrader and the Hendrick number 25 car.

Before the 1990 season, Rick wanted to run a Hendrick engine in our car every week, and me and Jeff Hammond agreed to give this a try.

Randy Dorton, who still leads Hendrick's engine program, was our in-house engine builder.

"Give 'em some feedback," Rick said, "and let's get it cranked up."

"We'll do it," Hammond and I told him. "We're all right with that."

The cars, though, never ran very well, and we always fought to find more power. Morale began to suffer as Hammond and I struggled to figure out how to improve the situation.

He and I had worked together for Junior, and eventually we made all of the decisions and did everything ourselves concerning the race team. Junior got the credit, though, rightfully so. Teaming with Hendrick was a step in the right direction, but because we worked out of my own shop, separated from the other Hendrick teams, and because we used Hendrick engines exclusively, we felt like stepchildren. We certainly weren't, but it felt that way as our struggles continued. We felt like there were too many cars on the multicar team and we were at the bottom of the heap.

We were so used to having success and being in control of our own destiny that we grew discouraged. Hammond and I did the math and realized that if he and I stuck together we might be able to do our own deal someday.

In retrospect, our problems were related to the fact that the Lumina just wasn't a very good race car. We had been so good in the Monte Carlo, but the new body style of the Lumina presented us with a lot of unknowns. But at the time none of this was clear to me. The more I thought about it, the more I believed it was time for me to do my own deal.

"We're doing all the work here. We have all the people here with us," I told Hammond one day. "They're employees of Hendrick, but they're 'our guys.' I own the building here. We're doing everything except making the money, ya know?"

Hendrick and Jimmy Johnson (not the driver) paid the bills, but we were in charge of everything else. We ran the team. I didn't see any reason why we couldn't do it on our own. I left my own team in '75 only because of the Grand Canyon of Debt, and I still believed I could do a good job as a team owner. I decided to start looking into the possibilities. Sponsorship wouldn't be a problem. Sponsors loved me, and Tide had even told me, "Keep us in the loop if you ever decide to do something on your own."

As the season wore on, we still thought we had better cars and better engines: Everything seemed to be in place. Yet we weren't up to speed. The team blamed it on the driver, and I blamed it on the team. I always knew what I wanted in the car, what I wanted it to feel like. The guys worked their guts out to make it better.

We kept making changes—change after change, springs, shocks, and anything else. But, for whatever reason, we never got the cars the way I liked them.

As April approached I had a sense that the race at North Wilkesboro, where I'd won numerous times, could be a turning point. It might be the weekend we got the team back in a winning state of mind. The car was great that day as I battled Earnhardt. We were leading, sailing to a victory, when a yellow flag came out near the end of the race.

This was before NASCAR used modern electronic timing and scoring, and there was a lot of confusion about who the pace car should pick up on the track. On a short track like North Wilkesboro, with almost 400 laps completed, things can become confusing, but there was no question we were leading.

For some reason, the pace car picked up Brett Bodine, who was driving the Quaker State car owned by NHRA drag racer Kenny Bernstein. Bodine had been fast all day, and had led some laps, but he had just made a pit stop, dropping him almost a full lap behind.

Since the pace car was in front of Bodine's green number 26, I was being scored second and Earnhardt third. Everyone up and down pit road knew Bodine was on the tail end of the lead lap, including Brett himself. "I'm not the leader," Bodine said on his radio.

My current broadcasting partner, Larry McReynolds, was Bodine's crew chief that day. He got on the radio and told Brett, "Shut up! You're in the lead and you have four fresh tires. . . ."

I was yelling and screaming on the radio, and Hammond was doing the same in the pits, although he did his best to calm me down, and he told me, "It's OK, we'll work it out after the race." But I knew better.

I was madder than a hornet, but before reason could

prevail, NASCAR threw the green flag and Brett took off. I was faster, but I was stuck dealing with Jimmy Spencer, who was four laps behind. Once I got clear of Spencer 20 or 30 laps later, I hauled after Bodine, and I caught up to him as the checkered flag fell. Now my only hope was that they'd get this figured out and prove we won the race. But they waved the 26 car into Victory Lane.

"The 17 car won this race!" we're yelling at anyone and everyone.

In the middle of the fury and confusion, I saw Bill France Jr.

"Will you please, PLEASE, straighten this mess out?" I begged him. "We won this race! Everyone here knows that man didn't win the race!"

France put his arm around me and said, "Darrell, how many races have you won?"

"Seventy-nine," I said.

France looked at me and said, "So you just leave that boy alone. He's never won a race, and you're gonna win a lot more races, so you just leave that kid alone."

"You mean you're not gonna do anything?" I shouted.

"No. No, I'm not. We're going to leave it like it is," he told me.

Had I known how the remainder of 1990 would go, I would have argued a lot longer and a lot louder. I didn't win a race in 1990, and it broke a string of winning at least one race for 17 straight years. I would have tied Richard Petty with 18 consecutive winning seasons had they awarded me the victory. Bobby Allison and I are tied for third in career Winston Cup victories, and Allison is always complaining about one of his wins that NASCAR failed to recognize, but at least I can always counter with the day NASCAR picked the wrong car at North Wilkesboro.

■ ■

A day or two after that race, I was still in a foul mood when the marketing people from Procter & Gamble (Tide's parent company) called. "We're doing a promotion with Ray-Ban sunglasses, and we need you to come to a studio in Charlotte so we can take some promo shots."

I wasn't at all happy about it, but I went down there. They were all ordering me around: Procter & Gamble people and Ray-Ban people and photographers and stylists and . . . I started to get very irritated.

"Do this . . . Turn that way . . . Try these glasses . . . No, they don't look good on you . . . Put these on . . . No, now try these . . . Turn sideways . . . Look tough . . ."

"What am I getting for doing this?" I asked.

"Nothing," they said. "You're not getting anything. It's in your contract."

"Wait a minute. You're bossin' me around and I'm not getting anything out of this? Somebody needs to call Rick."

They all stood there and looked at me like "What's wrong with this guy? DW's always been a team player." Someone called Rick, and he told me, "Yeah, it's part of your contract. You have to do it."

"All right, I'll do it, but I'm not very happy about it."

I had just lost a race I really won, and now I was forced to do this promotion.

We took a break from shooting, and I cooled down a bit. We all sat back and laughed about it, and I realized I was with the people that ran the Tide program—the PR and marketing side of the sponsorship. I realized this might be a good moment to see if they were serious about their interest in me if I chose to do something else.

I took them aside and asked, "Would Tide consider

backing me if I started my own team sometime in the future? How would Tide feel about it?"

"We'd take a look at it" was the answer.

"Are you unhappy with Hendrick?" someone asked.

"No! No, it has nothing to do with being unhappy," I insisted. "I have always wanted to have my own team. I started out on my own, and since then, I've wanted my own team when the time was right."

As soon as I left the studio, they dialed Rick.

Rick Hendrick is a cool guy. I mean, he rarely loses his cool. But that afternoon, he was as livid as I've ever seen him.

"What are you tryin' to do? Are you trying to ruin this whole deal?" he asked me. "My sponsor calls and says you wanna leave—you're not happy and you're starting your own deal. They said you were difficult to work with, completely arrogant! What in the world is going on?"

I thought I had asked them in confidence, and besides, it was merely a casual and hypothetical conversation. Rick was very upset about it, and I tried to explain.

"I was just asking their thoughts," I pleaded.

We needed to discuss the situation, and a few weeks later, Rick called and asked me to dinner at the Mayflower Restaurant in Concord, North Carolina. I knew I had to tell him the truth.

"I want to start my own team," I told him. "It's something I have always wanted to do, and I don't think I'll be truly happy until I do it."

Rick thought about it and finally said, "You're making the biggest mistake of your life."

"I don't feel that way. I don't see why I can't do it," I told him. "I've already got the building, and I think I can get my own sponsor. I'll buy all of the cars and all of the equipment from you."

"You don't like driving for me?" he asked.

I loved driving for Rick Hendrick. He was the best

car owner I ever had. Junior Johnson taught me about racing, but Rick taught me about business and how to run a race team. He was a multicar guy, and he ran the teams the same way he ran his car dealerships: You get a lot of 'em, run 'em right, and you'll be successful.

He tried to talk me out of it, but he knew it was something I had to get out of my system.

"I don't know, DW," he said with a sigh. "But I know how you feel. I worked at a dealership in South Carolina, and I always dreamed of doing my own deal. When I bought City Chevrolet in Charlotte, everybody said I was crazy. So I appreciate where you're coming from, and I'll help you any way I can."

"This is not a formal resignation," I said, "but I want you to know I'm gonna start testing the waters . . . just to see how things go."

He was disappointed, but he was understanding and supportive, and he kept his word. I know he would have been more upset if I had left him to drive for someone else, rather than my own deal.

That was in late May, and I started making contacts, very low-key. I'd done some commercials for Mello Yello, and Jim Bailey, the distributor in Charlotte, was a friend, so he helped me open the right doors with Coca-Cola. They were looking to do big things with their Mello Yello brand, and they were thinking about sponsoring a team. I met with them several times, and it looked like the perfect deal for everyone.

When we arrived in Daytona for the July race, I ran into Jim Foster, one of NASCAR's top marketing guys. I confided in him I was looking to start my own team.

"The Western Auto people are looking to expand their deal," he told me. "That might be something you could retire on."

Western Auto had recently signed on as "The Official Auto Parts Store of NASCAR." Before the season started, I was in a TV commercial announcing their new status, but that was my only limited contact with them.

I told him I was pretty confident I had the Mello Yello deal in place, but I'd be happy to speak with Western Auto.

"I'll make the call and see if they're interested," Foster told me.

Oh, by the way . . .

■■□■□

Rick Hendrick,
team owner and business partner

I was disappointed, but I did understand it from his side. It would have been worse if he had left to go to another team, but I knew he needed to do his own thing. I still found myself trying to talk him out of it. But he handled it like a gentleman. He told me he was going to do it, rather than try to keep a secret and do all of it behind my back.

He was a big help to the entire organization. I think he could have won the title in 1987, but we had failures and made mistakes an experienced team wouldn't have made. We weren't seasoned as a team, and if he had had the right mix behind him, we could have won several championships and a lot more races together.

The Crash That Could
Have Ended It All

*E*ntertainment Tonight was in Daytona to cover my
race weekend. It was going to be my 500th Winston
Cup start, so they were following me everywhere. I was always happy to work with the nonracing media. I was good
at describing our sport and talking to people who were not
race fans or had never been to a race. I was NASCAR's
ambassador, if you will.

The video crew shot some footage Friday morning at
our condo in Daytona. Simple stuff, like the three of us
eating breakfast together, and Stevie and Jessica sending me on my way and wishing me good luck.

When I got to the track, Winston arranged a big
media deal, complete with a cake and candles, congrat-
ulating me on my 500th start—which I hadn't even
made yet.

I should have known something was going to happen,
though. The awning on my motor coach fell, and here I
was, Mr. Perfection, climbing up to fix it. I got my thumb
caught in something and mashed that sucker bad. It
turned black, and I was forced to drill a hole in my
thumbnail to relieve the pressure.

The day before we had qualified fifth, but in the practice session that morning the car was dog meat. We were trying a new seat in the car. This was when some of the teams were starting to put leg braces in front of the seat to keep the driver's legs from being slammed around in an accident. The seat had been built specifically for me, and it tilted sideways, so I had a better view out of the top left corner of the windshield on the high banking at Daytona. Hammond had put the seat in, but he hadn't mounted the leg braces, because I wasn't sure if I was going to use them. A different type of seat is a major change for a driver, and I wanted to be certain I was comfortable before I started a race with it. I wasn't, so I told the crew to change back to the old seat when the session was done.

When I rolled back into the garage midway through the final practice session, it was not a pretty sight. The crew had their heads hanging down, moping around, looking at their feet. We hadn't won a race, we weren't running well, and the crew knew I was leaving at the end of the year. Morale was awful.

Hammond, Eddie Dickerson, and I leaned against the car, trying to figure out anything that would help. I was hacked off about the car, and they were hacked off about having to change the seat again. Change after change all season, and no improvement.

"Boys, I wanna tell you something," I said. "It can't get any worse than this."

Little did I know.

I changed out of my uniform and walked to the motor coach to watch the rest of practice from the roof. The guy from *Entertainment Tonight* was up there with me, and I was explaining why the cars were coming in and out of the garage, and why I was done for the day.

Then one of the crew guys ran over to the coach and yelled up at me. "They found out what's wrong with the car. We want you to come over and run two laps to make sure it's ready. But you have to hurry, because practice is almost over."

"I'm not taking that durned thing out again!" I yelled back down at him. "But I'm glad they found out what's wrong."

"No, we really need you," he said. "The motor guy changed the carburetor, and he thinks that's it. He needs to get a plug check, so you need to come over and make one more run."

Reluctantly, I climbed down from the motor coach, ran to the garage, and put on my uniform. As I fired the engine, they told me there were two minutes left in the practice session. I rolled onto pit lane just as a big group of cars zoomed past. It was 15 cars drafting in a pack. I started moving slowly down pit lane, timing it so I could blend into the pack on the next lap and make sure the car was ready.

As I came off of turn two, here comes the pack of cars, led by Earnhardt. But he wasn't in his own car, he was driving A. J. Foyt's car. A. J. had an Indy car commitment that day, and his guys needed someone to take out their car for a few laps. Dale agreed to do it at the end of the practice, once his own car was ready.

I blended in as we sped into turn three. Suddenly, the Foyt car blew an oil line. Oil was everywhere, and it was chaos. Five cars spinning . . . six cars . . . eight cars . . . There was nowhere to go; cars were wrecking everywhere. All I saw was smoke and debris, but somehow I made it through the first stage of the crash. I spun out but didn't hit anything. As I came out of the spin, the car was sideways, in the middle of the track with the left side facing traffic. Hammond was hollerin' at me on the radio to "crank that thing up and get outta there." Here comes Dave Marcis, sliding through the smoke. There I sat, sideways. His car hit me square in the door.

My left leg exploded, because it was extended, pushing the clutch pedal. I don't know if it would have made any difference if the braces had been in the car. My left arm was injured, because I was reaching up to crank the engine. I had no memory of any of it until I spun out a year later at Richmond. After I spun, facing traffic in turn four, I extended my leg to put in the clutch and reached for the ignition switch, and I had an eerie, chilling flashback. It was then that I knew what I was doing when Marcis hit me.

This was long before NASCAR qualifying and practices were televised, so I'm not sure if there would have been any footage of the crash if *Entertainment Tonight* hadn't been there.

Stevie was still at the condo, so Bobby Hillin called to tell her she'd better come over to the track because I had been in a crash. He tried to be reassuring, but she was so scared she made it to the track in record time.

My femur was the worst of my many injuries. It was broken apart in three places, and the bone had split open. It was like a war wound—but the shrapnel was from the bone itself. They transported me from the infield care center at Daytona to Halifax Hospital, less than a mile from turn four.

When we arrived at the hospital, a lot of people suggested that Stevie contact Dr. Terry Trammell in Indianapolis. He was a surgeon who worked with the Indy car community, and he was considered the top expert in reconstructive leg surgery.

Dr. Albert Gillespy was the orthopedic surgeon on call at Halifax. He eventually became dear friends with Stevie and me, but we didn't know him at the time. He insisted I was injured too badly to move, and that he needed to perform the surgery there. He and Stevie got on the phone with Dr. Trammell. Turns out Trammell and Gillespy had had much of the same training. Dr.

Gillespy described what my injuries were and how he planned to treat them.

Dr. Trammell assured Stevie I was in good hands.

Dr. Gillespy described my injuries to Stevie. He estimated it would be six months before I'd be able to return to racing.

"No!" she yelled. "You can tell him he has a broken leg. You can tell him he has a broken arm. Tell him about his concussion. Maybe mention the nine broken ribs. Tell him anything you want, but DO NOT tell him he can't drive the race car for six months. If you tell him that, the man will die of a heart attack!"

While all this was going on, I kept asking anyone and everyone, "What happened? What happened?"

The surgery lasted eight hours. My femur was shattered so badly, it took an 18-inch titanium plate and 18 titanium screws to put it back together. The plate was a big, scary, ugly thing. It looked like something built with bits and pieces from the hardware store where my dad bought our first go-kart in Owensboro.

I came to a weird, fuzzy consciousness the next morning. I was wrapped and patched up like a mummy. My left leg was in what they call a "constant motion machine." My leg was elevated and moving back and forth: *grrrrrnnn crack . . . grrrrnnnn creek . . . grrrrrrrrnnnnnnn crack.* My arm was propped up in a cast.

I had no idea how I got here, but I knew I was busted up. Broken arm. Broken leg. Broken ribs. Concussion.

Stevie, bless her heart, was right there. Flossie Johnson, Junior's wife, had come over to sit with Stevie while I was sedated.

This was when the July race was run on Saturday morning. I could not believe what I was seeing on TV: The race was getting ready to start! I can't tell you the feeling, but it was the worst thing in the world for me. One of my biggest fears during my career was not being able to get to the track when a race was ready to start. It was a recurring nightmare. I would be running for the championship and I'd think, "What if I got stuck in traffic? What if I missed the start of the race? What if something happened?" It didn't matter if I was only a minute late and drove 99 percent of the race. Only the driver that starts the race gets credited with NASCAR points.

Now I'm drugged and helpless at Halifax Medical Center. If the wind was right, I probably could have heard the engines from that hospital room. All I knew was that they were ready to race and I wasn't there.

I was 43 years old, and *busted up*. What was I gonna do? I had resigned from my ride. All I had was my wife and daughter, a race shop, and a contraption on my leg. I never thought I could get hurt. That only happened to other drivers. Well, at least that's what I always told Stevie. In those days, we really didn't know any better. Like all drivers, I felt as if I was invincible.

Jimmy Horton was in my car, and I was in tears. Like the three li'l bears: Someone's sleepin' in my bed. It was the worst feeling in the world. It was the first race I'd ever missed. Forget broken bones: I was crushed because someone else was in my car.

I had no idea at the time what had happened between the crash and the start of the race.

■□■

My car was wrecked so badly, NASCAR impounded it. It was a restrictor-plate race, and Hendrick engines had always been fast at those races. Turns out the engines had a floating block in the manifold that sat under the plate. The rule book didn't say anything about it specifically, but it was considered an "unapproved" part. When the carburetor was tightened, it released the floating block, and I'll bet it made 25 more horsepower.

NASCAR never knew a thing about it until they took apart my mangled machine.

I can only imagine how bad it was for my team. Their driver was in the hospital ("How bad is he hurt? Is he even gonna live?"), their car was destroyed, and, as soon as a NASCAR official took the restrictor plate off, there was a *clunk* in the engine. The inspector reached in and pulled out the block. Ah-haaaa! NASCAR went through the garage, checking everyone's engine. They made all the teams spot-weld the blocks into place.

Earlier in the season, Art Krebs, a NASCAR inspector, had come to me and asked, "Why do you think some of the restrictor plates come back with four small black circles around the intake?"

I had to think fast, because I'm sure the block was causing the circles. "It must be caused by the engine backfiring," I suggested.

"Yeah . . . yeah, that must be it," Krebs said, not realizing the plates with the black residue were all from the fastest cars.

It was a mess, especially for the Hendrick cars. We had all qualified to start near the front. Greg Sacks was in one of Rick's cars and had qualified on the pole. A single *clunk* had led to a series of cars starting the race with at least 25 horsepower less. When the race started, they were in the way. On the first lap, Sacks caused a high-speed traffic jam. He was a moving roadblock with no horsepower. All of the cars got bunched up, and there was a whale of a crash: 15 cars or so, including Sacks.

"See!" Stevie said to me. "If you would have been in that race you would have been in that wreck! You're crying, but you oughta be glad you weren't in there. Look at that! That's the worst wreck I have ever seen. Thank the Lord."

She was trying to make me feel better. That's what

she wanted me to believe, but I knew that, even if I was in that wreck, at least I would have been in the race.

That afternoon, so many people came to see me. Earnhardt came by, France Jr., a lot of people. Flossie was there, and then Junior came over after the race. I hadn't driven for him in years, but I was so happy he was there. I was drugged heavily for the pain, and I said, "Junior—who . . . who . . . who [I guess I stutter when I'm laid up] drives for you, anyway?"

"You know who," he said. "That Geoff Bodine . . ."

"Oh," I muttered. "Ya mean the guy you told me you didn't like. . . ."

◼◻◼

Because of the severity of my injuries, Hammond suggested the word *retirement.* Stevie was furious with him. "This is not how he's going to retire," she told him. "This is not the end of his career." I had an IV tube in my arm injecting morphine for the pain. It had a button you could press to allow more to drip into the tube. I was working that button overtime, almost to the point I'd pass out. On Monday morning I was moved from intensive care into my own room. No more morphine.

At the time of the crash, they believed I had broken my arm. I was lying in bed with a bar above me, so I reached to see if I could pull myself up. And I did, no problem.

"Please! Please stop!" Dr. Gillespy yelled when he ran into the room. "Your arm is broken!"

"I can't tell," I said. "I can lift myself with it. It doesn't hurt."

"I'm not hurt that bad," I'd tell Stevie. "Just get this thing off of my arm, I can drive."

Once I stopped the morphine drip, I began to come to my senses. That season, we had a weekend off after

Daytona, so I had two weeks before the race at Pocono. I was in the hospital bed, determining how I moved to get in the race car. If I could use my arm, that meant I could use crutches and start rehabilitation. If it had been as bad as they thought, I would have never made it out of bed.

I dropped only two positions in points even after missing the race. I was now 10th, and I was horrified about falling out of the top 10 in points. I had finished in the top 10 for 15 seasons in a row, still a NASCAR record, and I wanted that record to continue.

I'd never been hurt before, so I didn't know how badly I was injured. I thought it was as simple as climbing out of bed and into the car.

"I gotta be out of here in a week," I told Dr. Gillespy. "I have to be in Pocono in ten days."

He took Stevie out of the room and told her, "His head injury is worse than I thought. There is no way he can do that. He can't get out of bed for weeks."

I had a brainstorm, and I told Dr. Gillespy, "All I have to do is get in the car and do one lap. It's a piece of cake. Pocono is a big track, and I might not even lose a lap."

Remember, NASCAR awards points to the driver who starts the race, not the one who finishes it.

"No way," he said. "You have to keep that leg perfectly in line, or you'll damage it worse and you'll be right back here where you started."

I was lucky, because my brother Bobby was in Daytona with a show car—one of Michael's Pennzoil race cars. So I asked Bobby to take Dr. Gillespy to show him what it would take to get me in and out of the car. The doctor didn't know a lot about racing, and he certainly had never been in a race car, so he agreed to go only reluctantly. I'm not sure why. Maybe he knew I wasn't going to shut up until he had taken a look.

He looked at the car and started poring over it. He

took off his sport coat. He took off his tie and climbed through the door and down into the seat. As he was sitting there, he started to think, "Yeah, I think we can do this." Surgeons are a lot like race drivers: They love a challenge. And this was certainly going to be a challenge.

"I think I know what to do," he said when he got back to my room. He had a gleam in his eye like a crew chief who had thought of a new innovation. "I am not in favor of this, and I am not saying it will work, but we'll try. If you can get out of bed, get on some crutches, and start moving around, then maybe, just maybe, I can call my friends in Orlando. They might be able to build a cast that can be put on and taken off. As long as that leg does not twist, and we figure out how you can get in and out of the car, I might consider it."

That's all I needed to hear. These guys showed up from Orlando, made a plaster cast of my leg, then went off like mad scientists. Somehow, they concocted a huge contraption with Velcro straps. We all looked it over and realized it might work.

Several days later, I started smelling a familiar scent. They say the sense of smell is most closely linked to your memories, so, in my state of mind, I thought I was having a flashback. Or, maybe the Lord has taken me to heaven, and it smelled like a garage.

A few seconds later, this big ol' cowboy hat comes around the corner and into the room. It was Smokey Yunick. Smokey was one of the greatest mechanical legends of racing, and he ran a place in Daytona known as "The Best Damn Garage in Town." He smelled like carburetor cleaner. You could smell him long before you saw him.

"Durrrrrlll . . . ," he said slowly, "you done messed yourself up, boy."

Smokey hung around for a while, and now, whenever I smell carburetor cleaner, I think of him.

Mario Andretti called. A lot of people called in those first few days, but I remember speaking with Mario. We had become friends when we were in the IROC series.

"How are you doing?" asked Joe Carver, my business manager, when he called the room.

"They say I can go home later this week," I said, trying to look on the positive side of things, but I was feeling anything but positive.

"I hate to call you," he said, "but I have to. The Mello Yello people called today and said the deal is off."

"What happened?" I asked. I was shocked.

"The guy was very cold about it," Joe explained. "He told me they didn't want a 40-year-old driver with a broken leg."

"What are they going to do?" I asked.

"They signed a deal with Felix Sabates and Kyle Petty," Joe said.

(The irony of the situation is that Kyle was in a crash at Talladega the next season and broke his leg. So they didn't have a 40-year-old driver with a broken leg. They had a 30-year-old driver with a broken leg.)

It hurt so bad to hear those words. Now I was hurt more emotionally than physically. Whispers of my retirement were getting louder, and my dream sponsorship deal had fallen through. I felt sorry for myself more than ever.

This was only a couple of days after the crash, and I still didn't know if I was going to be able to walk. It was the lowest point in my career. Remember the 1958 Ford I brought to my first Daytona race? That's kind of how I felt: like they had gone to the junkyard and brought back all of these bits and pieces to put me back together. I certainly didn't feel like the Six Million Dollar Man. (Remember that TV show? *We can rebuild him. We have the technology. . . ."*)

Everything was falling apart. I felt like my world was tumbling down. Most people would have said it's a good time to quit and go home and play with your two-year-old kid.

For the most part, I agree. But champions don't quit. They rise up out of bed and walk on water. Or at least they think they can. In my case, I would have been walking on my one good leg. The pain of losing a sponsor motivated me, and I sat up in bed.

"I'm gonna tell you one thing," I said, more to myself than anyone else in the room. "I'll kick their butt with this broken leg. I'll wear 'em down with one leg."

■□■

I was in the hospital in Daytona for a week, then transported to Nashville. I went to Baptist Hospital, where their sports medicine specialists and their athletic trainers agreed to work with me. One of the trainers agreed to go to Charlotte to see if I could get in and out of the car. I was hurting. I mean, really hurting. It was at this point that the reality of my injuries became apparent to me. There was no part of my body that wasn't aching, but somehow I flew to Charlotte.

The plate was on one side of the femur, so walking on crutches or even standing up straight was not as critical as making sure my leg didn't twist side to side, which would have torn the bone away from the plate. Hammond and all of the guys at the shop got together with the trainer and worked out a plan to hoist me in and out without twisting the leg.

It took two crewmembers to lift me, but we came up with an efficient process. We even practiced it several times so the doctor could see. I was given the OK to drive one lap at Pocono. I tried not to show how agonizing it was to endure each attempt at transfer, but once I was in the car, I was all right.

Stevie was very supportive. I think she understood

how much it meant to me to do this, and she knew she couldn't talk me out of it. "I've got to do this!" I kept telling her—and myself. "If I don't do this, I'll be out of the top ten in points. If I miss all of the races, I may never get another chance. All I need is to do one lap, and then I'll get stronger and stronger each week. I can do this."

■ ■

When it came time to go to Pocono, the weather was awful. There were thunderstorms all the way up the East Coast. My pilot, Jerry VanDervlught, who has been with me for 25 years, did all he could—he deviated from the usual route to avoid the storms. Every time we hit a bump, it beat us around. It was a scheduled two-hour flight, but it took three and a half hours. It was miserable.

It was a welcome relief to get to the hotel. Somehow I crawled into bed, but I was a wreck. In the midst of all of this drama, Stevie had a herniated disk in her neck. She had gone to a doctor who prescribed an anti-inflammatory drug to ease the pain. Stevie took a pill before she went to bed. She's allergic to a lot of drugs like ibuprofen, and about an hour later she poked me. "I don't feel good."

I hadn't been able to sleep or relax, so I didn't feel any sympathy at that point. "You don't feel good?" I groaned. "Take a look at me over here."

"No, really, I don't feel right," she said.

I turned on the light, and I almost didn't recognize her. She had an allergic reaction to the medicine, and her face had swollen so big that her eyes were almost shut. I called Joe Carver, who took her to the emergency room in Wilkes-Barre. I was left behind while they went to the hospital. She didn't get back until 4 A.M.

The next morning, we had to go to the track for a news conference to talk about my injury. I have to laugh when I think about the look on everyone's faces when we came into the media center: me waddling on crutches, wearing my big Velcro contraption, and Stevie, a beautiful woman, looking like she had been in a prize-fight.

"What are these two thinking?!" they must have thought. "He looks like a ghost of his former self [I had lost almost 30 pounds in the two weeks since the crash], and who knows what happened to her!"

I told 'em I had a letter from my doctor to do one lap on Sunday. I had to show NASCAR how the team was going to get me in and out of the car, and then I had to run at least one practice lap on Saturday to be eligible to start on Sunday. I explained that Stevie had an allergic reaction to her medicine, and I'm sure there's never been a more sorry-looking duo in the history of NASCAR.

Dick Beatty told me on Saturday, "The *only* way I'm going to let you make a lap is if you start at the back of the field, stay all the way back, and don't get near any-one. You do one lap, come into the pits, and get out of that car. That is the ONLY way I will approve this."

When Sunday arrived, we started the process of slid-ing me into the car. I always felt most at ease inside of a race car, and this was no exception. I told Hammond, "I feel pretty good. I think I can drive to the first caution." Adrenaline is a wonderful thing.

Hammond said, "Remember, you pass one car and Dick Beatty will have us all in the big red truck."

As we came around to take the green flag, it was a shoddy start, with a bunch of cars straggling out of posi-tion. Pocono has a huge, long front stretch, and the field was out of formation. All I thought about was getting around the track, and getting to the pits as quick as I could so we wouldn't lose a lap. Before we even got to turn one, I passed about three or four cars. I needed to stay as close to the leader as I could.

As I came around, there was a crash in front of me. I couldn't believe it. I missed it completely, and I was so excited: I could come in under a yellow flag and let Jimmy Horton get in the car without losing a lap.

"See, I told you I could drive to the first yellow," I said on the radio.

It seemed like it took forever for them to lift me out of the car. As Horton was latching the belts, a NASCAR official walked over and held his hand up, as in "Stay right there." Dick Beatty had made me promise I wasn't going to get near any other cars, and he got so mad when I passed a few guys, he penalized us a lap. Whoooo, he was angry!

Horton ended up finishing 20th, three laps behind. But I was in misery, and after the race, reality finally settled in.

"That's the most ridiculous thing I have ever done in my life," I told Stevie. "I'm not going to do it again until I am healthy and really ready to drive the car right."

I know they never wished I'd been hurt, but when I announced I would stay out of the car until I was healed, the team must have been relieved to get someone else in the car. But they found out pretty quickly, once they got another driver in there (I should say a bunch of drivers in there), it got much worse. Other drivers were not such a hot ticket. Before a few weeks had passed, all of their cars were wrecked. Greg Sacks got in the car and finished second at Michigan, but other than that, it was a series of mishaps.

Even though I was leaving at the end of the season, Rick remained committed to me. He was under a lot of pressure from Tide to replace me with Ricky Rudd, but he kept his word.

"When you get well and you're ready to come back, it's your car to drive," he told me. "You're my friend, and you're my driver. I made that commitment to you."

It took almost three months, but I came back with a vengeance. I was in great shape. The staff at Baptist Hospital put me on a diet and a tough workout program. I came back better than I had been in years.

It felt great to get back in the car in Richmond, and I went out and took third in my first race. We also had top-five runs at the end of the year at Phoenix and Atlanta. It was such a crucial time, because I didn't know if I was ever going to drive again. Then I came back better than before I was injured. Despite missing six races (plus the one-lap mess at Pocono), I finished 20th in points. And I won the Most Popular Driver Award again. It was particularly heartwarming to have all of my fans rally around me after what I had been through.

I may have a slightly different walk than I once did, but the leg does not bother me today. After the operation, the hardware in my leg hurt like mad. It was the latest and greatest technology, and it did its job. But after two years I was still limping, and it hurt every day. I got into the best shape of my life, having spent countless hours working out. I never worked that hard in my life, but I couldn't help but limp. Every step, a jolt of pain. It felt like a shot in my rear every step I took.

I called Dr. Gillespy several times, and I'd say, "It's still hurting . . . something is really wrong."

"It can't be the hardware," he'd tell me, "because there's nothing there that could hurt."

"But it's pinching. Something's pinching all the time. What do I have to do to get this out of my leg?"

"Well, you would have to undergo the same operation as before, this time in reverse," he explained. "We'll have to reopen the same 18-inch incision to get it out."

I gave the go-ahead for him to cut the big gash, and he sliced me open from my hip to my knee. He found that the bone had calcified over the plate, so the muscles were like banjo strings. That's why it felt like a shock every time I walked.

Once they chiseled the plate out of my leg, I knew I wasn't going to spend the rest of my life limping. The minute I stood up, I knew I wasn't gonna limp anymore. My femur had been shattered, but you wouldn't know it today, even though I have a scar like a racing stripe down my leg.

Oh, by the way, if you'd like to see the titanium hardware, it's in the trophy case at Darrell Waltrip Honda in Franklin.

Oh, by the way . . .

■ □ ■ □

Stevie Waltrip

You'd have to be stupid to not think something could happen to your husband. I was honest about that, but I decided to leave him in the hands of the Lord whenever he climbed into that car. I had days of trepidation, especially at places like Daytona, Talladega, and even Atlanta.

CONTINUED

The day he was hurt, we were staying at a condo near the speedway. I got a call from Bobby Hillin. He was a driver himself, so he was able to be calm about it, and he sounded reassuring. He told me, "Darrell's OK, but he's been in a crash. You should come to the track." I got in the car, and I knew I had to get there as soon as possible. I knew traffic would be heavy, so I prayed. "Lord, please give me strength to choose the right path, and please don't let anyone get in my way, because you know I'll run 'em over." He must have heard me, because I didn't stop until I got to the care center.

As I got there, all I could think was to be calm, be strong for Darrell. His leg was awful: The bone never came through the skin, but it looked horrible. I knew he was going to be OK, because he recognized me right away. "Honey," he said. "What happened?" He would ask me every few minutes, "What happened?"

When we got in the ambulance, they made me sit in the front seat, but he could still hear me. "Honey, what are you doing?" he asked. "Singing a song," I said. I had been listening to Michael Card, our favorite Christian singer. I was singing one of his songs.

Kenny Schrader

When Darrell and I were teammates at Hendrick, we went to Chicago every year for a sponsor's dinner with Exxon. In 1990, before Darrell's crash, a group of us sat at the dinner and ordered quite a few bottles of wine. We all had our share of wine, Darrell included.

The next year, we went back to the same dinner. I ordered the wine, and Darrell said, "No. No, thanks. None for me. Since my accident, I haven't had a drink of alcohol." I looked at him and said, "Darrell, do you

CONTINUED

remember when I came to see you in the care center at the racetrack that day? All you could say was 'What happened? What happened?' Your leg was all bent, and the bone was sticking up. I decided right then I'd better start drinking a lot more!"

So I had Darrell's share of the wine. . . .

21

Western Auto Says Yes

Jim Foster had spoken to the people from Western Auto before my crash, and they were happy to meet with me after the Pocono race. I was in a lot of pain, but I was too stubborn to change the date, so we went ahead with the meeting at my shop near Charlotte. After Mello Yello backed out, this meeting became crucial.

I was barely able to sit upright. I had someone hide my crutches, and I stayed in my office chair with my leg hidden under my desk, but I still looked awful. They must have thought I was ready to die because I was pale and sweating, but I assured them I was all right. I was just hoping they wouldn't ask me to stand up!

The Western Auto folks were really superb people, but at first they were more like fans. They were new to the sport, so the only names they really knew were Richard Petty, Dale Earnhardt, and Darrell Waltrip. I had that in my favor. They told me they had seen me win a lot of races and knew all about me.

I gave them my best sales pitch.

"You can do whatever you want," I told them. "You can turn this place into a Western Auto store if you want! This can be the Western Auto Racing Team. You can put your name everywhere you want—this will be Western Auto's building. Whatever you want to do, I am all for it. I hear good things about you, and I'd love to be part of your team."

I even told them about going to my local Western Auto and buying that puny little jack for my very first Winston Cup race at Talladega.

I felt like they were excited about doing a deal with me. After the meeting, they thanked me and said they'd get back to me soon, but they had one more meeting that afternoon. They were meeting with Felix Sabates.

"You're meeting with Felix Sabates?!" I said, sweating even more now. "If you're going over there to meet with Felix," I said, mustering all the strength I had left, "I guarantee you'll be back."

I was so nervous and exhausted, I felt like I was going to pass out. I don't think I've ever been that nervous in my life. But, several hours later, the door to the shop opened and in walked the Western Auto guys.

It was a very good deal, a three-year package, with bonuses for top-10 finishes, bonuses for victories, and all of the perks we could negotiate. The sponsorship started at a little less than $2 million for the first season and was scheduled to increase every year. The total amount for the three years was a bit more than $6 million, so I guess, by then, I did feel like the Six Million Dollar Man.

The original guys I worked with at Western Auto were great. John Barlow and folks like Greg Trees and Terry Kuntz were a pleasure to deal with. They ran Western Auto. They were Western Auto. When you wanted something, you didn't have to go to the board of directors. You just called John Barlow. He was a great guy to have as a sponsor, and he turned out to be a good friend. He's with Safelite now—auto glass and wind-shields are his livelihood—and I still do business with him. Greg Trees is at Cash America. Sponsors kind of spread out, like drivers and team members do in racing, and eventually they all turned out to be friends rather than business partners.

I owned the building we were in, although I had been leasing the shop to Hendrick. I didn't own any of the equipment: race cars, tools, or anything else. I had already reached an agreement with Rick to lease engines from him for the following season, but we had not agreed on a price for me to purchase the cars and the gear.

I had offered a million dollars, but they wanted to send an accountant to the shop to do an inventory. He showed up and went through the place, piece by piece.

"Just put together a dollar figure," I said, "for all of it."

The accountant came back to me with a huge number: $3.2 million!

"Whoa!" I said. "That's way too much! What if I just buy a few of the cars and tools?"

He came back with another outrageous number. I was growing pretty frustrated, and the negotiations ground to a halt before I left with the team for an October test session in Phoenix.

I guess they didn't want to wait to settle the deal, because I got a call while I was there telling me they came by the shop and took all of my equipment.

I came back from Phoenix and headed straight for my shop. They had taken everything. *Everything.* They took the lightbulbs out of the fixtures. Any oily rag—gone. They even ripped the phones from the wall.

One room in particular had a huge hole in the wall. There had been a magnaflux machine (it's like an X-ray machine for race car parts) there, and the room had been built around it. It would have been too much trouble to dismantle the machine, so a big hole was cut in the wall to take it out.

I worked with what I felt like were the best people at Hendrick Motorsports, all of whom were told they would have jobs at Hendrick in the future. But, because of the way the shop was raided, everybody was ticked off and rallied around me.

"We're sticking with you," I heard again and again. "We'll work seven days a week, 24 hours a day, if that's what it takes for us to get ready for Daytona."

That's exactly what it took. We started with nothing but the walls and the roof over the shop. Not a single wrench, not a bolt. Everybody pitched in. We bought a new tractor and trailer. We bought tools. Of course, Western Auto was great because they had the Craftsman stuff, and they shipped tools left and right, everything in their inventory. Equipment came in bit by bit, day after day.

We were building pit wagons, benches, and race cars. In November, we had no cars. By the time Daytona came around, we had five cars: two Daytona superspeedway cars and three others for Rockingham and beyond.

We went to Daytona and ran really well. So well, in fact, we were in a position late in the race to win on fuel mileage, just like we had in '89. But someone spun, and it bunched the field. Kyle Petty and Rusty Wallace crashed in front of me, and I got clipped going by. We had to drop out with 10 laps to go. It would have been one heckuva debut, I tell ya!

■□

The deal I made with Hendrick to lease engines turned out to be good for everyone. The guys who were young and inexperienced when their engine program started had become better and more skilled, and they really had their act together that season.

The first year of the Western Auto deal, we won two races and finished eighth in points. The most spectacular moment of 1991, ironically, was an incident I don't remember because I was unconscious for most of it. As usual, it took place at Daytona, only one day from the one-year anniversary of my big crash. On lap 119 of the Pepsi 400, coming off of turn two, Joe Ruttman got into me and sent me into a spin. As I slid, I pushed the radio button, and the last thing anyone heard was "I'm in big trouble here."

Then there was silence on the radio as the car dug into the grass and began a series of 11 barrel rolls. There are photos of the car high in the air, with the body and the roof torn off completely, my right arm flailing out of the top of the roll cage as if I'm waving to the fans, pieces of debris flying everywhere. A rear spring here, a water bottle there, and huge clumps of grass flying as if a dozen of the world's worst golfers had just hacked huge divots. The sight was so spectacular, it received a two-page photo spread in *Sports Illustrated*.

Again, I was lucky to be alive. I was beaten and bruised all over, but, thankfully, I sustained no serious injuries. I was never so sore in my life, but we had a week off after the race, so Stevie and I spent 10 days in Nantucket, where I healed in peace.

The car was torn up so badly, I told Hammond I never wanted to see it again. It was taken directly to the museum at Darlington Raceway, where you can still see it today.

We had another good season in 1992, winning at Pocono, then winning back-to-back at the Bristol night race (my 12th victory at the track) and the historic Southern 500 at Darlington. The Southern 500 victory was ultimately my final Winston Cup win. We led only once for a six-lap stretch, but it was the final six laps before the race was called because of rain. As I received my winner's trophy, a huge rainbow stretched across the sky.

Davey Allison should have won it, as he was leading before the rain came. He was eligible to win the Winston Million, since he had won the Daytona 500 and the Winston 500. Davey had his first chance to win the million dollars at the Charlotte 600, but the week before the race he was injured in a crash with Kyle Petty at the finish line of The Winston, the first night race at Charlotte. He won The Winston, but was taken to the hospital instead of Victory Lane. It was quite a night.

Larry McReynolds was Davey's crew chief, and to this day, Larry says he could almost puke when he thinks about not winning at Darlington that afternoon.

During the race we could see all the rain clouds coming closer and closer. Hammond and I knew we could stretch our fuel mileage farther than anyone, and Allison needed to pit for fuel sooner than we did. McReynolds sent his shop foreman to check the radar screen to see if rain was approaching.

He came back to the pits and told Larry everything looked great.

Thinking the race was going to continue and not wanting to risk running out of fuel, McReynolds called Allison in for a pit stop for four tires and fuel. We stayed out, and were leading when the rains came in torrents.

After the deluge, McReynolds asked his guy about the radar. "I thought you said we were OK."

"It looked good," the guy answered. "The whole screen was green!" I guess that poor guy didn't know green was the color they used to signify rain. Green. Now poor Larry was green with envy after we won the race.

It was a great day for me and my team, but it would be the last time we would visit the Winner's Circle.

■ ■

After the 1992 season (when we finished ninth in points), I got a big head thinking about how well we were doing. I believed we might be even better if everything was built and prepared in-house. Have my own engines built right in my own shop. How cool would that be?!

It was the worst decision I ever made as a team owner.

I ended up spending about $2 million buying equipment, building engines, and hiring people. It's not as simple as throwing cash at it, and I never won another race after going away from the Hendrick engines. Ninety percent of my problems from that point forward were because the engines weren't very good. An engine with superior horsepower can sometimes overcome a poor-handling car, but if you are underpowered, you are in trouble. On top of that, the engines were unreliable, so we dropped out with engine issues more than we should have.

If I had stayed on the Hendrick lease program, I would have been all right. We would have continued to win races. It finally reached a point down the line when our engines ran well, but they were never as good as Hendrick's stuff, or close to any of the other quality teams. I guarantee you if I had stayed with the lease program, I would have finished my career with many, many more victories.

Oh, by the way . . .

Jeff Hammond, crew chief

We had a great relationship. We complemented each other, but he would cuss me up and down, especially during the races. We were emotional, and that's how it was. I think I had more success with Darrell as a crew chief because I could take what he would dish out. Whatever was said in the heat of battle was forgotten on Monday. He and I were able to really say what needed to be said to each other, but we didn't take it personally.

One day at Atlanta, he was so hard on me, he cussed me the entire race. Stevie heard it all—she sat on the pit box with a headset on—and she told me after the race, "You oughta go down and kick Darrell's butt for talking to you like that."

22

■■■■■■

Owner/Driver/Father/Husband

Leaving Hendrick and starting my own team was a
dream. It was a chance to have my own business
and control my future. It was more than just an opportunity to make more money. That was a part of it, but it
was a chance to build something that would extend beyond my driving career. The furthest thing from my
mind was retiring as a driver, especially before my injuries. Owning my own team was just something I had to
do at this point in my career. What can I tell you, the
timing just felt right.

Being an owner/driver is treacherous. There is a long,
long list of guys who were great drivers but were unsuc-
cessful as team owners. Buddy Baker, Cale Yarborough,
Bobby Allison, Bill Elliott, Ricky Rudd—the list goes
on and on. Each role requires a huge commitment, and
to do them both equally well is a rare thing. That worried me, because I had worked so hard to earn what I
had in my life with Stevie and Jessica. Having my own
team could be a path to the future, but I was also aware
it was a way to go broke in a hurry.

Stevie had been supportive since we first met. After
Jessica was born, we prayed and prayed because we had

decided we wanted to have a second child. In 1992, she became pregnant again and we had our second daughter, Sarah. Now we had two wonderful kids, and Stevie had tired of racing by that time. She never wanted me to have my own team, because she knew it would mean more time away from her and the girls in Tennessee.

Early in my Cup career we bought a second home, a little house in Charlotte. I was always in Charlotte. I stayed right there with the race cars. I worked on them. I slept with them. Those were my babies, but now I had real babies. She didn't want to drag the kids to the track every week. She wanted to have a home life. She had always been a home person, and had given up a lot to support me and my travels.

It made it difficult for me to manage the race team and stay on top of things at the shop. If I wasn't there, it didn't get done—or done the way I wanted. No matter what business you are in, absentee ownership doesn't work. It was a big struggle, which got worse as the girls got older. Stevie needed me at home in Tennessee. The guys needed me in North Carolina.

I tried to hire someone who could run the team the way I would, but I could never find that person. Early in my career, I struggled to find the right group of people with the same vision, the same drive to be champions. If you didn't understand or share that desire, you couldn't work for me. Now, after years driving for Junior Johnson and Rick Hendrick—guys who had worked many years to put their teams together—I was finding that my old problems had returned.

Hendrick fascinates me, because he makes you want to do things. He makes you want to work hard and do what you can to make the team a success. I think that's a huge part of why he has been at the top of the sport for so many years. He gets good people and he keeps them motivated and focused on winning. Junior Johnson is brilliant, and I loved driving for him because he looked at things as a racer. Rick was a racer too. He loved racing and he drove a little bit as well, but he would teach you about the business side. He taught you how to run the team, how to make a team run efficiently like any of his other businesses.

The one drawback to his openness was that it reinforced my belief that I could become a team owner again. I wanted to take his ideas and make them work for my own team. In retrospect, I could kick my own butt a thousand times for not staying with Hendrick. If I had stayed there, I am confident I would have ended my career with more than 100 race wins, and maybe two or three more championships.

■□■

It was the domino effect. Stevie wasn't happy, because I wasn't at home enough. I was trying to juggle all sorts of stuff and nothing was working. She wasn't happy. The race car wasn't happy. I wasn't happy. The sponsors weren't happy. Nobody was happy. It had gone sour, and it seemed like I couldn't stop it. Emotionally, it was getting worse, because I was torn between being a husband/ father and being an owner/driver.

I knew what I needed to be doing to make the team successful. I needed to be with that race car. I needed to be in that shop.

"When you come in for a week, this place runs like a greased wheel," one of my employees told me. "But when you leave, the spokes all come out of the wheels."

I tried to keep the guys happy, because they worked hard. We'd get the cars to run better when I'd hang around awhile, and I'd think we solved some problem. Then I would stay home for two to three weeks and we'd be right back where we were.

I hated firing people, but I fired Hammond. I had promised I'd take care of him for life, but I fired him because he seemed irresponsible when I wasn't around. I wanted to find someone who was more responsible. I hired Barry Dodson. I didn't like him either, so I fired him. I had a couple of other guys, too, but I never could find anybody to run the place.

For a long time, people looked at what I did and tried to emulate it. They looked at my teams and my cars and always said they wanted to do things like I did 'em. Once I got my own team, instead of being the leader I became the follower; I started looking at everybody else's stuff, and I started saying I need to be doing things like Jeff Gordon, Rusty Wallace, or Dale Earnhardt. We were behind the times. That's a lesson I learned—always be first, always be the leader—and I knew my team was struggling when we began following rather than leading. If you do what you've always done, you'll get what you've always got.

It got became too much of a headache. Eventually, the suitcase became too big for one guy to carry. It kept getting heavier and heavier. I often wonder: Would it have been any different if I had been running well? Winning cures a lot of ills, ya know.

The 1994 season started on a horrible note. Rodney Orr, a relative newcomer to NASCAR, and Neil Bonnett, one of the best, were both killed in practice for the Daytona 500. But the race went on as scheduled.

I'm a very emotional person, and racing is an emotional sport. There are highs and lows, like in other sports: the joy of winning, the disappointment of losing. But there's a deeper, more serious level of emotion involved in a sport where you see friends seriously injured or killed. The sport is so consuming. We have no time to grieve and we have no time to celebrate. We always have to pack up and move the circus to the next town.

It's a tragedy when someone is killed, but the attitude in the sport has always been "Man, that's the way it is. Sorry, but we gotta get to the next race."

Ready or not, the green flag flies with or without you. You get wrapped up in that attitude, and it makes you callous. It's like sweeping things under the rug, and we're all guilty of it. If you don't want to race, there are a lot of people waiting to take your place. It doesn't matter if your heart is broken, the race will go on. When you're competing, especially as a driver, you have to hide your grief and you especially have to hide your fear.

I don't recall the year, but before one of the races at Daytona, I made the mistake of confiding in Hammond and telling him I was scared.

I told him because I trusted him. We had a good relationship as friends, as well as a good working relationship. He went back to the pits and told the guys, "We're not going to have a good day today. Our driver is scared." My emotions affected my team and everything around me. We had an awful day.

Drivers have a great deal of fear. No matter how much they deny it, the anxiety is greatest in the buildup to an event. You worry about things that could happen. You think about horrible things you have seen. No question, there's a lot of fear. You're not human if you don't carry these emotions. You're a fool if you don't have some fear.

But you still climb into the car, strap the belts tight, and pull on the helmet. Once the helmet goes on, nearly all of the fear is gone. The helmet is your shield of armor.

When I flipped down the backstretch at Daytona in 1991, there were a lot of photos and video of my arms flying in the air, outside the roll cage. Yet, somehow, I was only bruised when the car came to a rest after flipping 11 times. I saw the replay and was amazed at how lucky I was. I could have lost both arms or, worse, been killed.

Drivers have a sense of denial, a way of putting it behind us. It'll never happen to me. Look how bad that crash was, and I'm all right. You block it out of your mind. After that one, I thought, "I'm OK. I don't have to go back to Daytona until next February."

Because the crash didn't kill me, I couldn't linger on it. I had to get back on the horse. Your concentration, your focus, the job at hand takes place over everything. Having some fear is no different from climbing into the car when you're hurt. Once you get in the car, the aches and pains go away.

People always asked, "How can you see your friends injured? How can you see a friend get killed? How can you get back in the car?"

I struggled to find a sufficient answer, but I usually said, "Driving a race car is what I do. This is how I make a living. This is what I get paid to do. This is what I've based by life upon. This is all I know. I don't wanna give it up."

Other than fear, the only word that comes to mind is *respect*. It's a fine line you have to walk. You have to respect what the car can do and what you can do, what the track conditions are. You can't take unnecessary chances.

If you go out there and drive without a fear in the world, you'll get hurt in a hurry. But if you sit back and refuse to take any chances, you can't expect to be competitive. To be successful you have to respect the danger of the sport, but you can't let fear dictate the way you drive. If you do, you don't belong out on the track.

■ □ ■

The '94 season had a tragic beginning, but later that spring, Jeff Gordon won his first Winston Cup race at the Coca-Cola 600 in Charlotte. After the win, Jeff was so happy he broke into tears. Dale Earnhardt made a big deal out of it, called him a crybaby, and wore the kid out.

I felt the opposite, and was glad someone was finally showing emotion.

You have to be a big man and have a lot of self-confidence to stand up and let people take shots at you if you let tears roll down your cheeks. It's not a sign of weakness. It's a sign of passion and satisfaction. I cried after I won the Daytona 500—and a few tears say you're a passionate person, you've got a heart, and that's the way I've always been.

When I started, it was just Stevie and me. Racing was everything. That's all there was. We had no kids. All my energy and my focus went into racing. That's what made me good. I had no outside interests. I wasn't interested in fishing. I never went hunting. I only played golf because I had to at charity events or celebrity tournaments. I loved automobiles and I loved the automobile business, but I didn't have time for that. I'm a pretty simpleminded person. I'm not good at multitasking. I can do one thing at a time, and my 'sperience proved to me that if you do one thing with all of your heart, you'll be a success.

When a driver gets to a point in his life where he's made a lot of money, is secure, and has a family, that's when a driver doesn't perform like he did in his early years. That's why Junior Johnson looked for that driver between 29 and 30.

Having children when I was older impacted me more than if my daughters had been born when I was younger. By the time they were born, I had already accomplished a great deal. The only thing I hadn't accomplished was being a dad. I hadn't yet had that privilege. But once my daughters did come along I didn't want to jeopardize my life, so I'd take fewer chances on the track.

I drove according to the situation. If I had a car that was capable of running up front, that's where I'd be. But if I had a bad car, and I was fighting for 20th place, I wasn't going to risk everything trying to move up to 19th place. Winning is the only thing that mattered, and I didn't see much difference between second place or 20th place.

■□■

The 1995 season started really well for the team, and it looked like we were on the right track. I almost won at Martinsville, where Rusty Wallace beat me. I had a great day at Talladega, finishing fourth, and coming into Charlotte, we were back in the top 10 in points and it seemed as if the team had cleared some imaginary hurdle. We were starting to click, and the results marked our growth and momentum.

We were really fast in The Winston, and I thought I was on my way to win the big money, but Earnhardt pretty much put an end to my year when he made a banzai move under me in turn four. He got loose and slammed me into the wall. Somehow I got out of the car and managed a weak wave to the fans, but I knew I was hurt.

The crash broke several ribs, and caused some internal injuries that meant I couldn't drive. The crash even tore my rotator cuff. I was busted up, and I had to let somebody else drive my car for at least six weeks.

While I was hurt, we didn't run well, and morale suffered. Several other race teams were looking for good people, so one of my crew guys was hired away. Then another. When I finally got back in the car, I had lost most of my best people. A season that started so well ended in shambles.

I felt like that woman in the TV commercial who says, "I've fallen and I can't get up." If I could just get up, I'd be all right, but nobody offered a hand. I'd been around a long time, so people pretty much said, "You've had your time. Why don't ya quit? Go do something else."

No matter what age, you can be a good team owner or you can be a good driver, but you can't be a good team owner/driver. You gotta make up your mind. It's one or the other. I was struggling to do both, as well as trying to be a good husband and a good father. The guys from Western Auto finally sat me down one day because they were concerned with the lack of results.

"Darrell, we have never questioned your ability as a driver. You're one of the greatest drivers of all time," they said. "But you're a terrible owner."

That really opened my eyes. It was another lesson learned.

I became more and more worried about all of the money I was spending on the team. I knew I couldn't fall into the trap of running the team like a racer. A racer will spend every dime he's got. You'll spend all you've got and then borrow more from somebody else, like an addict.

My wife never wanted me to start my own team. Women are intuitive. She told me, "This is the biggest mistake you could make. Why do you want to do this?"

I told her I wanted to control my own destiny, and

while she understood, she knew it was a mistake. I wasn't in a position to risk everything I had earned personally, and even though I was determined to make it work, I just couldn't.

My thinking was that I was going to drive the car myself. I would use my reputation and ability to build my team. My name still had a lot of credibility and value. I'd build this thing up, and when I was ready to retire as a driver, I'd sit back and be an owner. I'd get somebody to drive and I'd live happily ever after. That was my intention. I was running out of time, but I also didn't want to leave the sport. I didn't want to park the car one day and say, "That's it, I'm done," and have no place to go.

By the 1995 season my goals were farther from my reach than I had thought. That season was marked by an incredible leap in technology and the large sums of money people like Rick Hendrick and Jack Roush were willing to invest in their teams to take advantage of the technological breakthroughs. As a single car owner, I couldn't keep up financially with these teams and the investments they were making. It became a vicious cycle: I couldn't keep people because I couldn't pay them as much, and I certainly couldn't perform at their level on the track because I didn't have the kind of money to improve my equipment. And because I wasn't performing well, I couldn't go to a sponsor and ask for more money. They would have looked at me like I was crazy. Visions and fairy tales don't always come true.

My team struggled so much that the highlight of 1996 for me was when my brother Michael started at the back of the field and then blasted past everyone to win The Winston. It was his first Winston Cup win, and we had a joyous, tearful time together, celebrating in Victory Lane. Michael took his winnings from that race and built a house for my mom and dad to live in near him at Lake Norman.

We really struggled with qualifying. NASCAR had already created a system of provisionals in which they held six positions at the back of the field for their full-time teams that weren't fast enough to qualify in the top 36. A team could make the starting lineup with a provisional spot even if they suffered a bad qualifying effort. But Bill France Jr. created the champion's provisional for me.

He tried to think of something since Richard Petty started missing races at the end of his career. It was a big deal—the King going home. Imagine if you're a Richard Petty fan, buying your tickets months in advance, and when you showed up on Sunday, he wasn't even in the field?

I called France Jr. and said, "You have to help me here. I have this sponsor that helps the whole sport. We're working around the clock getting these cars built, and I am out on a big limb. And I can hear everyone starting the chain saws. This is my money, my deal, and it will ruin me if I don't make a race. What if I miss the Daytona 500?" That's every racer's nightmare. No one wants to miss the biggest race of the year, going home with your tail between your legs.

"I am working without a net," I argued, "and we need to figure a way to develop an exemption. I can't afford to lose their support, and NASCAR can't afford to lose them. There has to be a way to avoid what happened to Petty."

That's when France came up with the idea for the champion's provisional. If you were a former champion, NASCAR would hold a spot for you at the back of the starting field.

So Richard Petty's misfortune helped me, and luckily

NASCAR saw the merits to my thinking. It was a great insurance policy, and it helped ease my fears, knowing I had this Get Out of Jail Free card in my back pocket.

But in the long run, it cost me. It damaged my image and did a lot of harm to my reputation as a driver. I relied on the exemption too much, and it became known as "the Darrell Waltrip provisional." Initially, it was a great deal because we weren't concerned about qualifying. The teams with the biggest budgets would bring qualifying engines each week. They were light and fragile, designed to go very, very fast for only a few laps. We wouldn't even bring a qualifying engine, and we didn't have to worry about a qualifying setup because we had the provisional crutch. We didn't use it every week, but when we were struggling, it helped to know we were in the race.

Things were tough, but for the 1997 running of The Winston we decided to have some fun. I've always liked slick cars and I've always liked chrome, so we did up the race car with an all-chrome look. Under the lights, that baby was gleaming. We called it the Silver Bullet! I even had a driver's suit that looked like some sort of cross between Elvis Presley and a Martian suit—all silver and shiny. I wore it for the prerace introduction and hoopla, then slipped into my real driving suit for the race itself. It was all in the spirit of The Winston: No points on the line, so let's have some fun and let it all hang out!

But the fun didn't last. Later that week, during qualifying for the Coca-Cola 600, Terry Labonte ran poorly and failed to qualify, which was surprising because he had one of the fastest cars in practice. Because of how the starting field was aligned, if Terry took one of the six regular provisionals, it would knock his Hendrick teammate, Ricky Craven, out of the race. If Terry took the champion's provisional spot, then his teammate would gain the last regular provisional spot. Long story short, Terry used the champion's provisional and I was forced to miss the race. I don't blame him—I'd have done the same thing—but it hurt me to the core to sit out.

I wanted to go home, but because we were in Charlotte, I had a fan club meeting the next night, and I was also scheduled to be a guest analyst in the TV booth during Saturday's Busch race. Stevie and I got in the car, drove out of the tunnel at the speedway, and went to Frank Liske Park. We sat on the bank of a small pond. We threw rocks in the water and we cried. She said, "Let's just go home."

"I wanna go home," I said. "I want to go hide somewhere. But I can't do that. Champions don't go home."

We had our fan club meeting Friday night, and it was difficult. I did television on Saturday, and it was just as hard. Then we finally went home after the race on Saturday. I wanted to be anywhere but at the racetrack on Sunday, because they were starting without me.

In 1998, we struggled almost every week, and I think I used that darn champion's provisional something like 20 times. I started getting letters and e-mails saying you're just taking up space out there . . . you're washed up . . . you're taking the place of someone else in the field.

By the end of the season the backlash was awful, and it really hurt me. NASCAR felt we were taking advantage of the rule, so they changed it. The new version allowed the use of the champion's provisional only four times each season. That year, 1999, I was driving for a new team with poor equipment, and I used up my freebies very quickly. Once we started missing races, things began to snowball, and I failed to make the starting lineup for seven races that season.

If I could have predicted the harm the champion's provisional would bring me in the long run, I would have reconsidered ever using it. Add that to the list of hard lessons learned: Be careful what you wish for.

Oh, by the way . . .

■ ■□■□

Michael Waltrip

It was a great moment when he came to see me in the Winner's Circle at The Winston. There are some great photos of that. I remember the TV guys were trying to interview him after the race near the gas pumps, and he was so excited for me, he drove off with his trunk still open. . . .

I have really enjoyed the last few years with Darrell. We've come a long way as brothers. I had admired him from afar, and now it's gotten to the point where I know him more as a brother than my idol. Now, we're working together and getting closer all the time.

Joe Carver, business manager

It broke his heart to hear the people from Western Auto tell him he wasn't as good of an owner as he was a driver. Darrell really took his team to heart. He budgeted a certain amount for his salary, but he never took anything close to that amount. He only paid himself what he absolutely needed. The rest of the money—sponsorship, winnings, souvenirs—went directly back into the team. He really felt obligated to the people who

CONTINUED

worked for him. Those people and their families were very, very important to him.

Jeff Hammond, crew chief

It was a question of focus. Darrell had so much in front of him. He said it used to just be him, Stevie, and their dog, but now he had his own team and his kids. It's a lot of responsibility, and a lot of accountability for one man. It's difficult to point to all of that and say, "He lost his killer instinct." He could still drive, and he could still be very successful, but it was too much.

It was a bad time for all of us. Things were in disarray. It was a mess. I wrote a letter to Darrell saying, "Here's what we need to make this team successful." But he was just being pulled in too many directions to do what needed to be done to make the team a success.

23

Selling My Future

After a disastrous season in 1995, Western Auto informed me they were not going to renew their sponsorship at the conclusion of 1996. The stores had been renamed "Parts America," because it was a name that would play better in the South or northeastern regions of the country. I didn't think it had the same ring as Western Auto, but I hated to lose such a great sponsor, so we came up with the idea for "Darrell Waltrip's 25th Anniversary Tour 1997."

"Look, we have a plan," I told them. "We're going to get more media attention than you ever imagined."

It had been 25 years since my first Winston Cup race, and Hammond and I had the idea of painting the race cars in a series of color schemes to look like all of the combinations I had driven before. The car would still say "Parts America," but at one race it would be in the white and green colors like the Gatorade car, then we'd do another race with the car painted red and white like the Budweiser car. It would be like a rolling memory lane for me and my fans. We also decided, since 25 years is known as the silver anniversary, we were going to do several races in a chrome race car. That baby was going to shine. We'd need sunglasses on a bright day, because it was going to be sharp.

Parts America liked the idea, so they agreed to extend their sponsorship through 1997.

"A Major Announcement," the invitation read when we scheduled the news conference. We had a big dinner in Charlotte and I had the ol' Mercury on display, restored and looking better than new. What I hadn't expected was the reaction. Based on the tone of the invitation, and the headline, everyone assumed I was going to announce my retirement.

The turnout was huge. We had more than 300 people in attendance at the First Union Plaza in downtown Charlotte. The media were packed in there, maybe because of the free food, and also because they assumed I was calling it quits. Anyone who was anything in NASCAR was there: Bill France Jr., my brother Michael and his wife Buffy, David Pearson, Richard and Linda Petty, Brian France, Bruton Smith, Humpy Wheeler, and Ned and Martha Jarrett. They wanted to be there when I hung the helmet up for good.

Me, Stevie, and the girls rolled up in a big black limousine.

You can imagine the reaction I got after announcing I was going to do a bunch of cool old paint schemes.

Maybe I should have taken everyone's less-than-enthusiastic reaction as an omen.

I think we brought in $7 million from the entire 25th Anniversary plan, between the sponsorship, prize money, and souvenir sales that year. I spent every bit of that and more on the team, buying equipment like a CNC machine (that stands for "computer numeric control," in case you were wondering) to make our own parts with precision within fractions of the width of a strand of hair. Long gone were the days when I'd mark my favorite set of springs and then pull them out the next time we went back to that same track. Now I was building an addition to my shop, constructing the finest parts, trying to upgrade my team, because that was the only way I was going to be competitive enough to draw another sponsor for 1998.

The Silver Anniversary Tour was great fun. The all-chrome car was the hit of the season. Everyone loved it. I was competitive and was in or around the top 15 in points throughout the season. We had special events at the tracks where we ran the commemorative painted cars, and we brought a number of country music stars to be our guest for those events. Stars like Lorrie Morgan, Charlie Daniels, Lee Greenwood, and others hung out with us in the pits and sang the national anthem at some of the races.

Earlier in the year, Glen and Ned Jarrett tried to help us secure General Mills sponsorship for 1998. We hosted the General Mills folks at our shop one day. Lorrie Morgan was our country-and-western star guest that weekend, and she just "happened" to stop by while they were there. Unfortunately, we soon learned that General Mills wanted to invest in a young driver starting his career and not a veteran driver nearing the end of his career. General Mills decided to go with Johnny Benson and the Jack Roush team for 1998.

In June, we began speaking with the executives at Pennzoil about sponsorship for the future. We spent the next two months talking to them. By August of that season, I believed I was going to sign with Pennzoil. I had everything in hand except the contract. We had a great meeting in Loudon, New Hampshire, with them. In fact, they told Van Colley, my marketing director, they would have a letter of intent ready when we got to Indianapolis for the Brickyard 400. I was parked right next to the Pennzoil motor home inside the speedway when the race week began, so I was pretty happy about how the whole thing was shaping up. We set a meeting for eight o'clock on Saturday morning to finish the deal.

All of their executives had been to my shop, including Johnny Rutherford, whom they called "Lone Star J. R." Rutherford was a Houston hometown hero because he had won the Indy 500 with Pennzoil sponsorship. They said they liked what I was doing.

Saturday morning came around, and Van and I went over at eight o'clock sharp. Man, I was itching to get over there—and when it was exactly eight, we walked only a few feet to the next motor coach. The second we walked in, I knew it didn't feel right. Everyone was talking about everything except the contract. I couldn't mess around very long, because it was race day and I had to get ready.

"What about this letter of intent?" I asked.

"Well, uh, we need a couple of more weeks," they said. "Some things have come up and we need a couple of more weeks."

"All right," I said, taking a deep breath, knowing that "some things have come up" is not a good sign—like when your wife or your boss says "we need to talk." That isn't a promising sign.

"Is everything OK?" I asked.

"Oh yeah, we think everything is great, but we're just taking a look at some other things."

My dad called me Monday morning.

"Son, I thought you told me you had the Pennzoil deal?"

"Dad, I was going to sign Saturday, but for some reason they put it off for a couple of weeks."

"I know why," he said.

"You know why?!" I said. "What do you know that I don't?"

"I heard Dale Earnhardt got it," he said. Earnhardt was starting his own full-time Winston Cup team, and his driver was going to be his current Busch Series driver, Steve Park.

"There ain't no way, Daddy!" I told him. "They already told me they weren't going to mess with another rookie. They had some young guys before and they didn't want to mess with a rookie driver, so I find that hard to believe."

"I'm telling you, I was in the Cracker Barrel," Dad said. "I'm sitting at my table and there are two guys behind me from Pennzoil saying that Dale and Don Hawk [Dale's business guy] had flown down to Houston and had signed a letter of intent with them."

I never thought about sending a plane to pick up the president of Pennzoil. I never thought of flying him to a race. I was worried only about getting me and my team to the race. That's how Dale shot me out of the Pennzoil deal. He flew to Houston and went hunting with the president of Pennzoil. I always thought like a driver, not an owner. My approach was: If you wanna go hunting, fine. But I'm racing, I'm thinking about racing. And that hurt my business more than once.

I thought I was going to throw up. I called Van and asked him if it was true or not. Sure enough, it was true. I couldn't believe it, because I had banked heavily on the deal. But Dale had flown down there in his plane and swept 'em away. As a car owner, I was never good at that kind of grand gesture.

Then we were working on a deal with the FOX network, believe it or not. This was several years before there was any talk of them bidding for the NASCAR telecasts. *America's Most Wanted* was looking to sponsor a car to help promote their show. We designed a car for them, painted it, and even hauled it to New York to show it off. They loved the car! It really created a stir around the offices. All we needed was someone to sign off on the deal, but it became a situation where we couldn't figure out who we were dealing with, the network or the production company that does the show. They all liked the idea, but no one was willing to write the check. Finally it got down to November, and the FOX people were ready for the Super Bowl in January. They told us they weren't in a position to make a decision until after the game. That was too late for us.

It's November, and Daytona was only three months away. I had no sponsor, and the biggest race of the year was coming soon—very soon.

Out of nowhere (well, actually Ohio), in walks a guy with a company called "Speedblock."

Keith Waltz, who handled public relations for my team, had heard from a buddy of his who worked for a guy who knew about a company interested in signing with a team right away. It was one of those "I know a guy who knows a guy . . ." deals. After 30 years of racing, I should've known right away: If it's too good to be true, then it's too good to be true.

Speedblock was a company with a system to build houses out of concrete. It was a big deal in Europe, where, instead of wood, you use concrete to construct walls, and they were bringing this process to the United States.

They came in and presented a package where all of the companies that were a part of the Speedblock plan had a piece of the action. We were given a list of all of the vendors that they were working with: Whirlpool, Maytag, Kohler. These companies were pooling money into the program, and they wanted to sponsor a car to promote Speedblock. The concept was similar to the format Western Auto had used to include their retail vendors.

Dick Haas was the owner of Speedblock, and he was going to give us a \$4 million base sponsorship package. Then we were going to get a percentage of each house he built, which he projected would be somewhere in the neighborhood of 1,000 houses a year. The sky was the limit! He had his vision—a real turnkey deal: Here's the lot for your home. Pick out your home design, pick out your appliances. We'll build it, we'll finance it. One-stop shopping! Everybody's happy!

We projected and analyzed the numbers, and it looked like it was going to be a pretty darn nice deal.

We had very little time to get ready for Daytona, but we worked everyone overtime to paint cars and trucks and order uniforms and everything else that goes with a major sponsorship change. I called Dad to tell him the news.

"How much money did the man give you?" was his first question. "Who's paying for all of this stuff?"

We were spending money like crazy.

"We're paying for all of this right now," I explained, "and he's going to reimburse us with our first payment on January 15th."

Every January, Lowe's Motor Speedway brings the motorsports media from across the United States to Charlotte to visit with the major teams before the season starts. We were happy to be a stop on the tour, and we were excited to announce the sponsorship and have the new car on display.

I had never met Dick Haas until that day, but I knew the moment I shook his hand that something wasn't right. You know when you shake someone's hand and they give you the ol' dead-fish grip? All clammy, floppy, and lifeless? I hate that.

He was talking 190 miles per hour. He had a couple of cronies with him, and he was the king of the show. There wasn't a whole lot I was going to say to get in his way, but I just figured we'd get past these annoying personality traits. The problem was there was no check.

"We ran into a couple of problems with some contracts with a vendor or two," he said. "We should have it resolved by the end of the week, and you'll have your check Monday."

I was as pale as a ghost, because I'd seen this happen in racing a thousand times before. If I'd met that man before we did this deal then I would've known, but I never met him. How could I have been so blind? I really thought this was for real.

But it was too late. I'd already announced this new sponsor to the world, and the only choice we had was to go to Daytona and race.

At this point, a small part of me was still hopeful, but my bad feeling continued to get worse. We packed the team and headed south to Speedweeks at Daytona, money or not. We'd called the guy every day, and somehow we finally got ahold of him.

"I'm sending you a check tomorrow for $250,000," he told us.

The next day a check came via FedEx—made out for only $25,000. We rushed it straight to the bank to deposit it. Any little bit will help. From January through March, we received four payments for fractions of what was promised, and one of the four payments bounced.

That's the last anyone ever heard from him. We tried to track him down again and again. I had my attorney run all kinds of checks on him and his company. The company didn't exist any longer. I was so angry with myself, because I had never gotten stung like this. I'd always checked people out. If I didn't know them, I had them checked out before I did a deal. I didn't care what it was—endorsements or whatever. But everybody was so anxious, and I was getting so nervous that we weren't going to have a deal for Daytona.

All my life, I had been focused on one thing: driving that race car. And now my desire to keep driving blinded the part of me that should have known better. We took the deal and ran with it. We had a contract, but there was no recourse. It wasn't worth the postage it would take to send it back to my attorneys.

After that nightmare, the on-track stuff is kind of fuzzy, but I wrecked in practice and we had to race the backup car. We finished 33rd. Next we went to Rockingham, where we were 41st. It wasn't much better at Las Vegas, where 35th was the best we could do. After that, I knew Darlington was my last race. I didn't have the money to go any further. Just so I wouldn't be so depressed driving out there with a plain white car with no decals, I ran a vintage look. I painted my ride to look like the number 300 car the great Tim Flock drove in the early days of NASCAR. We were trying to find deals, but there were none to be found. It was costing me $450,000 a month to pay 55 employees and try to race.

I still had my Craftsman Truck series team, and Rich Bickle had driven the truck for me the year before, and he finished second in the championship. He won three races and four poles with DieHard Batteries as the sponsor. DieHard was part of the bigger Sears/Parts America corporate family, and I had a real good team. We darn near won the championship in 1997, but Jack Sprague beat us.

I had hoped to put a deal together for Bickle to move up to Winston Cup, and we planned to run two cars. I ran him at Indy in the Kentucky Fried Chicken car the year before, when he qualified 10th and was running in the top 15 with just a few laps to go when a tire went down and he crashed.

I didn't have a sponsor for my own car, so certainly I couldn't run him. He got mad at me and stormed off. That didn't sit too well with the folks at DieHard.

"I don't know" was the response from Paul Baffico at Sears. "We've had a lot of drivers. Every year we turn around, it seems like we have a different driver. Let me know what you're thinking, but we're not very happy changing drivers all the time."

"I'll find somebody," I promised, "as good as or better than he is."

The best guy, or more accurately the *only* guy, who was available at that late date was Phil Parsons. I figured he had run pretty well in the Busch Series, so soon I had Parsons sitting in my office, ready to sign a contract to drive my truck.

There was only one piece left to confirm, so I called Baffico to tell him we had a driver.

"Paul, he's sitting here right now," I told him, "so all I need is your commitment. I can sign him right now and we'll get started testing immediately."

"Darrell," he replied, "we've decided that we're not going to be in racing anymore."

It was another one of those drop-my-jaw-to-the-floor moments. DieHard was going away, Speedblock was the worst disaster ever, and everything was disappearing before my very eyes.

Every direction we turned, it was a mirage or a dead end. I really thought we were close with Pennzoil, and the *America's Most Wanted* project was a ghost chase from day one. Now this was the final blow.

I called Rick Hendrick before I went to Darlington and offered to sell him my share in the auto dealership to keep my team afloat.

"No way," he told me. "That dealership is something you can make a living at. You should sell the team instead."

"Rick, do you know anybody, among all of your buddies, all your dealings, that might want to buy a race team?"

"No," he said. "I don't know anybody. I've got some that I'd like to sell!" I didn't know if he was kidding or not.

"I'm either going to have to sell," I said, "or I'm going to lock the doors and send all the people home because I can't keep doing it."

A couple of hours went by, and Rick called me back.

"I did think of one guy down in Tyler, Texas," he said. "He always said that he wanted to be in the racing business. Tim Beverley is his name. He was in on another deal, but it didn't work out. Do you want me to call him for you?"

It wasn't 30 minutes until Tim Beverley called me.

"I want to come down and look at your place," he told me. "I've wanted to get into racing, and I was going to go into business with the number seven team, but I don't like Fords and it's not going well."

"I have to go to Darlington," I said, "but I'll be here Monday and I'll show you what I've got." He said he would come in from Texas in his Falcon 20 jet, and I agreed to be there to meet him.

After the plane taxied in, a young guy got off the plane who I thought was the pilot.

I wondered why only one guy was getting off the plane.

Well, Tim Beverley was the pilot. That was his business. He sold jets, and that's how he knew Rick and a few other team owners.

I first thought he was a bit too cocky. He was a good-looking guy, but he looked young, maybe no older than 35. "Here we go again," I thought.

It was hard to get excited or feel optimistic. The thought of selling my team . . . everything I had worked to build, all of my dreams, my hopes and my future . . . I couldn't believe things had become this desperate, but I had people relying on me to write paychecks, so I had to do something. I had no choice. I was going through my cash like it was water pouring into the ground. It ripped my heart out to sell the team. Stevie was happy because it was like an albatross around our neck, but that didn't make it any easier on me.

I showed him everything I had. Then we drove over to meet with Hendrick to discuss the possibilities. I told Beverley my price.

"For that amount of money," I told him, "you can take it all. Just take my name off the property, the building, the people, and put your name on it. Everything."

Rick looked over the details and assured him it was a good deal.

"The cars there are good," he explained to Beverley. "This would be a great opportunity for you. You're getting ten acres of real estate, a good shop, and good people already in place."

Beverley and I got back in the car to take another look at the shop. He stuck his hand out and said, "I'll take your deal."

His handshake was strong.

"There really is a God," I thought. "And He has answered my prayers—again."

"I think you'll be happy with that decision," I told him. Me, I was happy, sad, relieved, crushed, depressed, and elated all at one time about Beverley's decision.

"Get your attorney and everybody you need to get in touch with," he said. Then he gave me his card. "We'll get the ball rolling."

Oh, by the way . . .

■■□■□

Van Colley, marketing director

Not getting the General Mills deal hurt, but we never recovered from losing the Pennzoil deal. They weren't upfront with us, and then to have Darrell's dad Leroy hear the "real deal" at the Cracker Barrel only added insult to injury. Those were dark days.

I've never seen DW so hurt as when he had to sell the team. Beverley came in and gutted the place. All the people DW had taken care of all those years were being fired, and it broke DW's heart. But there was nothing he could do to stop it. It wasn't his anymore.

24

Driving for Dale

While I was struggling with my own situation, completely immersed in my problems, Steve Park had been hurt in a crash during practice for the Atlanta race. He crashed hard in Earnhardt's Pennzoil car and was going to be out for at least a couple of months with serious injuries, primarily a broken leg.

Earnhardt, who made a mint driving for Richard Childress for many years, was trying to build his own team just like me. He still drove Richard's black number 3 car, but he wanted to get his own team going with another driver. This was their first full Winston Cup season, and it had been a rough start with a rookie driver and a new team.

The week after the crash, Ron Hornaday drove the car in Park's place at Darlington and didn't make the race. I made the race in my own car, one day before I met with Tim Beverley, and finished 30th. The race after that was Bristol, and even though I had been struggling, it was pretty clear that I could still get around Bristol as good as anyone.

After Beverley left Charlotte on his jet, with our deal agreed upon, Don Hawk, Earnhardt's business manager, called to find out what I was doing with my team. I told him that a part of my deal for selling the team to Tim Beverley was that I'd drive the car. He wasn't going to buy the team unless I agreed to drive.

"I gotta honor that commitment," I told him.

Then my brother Michael called. He and Dale were in the Bahamas, relaxing and getting a suntan out on a boat. Well, not just any boat, but Earnhardt's yacht, *Sunday Money*. Calling it a boat was like calling Lake Michigan a pond. Michael and Dale had become very close friends over the years, and for me, it was exactly like when Michael went to live with the Petty family. It hurt me knowing that he was finding friendship and advice from my biggest adversaries.

"You need to get in Dale's car. Dale really wants you to drive his car," he told me.

"I don't believe you!" I said. "If he calls me himself and tells me he wants me to drive his car, then I'd believe you. I want to hear it from Dale directly."

It was about pride more than anything. If that scoundrel Earnhardt wanted me to drive his car, he'd have to pick up the phone and call me himself. Especially after he had signed the sponsor from right under my nose, on top of all that we had been through as rivals. We always had a lot of respect for each other, and as our careers progressed, we slowly became friends. "Frienemies" is probably the best way to describe it. Friends and enemies at the same time.

Michael's call was on Monday night, and early Tuesday morning, I hosted a Bible-study group in the basement of my home. The group consisted of about 100 men, and we'd been doing it for almost 20 years. They're my friends, and I trusted them to tell me the truth when I had a problem. They had been very supportive as I struggled with the team and the business.

"Look, guys," I said right off the bat. "We need to

pray, because I have this dilemma. I've sold my race team and that was an answer to a prayer, but Michael called to tell me Earnhardt wants me to drive his car. I told the guy who bought the team that I'd drive for him. I'd really like to go drive for Earnhardt, because I think it would be a really cool thing to do. I battled and battled against that guy for years, but now I think it would be a great thing for me."

The Bible study began at 7 A.M. A few minutes later, Stevie ran downstairs and grabbed me by the arm.

"You have to come upstairs. Dale's on the phone."

So I excused myself from the meeting and walked upstairs to pick up the phone.

"Zip!" he said.

He called me Zip. That's a nickname I got way back in Owensboro. They called me that when I was on the track team in school because I was pretty quick. Somehow Earnhardt found out and he thought it was funny, so he always called me Zip.

"Zip! What are you doin'?" he asked.

"Meeting with all of my guys," I said.

"I need your help," he said.

"You what?" I said, kind of needling him a bit. Earnhardt loved you to death when he needed you, but you were nothing to him if he didn't, so I figured I'd take advantage and savor the moment. "So what's the deal?" I asked.

"I need you to drive my car for about three to four months until Park gets well," he said. "I know it's not your car, but I need you to drive it for me. It's a new team, and already I've got eight wrecked race cars and a hurt driver. Pennzoil's on my case, and I'm afraid I'm going to lose this deal if I don't do something. I called them and told them that I might be able to get you. Pennzoil said, 'If you can get Darrell Waltrip, then that would make us very happy.' I'm at your mercy," he pleaded. "Tell me what you want to drive the car and I'll give it to ya."

We discussed the details, and he told me what he would do, and I mean it was very generous, very generous. Especially from Earnhardt! I was shocked, because he had a reputation of not paying his people very well.

"Dale," I said. "I would love to do this, but I have a commitment to Tim Beverley. If I don't drive that car, my deal doesn't go through."

Our conversation ended, and I know we were both disappointed.

I walked back downstairs, where the meeting was still going on.

"Dale called, and he wants me to drive his car," I told them, "but I can't do it."

The sentence had barely left my lips when Stevie grabbed me again.

"You have to come upstairs," she said. "It's Tim Beverley on the phone."

"What are you doing?" Tim said.

"I'm just having a Bible study at the house," I told him.

There was kind of a pause, and then he started with hesitation.

"Let me ask you something," he said. "How upset would you be if we shut the race team down for three to four months?"

"Why?" I asked.

"Because I want to totally rebuild it," he answered. "I've been here this morning. I've looked the place over. We've got work to do. We're not ready to go racing."

I couldn't believe what I was hearing.

"If you can find something else, whatever you want to do, I'll understand," he said. "If you can give me about three to four months, I want to rebuild this thing and make some changes."

Within an hour, I had been offered a great deal that I

couldn't take, and then the guy who bought my team had called to say he would understand if I found something else!

Before Dale could call another driver, I called him back and yelled, "I'll take the deal!"

I had been losing hundreds of thousands of my own dollars each month trying to keep my team afloat. Now, all of a sudden, somebody was paying me to buy the business, and someone else was going to pay me to go drive their car?!

It was crazy. I ran downstairs and I cried.

"This is what we prayed for," I said. "One hundred men saw prayers answered just like that. It may not happen very often, but it happened this time!"

■□■

Dale and I met a day later in what is known as the deer-head shop. This was Dale's own personal little garage, and it still sits behind the huge DEI complex. There are God knows how many stuffed animal heads mounted on the walls. Deer, elk, moose, whatever he hunted, there was a big ol' head mounted on the wall around this shop. It was where Dale would go to relax at night, and he'd work on his street cars or even let Dale Jr. work on his late-model race cars before Junior moved up to the Busch Series.

"Let's go over to the new shop," he said after we talked awhile. "Let's look at the car we're working on for you to drive at Bristol."

It was an old race car he had bought from Andy Petree. To be polite, it was a piece of . . . junk. They were thrashing on it and the team wasn't even close to having it finished. They were still working on everything. Before the leap to Winston Cup, DEI had been a Busch Series operation that had run only a few Cup races. It was a brand-new team with a rookie driver, and as usually happens in that situation, they had wrecked every car Dale had—all eight of them.

The crewmembers were all down in the dumps. Phillippe Lopez was there as crew chief, along with people like Ty Norris, still one of the top executives at DEI. Good people, but the whole crowd was walking around like zombies.

Dale assured them we were all gonna work to get this deal together, and they seemed pretty happy I had agreed to come aboard.

But the car they had for me to drive at Bristol . . . whoa, I couldn't even get in it. The seat wasn't right. It was like an old beat-up shoe they were trying to polish up and make look nice. As I struggled to get out, I got an idea. My team—well, at least what had been my team—had a car ready to go to Bristol.

"Why don't we call the guy I sold the team to and tell him we want to lease the car?" I suggested. "It's sitting there ready to go, and it's a car that has been great at Bristol."

Everyone agreed on the deal pretty quickly, so we drove to my old shop, picked up the car, painted it yellow, put a red number one on it, and off we went to Bristol.

What made the race memorable was racing so hard with Dale near the end of the event.

"Richard!" Dale called on the radio to Childress. "Tell Ty [Norris, who was my spotter] to tell DW to move over and let me by!"

Oh man! As soon as he said that, Phillippe came on the radio and said, "If you even think about moving out of his way, you're going to have all of us on your case when you get in here!"

So I didn't.

"I'm running for a championship, he's not!" Dale's

yelling. "That might mean something at the end of the year!"

There was a late yellow flag, and Dale did go past me. We didn't run that great, but I finished 23rd, right behind Dale. The key was to just finish the race with the car intact. But on Monday morning, the whole team went into the office and told Dale, "Don't put us in that position anymore. We're racing you just like you're racing us, and don't ask us to move over, 'cause we aren't going to!"

And that was the start of a great couple of months. It gave me so much satisfaction, because I had left my own team under the worst possible circumstances. I was really at a low point. I wasn't competitive. I was depressed. Then, driving for Dale when I went over there, it was like I had been released out of a cage.

Before then, I felt I was useless. I had seen my plans for the future go up in smoke, and worst of all, no one thought I was capable of driving at a competitive level anymore. But after I walked into a situation with Dale and his team where everyone was glad to have me on board, it was like a drug. I hadn't felt that good in a long time. It was really an ideal situation, and it worked out well for everyone. Everybody was happy. Heck, we almost won two races.

It was important for me, and for them, to qualify well. I had used provisionals way too often with my own team, but I think we used only one in eight races I drove the car. We almost won Pocono. We almost won California. They got all their cars fixed and rebuilt. We tore up only one car while I was there. And when Park came back, the team was better in many ways than when he left. They really improved after he got back, and Park ended up winning several races before he was injured in a bad crash in a Busch race at Darlington in 2001.

If I had known then how much I would struggle to get myself into a good car for the rest of my career, I probably would have tried to break Park's other leg so I could have stayed a little longer, maybe won a race, and then found another, competitive ride. But I always say I have brilliant 20/20 hindsight.

I tried every way I could think of to get Dale to run a car for me the next year. He was close, but his business was still new and he wasn't quite there yet. He was bringing Dale Jr. along from the Busch Series to Winston Cup with Budweiser backing, and he even spoke with NAPA Auto Parts about putting me in a car. His vision was to bring NAPA from a Busch Series sponsor up to Winston Cup, but we never could put all of the pieces in place.

"I'm just not ready," Dale finally told me.

Oh, by the way . . .

■ □ □ ■

Ty Norris, Dale Earnhardt Inc.

We were in total disarray. Our driver was hurt, and we missed three out of the first five races. Darrell walked in with a swagger and a sense of humor and said, "Boys, you're going to be OK." And we all believed him. The next few weeks were the most fun I have ever had in our organization.

The first race was at Bristol. Dale cut a tire down and had to pit. Then there was the discussion about Darrell

CONTINUED

moving over for Dale. After the race, Darrell got out of the car and said, "If I'm going to have to pull over to finish one position behind the boss, I want a faster boss. I'm not pulling out of the way for 22nd position again." It made light of a tense situation.

When we finished in the top five at California, it felt like we had won the Super Bowl. Here's Darrell Waltrip, a man many thought was through, finishing in the top five at one of the fastest tracks on the circuit. Then we almost won at Pocono. Darrell gave a great emotional interview after that race, and we have all loved him since.

25

I Should Have
Walked Away

I was out of the Pennzoil car once Steve Park was healthy again. I had done a good job, so at least it was something to build on. But then I stepped into what is known as the Tabasco Fiasco. Bob Hancher was the car owner who brought Tabasco into NASCAR. He seemed more interested in his Indy car team, but he convinced Tabasco to also back a NASCAR effort. It was a heck of a deal, rumored to be at the seven- to eight-million-dollar level. Todd Bodine started the year with them, and I ended the season, but the team was dog meat. And, even with a lot of Tabasco sauce, dog meat doesn't taste very good.

Tim Beverley was involved, because he was trying to get the Tabasco deal for himself the following season. I lost count of how many times we went to Avery Island, Louisiana, meeting with the Tabasco people, but they decided not to sponsor a race team the following year.

"I've had it with this team," I said. "I am not driving for this team anymore."

As far as I was concerned, I was done at the end of '98. I didn't know what I wanted to do, but I wasn't going back to that team. Then I got a phone call from Todd Parrott at Robert Yates Racing. I had worked with Robert back in the DiGard days, and since then he had built what was considered one of the top teams. I had also worked with Todd's dad, Buddy.

"We wanna know if you want to drive the 88 car," Parrott said.

I almost fell to the floor. This was a prime ride! Dale Jarrett was great with the team, and I couldn't believe what I was hearing. I had heard rumblings that Jarrett was having back trouble and was due to have some kind of surgery.

"What are you talking about?" I asked, thinking this is a dream come true. "You want *me* to drive the 88 car?"

"Yeah," he said. "In Japan."

Awww . . . The wind went out of my sails quick. NASCAR had taken teams to Japan for an exhibition race for several years, and Jarrett was having surgery so he couldn't drive in the event, let alone fly over there.

I went to Japan and drove the 88 car. It was nice, and even though it was an exhibition, it was another chance to show I could still wheel it. I qualified fourth and was running well, but Bobby Hamilton spun and put me in the wall.

It was going to be a long, sad flight home. But someone asked me, "Have you talked to Travis Carter?"

"Nope," I said.

"Well, he's working on a deal with Kmart, and I hear it's pretty big," they said. "They don't have a deal signed yet, mainly because they don't have the right driver. You should call him."

"I don't know. I might," I muttered.

It was an endless ride home from the Orient, and I had a lot of time to think. Maybe this was something I should explore. So I asked for his phone number and called from the airplane.

"Travis, where are you on that Kmart deal?" I asked him right away.

"It's falling apart!" he told me. "They didn't like the drivers I've been talking to. It may be too late to put the deal together."

"Well, I was just thinking," I said. "If you wanted to get something going, I wouldn't mind driving for you."

"You'd drive for me?!" he asked, in a tone that should've told me I was making a mistake.

"Yeah, I would." I said. "If you get a deal together, I'd like to drive a couple more years and do my farewell tour. Kmart would be perfect for it. Go to all of those retail stores. The whole nine yards. It would be a perfect deal for me."

"Call me tomorrow," he said.

I got home and called.

"I mentioned your name to the sponsor, and it was like magic!" he said. "The deal is back on. But you need to call Carl Haas [Carter's co-owner]. Carl is not sold on you. He says you're too old. You need to call him and tell him you can get the job done."

As a car owner in Indy cars, Carl Haas has won a lot of races paired up with Paul Newman as co-owner and Mario and Michael Andretti as his star drivers. But Haas was a bizarre individual. Before every race, he kneeled down, touched every part of the car, and talked to it. Seriously, he talked to the car. Either he was senile or eccentric, I wasn't sure which. I had never met him, so I called to talk about the deal.

"This is Darrell Waltrip, and I hear you and Travis Carter are putting a deal together with Kmart," I said. "I want you to know I'd like to drive the car. I'm 50 years old, but if you give me a good car I can still get the job done."

I'm going on and on. But it was like no one was on the other end of the line. When I stopped talking, there was an awkward silence.

"Who is this?" he asked.

"This is Darrell Waltrip!" I answered.

"I thought Michael wanted to drive the car," he said, I suppose referring to my little brother.

"I don't know anything about Michael," I said with a laugh. "He has a ride! I'm calling to tell you that if you put the deal together, I'd like to drive the car."

Long pause.

"I gotta call that Carter Travis," he said. I swear he called his partner "Carter Travis." "And I'll find out what the heck's going on."

Then he hung up the phone.

I called Travis and said, "I don't know what is going on."

"That's the way Carl is." He laughed. "He'll call me, and I'll get it straightened out."

We made our deal, and Kmart came aboard.

I went to meet Travis and see the shop. Travis and Jimmy Spencer had been running as a single-car team, with Winston as their sponsor. For the most part, they ran pretty well for a single-car team, and I thought the second team would be a good addition. They had good cars and good guys like Cecil Gordon and Donnie Wingo, guys who had been around. I thought it would be kind of fun being a teammate with Spencer, who was often as outspoken as me.

I met Travis Carter in his office in a pretty nice shop where the team prepared the number 23 cars for Spencer.

"Come on," he said. "I'll take you over to the other shop."

We drove to a warehouse. Not a shop, a warehouse. They put a tarp in to make a paint booth. Junk was piled everywhere. Someone else had owned all these old cars.

Ernie Irvan and Todd Bodine had driven them. Greg Sacks had driven them. Every Tom, Dick, and Harry had been in one of them. Just hodgepodge cars everywhere. Seven of them, all junk. My stomach sank.

"Who's the crew chief?" I asked.

"Well, we don't have one," he explained. "We have to hire the people. We were waiting to get Kmart as a sponsor."

I should've quit right there. I shouldn't have gone a step further. I should've turned around and taken my little butt back to Tennessee. I should have ended my career at that moment. But I didn't want to quit driving. I didn't have enough guts to say, "Hey, this ain't no good."

I told myself, "I know these cars are lemons, but I can make lemonade. I've always been good at that. Throw me in a briar patch and I come out in pretty good shape."

I was still a really good race driver, but I didn't have anything left to prove. I wasn't as aggressive or as hungry as I once was. The short time I spent in Earnhardt's Pennzoil car was the only time I was in equipment where I could show I was still fast. I should have looked at the Travis Carter deal and said, "This isn't good enough for me." I should have turned around and walked out, but . . .

If this is all that's left, I'll take it. I can force it to work. Something wasn't letting me say, "If I can't be in a car with the number 17, in a first-class ride with a first-class team, then I don't want to race."

The Kmart car was number 66 because Route 66 was the clothing line they were promoting. I did a fun TV commercial or two for them, but other than that, I hated 66. I hated that number. They were a relatively new sponsor that didn't know the sport. They didn't know me, and they didn't care I was known as number 17. At that time, I didn't fully understand the equity I had in the number until I lost it. I had been 17 forever; people recognized me for that. I should have fought harder to keep that number on my car.

All of the identity and all of the equity I had, I couldn't carry into my last two years. The 17 slowly slipped away from me. After I stopped racing in the Busch Series, Matt Kenseth came along as a young hot-shot from Wisconsin, and his team, owned by Robbie Reiser, started running the number in the Busch Series. That wasn't such a big deal, but then Mark Martin bought a portion of the team, along with Jack Roush, and they planned to move Matt to Winston Cup. Mark came to me and asked if they could use the number in Winston Cup because I wasn't using it. He had gone to NASCAR, but they told him he had to come see me if he wanted the number.

NASCAR says you have one year to use it, and I wanted to race it again, even if only as a car owner, but I had hung on to it as long as I could. Mark and I have been good friends, and he asked if I was gonna use it.

"Man, I want to hang on to it so bad," I told Martin. "I'd like to tell ya I'm gonna use it, but I can't lie to ya. I don't have any prospects to use it. You can have it, but on this condition: You will make a big deal out of me letting you have it. You know: 'This is carrying on with DW's number, carrying on a tradition . . .'"

They mentioned it, but that was about it.

Carl Haas came to Daytona for the first race, and when I met him for the first time, he had a soggy, unlit cigar in his mouth. Turns out he always has a cigar with him. I'm not sure how often he grabbed a new cigar, because he didn't smoke it, he just chewed on it. Before the 500, he got down in front of the car and spoke to it. He must have scared the daylights out of it, because it didn't run worth a damn. I think he put a hex on the car. And that hex lasted the entire two years I was with the team.

The first year was a nightmare, and we raced out of the warehouse as well as we could.

Before the next season, we were testing at Talladega when I learned that my dad, Leroy, had passed away. Dad had been in chemotherapy and radiation therapy for a few months at Carolina's Medical Center, and he had several months of fair health before he passed.

Throughout my career, he and Mom had attended as many races as they could, and it always meant a lot to me. Dad loved coming to the track, but he especially liked coming along when I went to non–Winston Cup events, where the mood was a lot lighter and a lot more fun. He especially loved places like Milwaukee and Topeka, Kansas, where I'd race in Busch or ASA races each year.

I was heartbroken, but I hoped a better performance on the track would make me feel better. The team built a new shop beside the main shop, so we were no longer working out of the warehouse. Things were looking up. We also hired crew chief Phillippe Lopez away from Earnhardt and the Pennzoil team because we had worked so well together in 1998.

But it wasn't the same. The magic wasn't there like it had been when we were working for Earnhardt. Phillippe quit pretty quickly when things continued to be so hapless, and we were back to no crew chief again. Larry Carter, Travis's nephew, became the new crew chief. He had never been a crew chief. His qualifications: He had run a lawn service two years before.

The only on-track highlight of 2000 was qualifying on the outside pole at Indy. We really hit on a setup, and I had a fast, fast hot rod. The best memory of my final two years was getting out of that car after my qualifying lap, looking at the tall pylon at Indy, and seeing my number at the top. I did a little Ickey Shuffle and hugged Michael. It felt so pure, so good. The crowd cheered, and it felt like the good ol' days for a second. Then Ricky Rudd beat us for the pole by something like two-hundredths of a second.

If I had a chance to run one Winston Cup race, if I could choose to run a single race at any track, I'd probably choose Indy. When I was a little kid growing up, it was THE place. It seemed like the logical place where I would look to end my career. The center of speed. It was such a magical, historical place, and I loved racing there.

I had a fast race car when the race began, but bad pit stops killed us. We came in running seventh, came out running 39th. I'd get back to 11th and then I'd lose it all again on the next pit stop. I passed more cars than anybody, but it was the only good car I had all year, and we finished 11th.

Every week, I would come home after one disaster or another, and I would tell Stevie, "I can't believe I spent 30 years building a career and this is the way it's going to end." I started doubting myself, the team doubted me, and it all picked up speed like a snowball rolling down a big hill.

▬▭▬

I have 105 significant victories—that includes the Busch Series, IROC, USAC, ASA, 17 wins at Daytona, and so on. While you are in the middle of your career, the two most significant are the first one and the last one.

When you start in the Winston Cup series, no matter how confident or cocky you seem, there is a part of your brain that wonders if you'll ever win a race. It must be the same in any major sport. It doesn't matter what you did in the minor leagues or if you were the stud on the college basketball court. When you get to the top level, there is a small place in your mind with doubt about your ability to win. So much depends on the team around you—you can't do it all yourself, even though the bravado of youth may hide that doubt. If you're the star quarterback, like my buddy Terry Bradshaw, you may be able to throw that thing 100 yards. But you can't throw it and run down and catch it yourself. He had Lynn Swan and John Stallworth to catch it, and Franco Harris to run it. He also needed those big linemen to block so he had the time and space to throw it. You need the team around you, and in racing it's as critical as in any other sport.

When I was young, I'd tell my crew chief, "Don't worry. I'll carry that car around the track. I'll *will* it to victory. Just strap it on my back and I'll carry it." And when I was on top of my game, I believed I could actually carry that thing around and wear 'em all down. But when you first start out, you're haunted by the fear and anxiety of winning your first race. Then you win one, and it's not only an outburst of joy but a sigh of relief. Once you get the confidence from the first one, it actually gets easier to find Victory Lane.

Man, when I was winning 12 races a year and winning championships, it felt like it would go on forever. But, all champions have their era, and that era always comes to an end. As you near the end of your career, doubt begins to creep into your brain like when you were young.

"Will I ever win another race?"

You start off your career wondering, and you end your career wondering. The difference is, when you're starting off, you think you've got all of the time in the world. As you reach the end, you know that you don't have much time left to win. Your numbers are limited. Your opportunities run out. As I got older and more experienced, I knew I needed the car to be right, the team to be right on every pit stop. I could still carry the car around if needed, but as the competition continued to get stronger, it no longer seemed possible to do it all myself.

There are so many things that can prevent a victory. The car can blow up in a huge cloud of smoke and flames, or a small, simple part you never thought about will fail. You lose a million-dollar race because of a two-dollar part. Your car can be the fastest, but your pit crew may screw up. As a driver, I might be perfect for 499 miles, but if I make a little mistake in the final corner, I could crash and never see the finish line. When you crash, it's not like baseball where you get three strikes. In racing, one strike means you are out. Maybe permanently.

There are so many things that can stop you, and it's not like it happens occasionally. Even for a great team, problems can happen every week, and that's what you worry about. If none of those things stops you, you might have a chance to win.

Occasionally, I'll look back through the records and see where somebody lucked into one—maybe a driver with only one career victory—because everybody else crashed or broke and he was the only fast car rolling at the end of the race. There are occasions like that, but it wouldn't take me long to count 'em. You need more than luck to win in Winston (Nextel) Cup.

Am I ever going to be able to put it all together again? That became my mood at the end of my career, a constant, gnawing doubt as the results began to fade.

I was glad when the end of the 2000 season finally arrived. It was a relief, but it still broke my heart at Atlanta, the last race of the year. It had been the "DW Farewell Victory Tour" all season, and this was the finale. Ed Clark and the people at the Atlanta track did a good thing for me. They were very kind. The race was rained out on Sunday. It was cold and rainy, and they had planned a ceremony on the front straightaway with all of the former Winston Cup champions. But when it rained, they moved it into the media center. It turned out even better than expected, because we had some time. We had all day, and we weren't in a hurry. Dale, Rusty, Bill, and Jeff came, Michael and all of them. We sat and told stories and laughed all afternoon.

When the race finally started on Monday morning, they had a surprise for me in the main grandstand. The fans held up cards that spelled out "THANKS DW." The crewmen from all 43 teams came out on pit lane and gave me a big send-off. That day was great, but the season was awful. It's hard for any athlete to quit, but I was frustrated from not being competitive. Because of that, I didn't capitalize on my last year like I thought I would. My victory tour didn't turn out too well. No victories.

Oh, by the way . . .

Stevie Waltrip

The last two years were worse for me than when he lost the team. He was doing it for the money—he wasn't doing it to win races. The team wasn't prepared to win races. Darrell asks and requires excellence of the people around him, and he got so much less. They used him, but he used them too, because he wanted to stay in the sport. I think God helped him through the pain and humiliation and made him a better, stronger person.

CONTINUED

Van Colley, marketing director

I was praying Earnhardt would put a deal together for DW to stay at DEI. When he climbed into Big E's number 1 car, he was rejuvenated. He made the critics eat crow. He showed he could still run with the best with good equipment and a team that believed in him. He was the "Darrell of Old," not "Old Darrell."

Sadly, it wasn't meant to be. DW is fond of saying, "The hits just keep on coming." Unfortunately, we would learn they weren't going to be good hits.

26

The Biggest Moment

The first NASCAR banquet in New York City in 1981 was a big deal. A really big deal. It was big for NASCAR, for Winston, and for Bill France Jr., because the sport was in the center of the media universe to celebrate. It was a big deal to me because it was my first title, and winning it with my team owner, Junior Johnson, was particularly gratifying. It was also a big deal because my mom and dad came along for the week. It was extra special for my mom, because it was her first trip to New York City.

When I got up to accept my awards, I received a check for $150,000, a great big belt buckle, and a dinky ring that looked like a high school ring.

I was back home from New York with all of my stuff on Monday, and Bill France Jr. called.

"What do you think about that?" he asked. "Pretty cool, huh?"

"I liked everything about it," I told him. "The money was great. The dinner was great. Black tie, Waldorf-Astoria, everything was cool. But that ring wasn't much! I thought it'd be more like a Super Bowl ring."

"I beg your pardon," he said.

"The ring is not Winston Cup caliber! That ring is pitiful," I said. "I can't wear it. I've got a high school ring that looks better than that."

You can just imagine—France was ticked.

"So you don't like the ring?" he asked. "I'll tell you what we'll do, Mr. Big Shot. You win the championship again next year and you can pick the ring."

Of course, we did win it again in 1982, and they sent the catalog over. I picked out the ring, and it was a sharp one. From that year on, everybody who won the Winston Cup title got one of those rings.

I really didn't want to go to the 2000 NASCAR banquet. I had been the first champion honored in New York, and after the last few years of my career, lemme tell ya, buddy, I didn't particularly care to attend and see someone else get the ring I had picked out two decades before.

Late in the 2000 season, when most of the tracks were presenting me with a gift or an honor to commemorate my last race there, Joe Carver told me I was going to get some sort of NASCAR award at Homestead.

Homestead came and went. Nothing.

The day after the race, someone at NASCAR called Van Colley at my shop and told him, "We are going to give him an award at the banquet, but it's top secret. Do you understand? No one is to know anything about it." So he tried to make sure I was there.

I decided to go to New York for some of the events and festivities, since I would be working for FOX TV in 2001, but I didn't want to go to the banquet. I told NASCAR I might agree to give the invocation, but then I wanted to take Stevie to a show.

"DW!" Van scolded me. "It's the banquet!"

"Nahhhhh . . . Get me tickets to one of the Broadway shows," I told him.

This went on for a week, so Van had no choice but to bring in the heavy artillery. He called Stevie.

"This is a big deal," he told her, "but DW can't know anything about it."

Bobby Labonte was the champion that year, with the Joe Gibbs team. Bobby and I always liked each other, so Van and Stevie knew it was the best angle to convince me. Bobby used to wear one of my Mountain Dew team T-shirts when he was a kid, and he still has it! Stevie knew I thought so much of Bobby and Coach Gibbs, and she had little doubt she could convince me to be there to celebrate the championship with them.

"Leave it to me," Stevie said. "Give me a few days."

She didn't need that long. The next day, I called Van and said, "OK, cancel the Broadway show. I'm going to the banquet."

When the banquet began, Stevie and I ate dinner with George Pyne of NASCAR and Fred Wagenhals, the top guy at Action Performance, the company that makes all of the die-cast cars and souvenirs. We were having a nice time enjoying the rubber chicken as much as possible.

I wasn't paying attention, half listening at most. Then a video began to play, and it's a capsule of my career featuring a lot of highlights. I thought they were being nice. You know, it was my last year, so they're being nice to ol' DW. Giving me a round of polite applause before they kick me out the door.

Slowly, it started to dawn on me.

"Honey," I whispered, "they're talking about ME!"

The TV cameras were zooming in on me, and I started to tear up.

I walked to the stage, and for the first time in my life I was speechless. I had won the Bill France Award of Excellence.

I looked down from the podium, and there was Bill France Jr. in a wheelchair. He had been fighting cancer, and I hadn't seen him since July, when it became known he was gravely ill. The doctors thought he was going to die, and I went to Daytona to see him. I know Earnhardt and a few other guys went to see him as well. He had been in a hospital in Jacksonville, then he was transferred to Halifax Hospital in Daytona to be closer to home and family.

Mike Helton, who took over France's position as NASCAR's president, took me to the hospital, and I will never forget Mike turning to me and saying, "Be prepared, because you won't recognize him." I walked into the room, and Bill was so very sick, I almost couldn't tell who he was. The man lying there was not the tough guy I had known. He was so frail, the doctors did not believe he had the strength to live through the cancer treatments.

I'm not sure if he is a very religious man, but I prayed with him that day. I prayed for him, then hugged him and leaned over to kiss him on the forehead. I thought it would be the last time I'd see him.

Bill France Jr. took over NASCAR the same year I drove in my first Winston Cup race. As my career began to blossom and the sport became more and more successful, I became one of his "go-to guys." That's what he called a competitor he trusted. He would call me—very confidentially, of course—and when he called to ask my opinion about an important issue, those conversations stayed between us. I didn't go around the garage area blabbing everything I knew. Oh, I wanted to a lot of times, but I never did because I wanted to have his confidence. It meant the world to me.

One of my most memorable conversations with France was before a race at Nashville in 1982. I won 12 races in 1981, and even though it was early May, I had already won four times in '82. I won the pole, and right before the race, I was adjusting my belts, getting strapped in. France walked down the track and knelt beside my car, leaning in the window.

"How's your car?" he asked.

"Haulin' butt," I said. "I'm going to lap these guys."

"That's a problem," France said.

"What do you mean?" I asked.

"We're going to have to do something about you," he said. "We're going to have to slow you down. You're stinking up the show every week. You should at least take it easy."

I shouldn't have been surprised. NASCAR wants "the show" to be good no matter what.

"All right," I said. "Tonight, I'm going to take it easy."

He walked away from the car.

"Take it easy?" I laughed to myself. "Just watch me."

The race was 420 laps, and I led 419 of them. Harry Gant led one lap when I came in for a pit stop, and that was it. I won by more than a lap, third place was two laps behind, and Earnhardt was five laps behind in 10th place.

In 1998, before the race at Phoenix, France approached me in almost the exact same manner. "We're going to have to do something about you," he said.

"What are you talking about?" I asked him.

"Why do you keep driving this race car?" France asked.

"What am I supposed to do?" I laughed. "I'm getting paid a lot of money to drive this car."

"You're stinking up the show," France said. "You need to get out of that car and get your butt in the TV booth."

Only he knew network negotiations would begin the following year, and he knew I could do the most good for the sport from the booth.

He wasn't always so blunt, and there were times he was actually quite funny. He called me in 1995, a day after I finished fourth at Talladega. I had led the race, and I ran near the front most of the day.

"Were you there yesterday?" he asked.

"What?! Didn't you see me?!"

"No," he said. "I saw your car, but you couldn't have been driving it the way it was running."

I used to argue with France, telling him he had it in for me when he announced the schedule every year. I dominated at Nashville, so they took Nashville off the schedule. I dominated at North Wilkesboro, and they took Wilkesboro off the schedule. I dominated at Riverside, so they took Riverside off the schedule. The old Richmond fairgrounds? I was great there, then they changed the track dramatically. He and I laughed about it, because it seemed as if he was taking races away to slow me down.

I don't believe France trusts a lot of people. He has a small circle of people he confides in. I feel as if I was in the small group that has earned his trust—"the inner circle," I called it. But I had to work hard to earn that respect. When I won my first championship, I became the man, almost like NASCAR's spokesperson. The champion was the PR guy for the sport. You could either take advantage of it or you could walk away from it. I wanted to grab every bit of it.

When I started, there were five guys in the inner circle. They won all of the races, and they controlled the sport. It was a closed fraternity. They had things the way they wanted, and they didn't want to let a smart aleck from Kentucky bust into that circle. I wanted what they had.

I can't tell you how envious I was of Richard Petty. I wanted everything he had. He was the most popular, and he had the most wins, the most championships. He was Mr. NASCAR. I knew I had the ability to win, more ability than the guys I raced against, but I also had more of an ego. My ego, which was connected directly to my mouth, got me in a lot of trouble.

They didn't know what to do with me. When Cale Yarborough called me "Jaws," I thought it was funny. I loved it. I didn't care what they called me. Whatever they could dish out, I could take. I dished a lot more back. They didn't like anyone breaking up their private party. I became a constant thorn in their side, and they tried to run me off, but I was determined to not give up. I wasn't goin' away. I could be charming and persuasive, or I could be rude and obnoxious. Whatever was necessary. We could be friends or enemies, but I was going to make my presence felt.

Now, as I received this award, I realized I was no longer the troublemaker. No longer the thorn in their side, the guy who always asked "Why." I was not "Jaws," the driver everyone loved to hate. I wasn't the aging past champion taking up space at the back of the field. I had lived my dreams, after promising myself I was going to wear 'em out when I grew up. I won three championships and 84 races, and earned my way into the inner circle.

After winning my first title, I earned France's respect. He was always trying to figure everyone's intentions. He was always suspicious. It was hard to have a close, personal relationship with the man when you were involved in NASCAR, because he always suspected you were trying to get something. Occasionally, he dropped his defenses and had a real conversation with you, or took your advice. Only occasionally, though.

I think he trusted me to give my heartfelt, honest opinion of a situation. And I know he felt the same way about Earnhardt. He could call and talk to me about rules or decisions, and I took it very seriously.

France led NASCAR through what will be known at the Winston Cup era. Now, with Nextel coming aboard, the sport continues to adapt and grow. Bill Jr. has even turned over the reins of the sport to his son, Brian, beginning in 2004.

Most of the people who come to the races now think racing started in 1992. That's all they know. It's been the case since Jeff Gordon came on the scene. The youth movement helped move NASCAR from a sport that had a limited audience—old guys with grease under their nails—to a younger, more mainstream sport, a sport that appeals to a huge audience. I think I had a lot to do with the growth. When I became champion, it wasn't as big as it is today, but I did my fair share of lifting the load and exposing a lot of new people to the sport.

That night, I had no idea what the road ahead looked like. I don't know what I would've done if the opportunity to become an analyst with FOX Sports hadn't come along. Maybe I would've scrounged around and found a ride. I couldn't have handled being away from the sport. I would have ended up getting a Busch ride or maybe something in the Craftsman Truck series to stay connected. Now I'm connected in the best way.

From 1995 on, I got sick of hearing the same question: "Why do you keep racing?" My reasons were selfish: I liked my lifestyle. I liked going to races. I liked being in the race car. I liked people screaming my name. I needed it. If I gave up driving, what would I do? I would lose my identity. But that's the beautiful thing about the TV deal: I didn't lose my identity, I gained a new one.

People used to ask, "Hey, buddy, are you with the show?"

"I AM the show," I'd answer.

With my new career, I get to be the show every week. I have had so much fun with my new role; it would make a good book. Hey, wait a minute. That's a good idea . . . (My first week as a FOX commentator ended with my brother Michael's first Daytona 500 win and the death of Dale Earnhardt. I call it "Black Sunday," and I could probably do an entire book on the emotions of that week alone.)

As a driver, did I inspire kids just as G. C. Spencer and his Flying Saucer car inspired me as a young boy? How many people were like Granny, smoking her cigarettes, yelling and screaming for me and at me from the grandstands? How many young racers wanted to put "17" on the side of their first race car?

Those were some of the many, many thoughts racing through my mind as I stood on stage at the Waldorf, looking down at France in that wheelchair. I couldn't believe I was receiving the Bill France Award of Excellence. The passion and the magic I felt as a six-year-old holding Granny's hand was still there.

I looked at my beautiful wife in the audience. The Red Head. How many times had I been exhausted and dejected after a day that was less than perfect, only to have her come over, give me a hug and a kiss, and say, "You'll get 'em next week"? Nothing could come close to making me feel better than to hear that from her. And now she was here with me, sharing my biggest moment.

Reflecting on my career, what stands out? What is the most significant moment or milestone? Nothing stands out, because I see my career as all-encompassing. It's a whole. There are a lot of things that were defining: the first guy to win a million dollars in a career; the first to win $10 million in a career. Those are the things a competitive person looks at. That's what's made me and Dale great rivals. That's what made my rivalries with Bobby Allison and Richard Petty and Cale Yarborough so intense. We all badly wanted to be first at everything.

And, more important, we wanted to be better than everyone else.

I look back on my career and say, "OK, here it is. You lay it out and you write a book." Hopefully, I've done enough to write a good one.

When NASCAR celebrated its 50th anniversary, they created a list of the 50 greatest drivers. I'm glad to be on the list—it means a lot to me. But, among the 50 greatest drivers, which one am I? Am I number one? Am I number 49? A more rewarding feeling is knowing I was the best in my time. That's what matters. The 50 greatest drivers, the driver of the decade, the most popular driver . . . I've been inducted into a series of Halls of Fame and received many, many awards. They are all precious to me, and they mean a lot, but this was the top of the heap. The best award possible. The ultimate NASCAR award.

Granny Oda would be proud.

When I came into the sport of NASCAR racing, I was a young upstart with a cocky attitude. Combining heart, desire, passion, and a God-given ability, I was able to reach all of my goals, both personally and professionally.

There were a lot of sacrifices. But I was able to get through them with the love and support of my family—my loving wife, Stevie, and my two beautiful daughters, Jessica and Sarah—plus my strong Christian faith.

And along the way, I needed the steadying hand of people I looked up to. It started with my racing hero David Pearson. Junior Johnson molded me from a race winner into a three-time Winston Cup champion. Rick Hendrick showed me how to be successful on and off the track.

And I would be remiss if I didn't mention Bill France Jr. He took over the sport of NASCAR the same time I entered it. Needless to say, I was his first problem child. His strong leadership was a good example for me to follow. It's been said that we both have made significant contributions to our sport. And guess what? We will continue to do so!

—*Darrell Waltrip*

While working on the text of Darrell's book, I found I was constantly using CAPITAL LETTERS and *italics* for emphasis. DW is a man who talks in italics. Words and emotions jolt out of him like bolts of lightning, transcending the printed word. He tells stories with such verve and joy, it was a challenge to translate the energy and spirit to the page. Writing about auto racing is like trying to write about rock and roll. You need to see, feel, and hear it in person to fully appreciate it, but I hope I've captured a small part of the essence.

Thanks to Darrell. I can't imagine a more fun time putting this together. Thanks to Van Colley, who made the first phone call, and to Stevie for her hospitality in Franklin. (Smitty: Thanks for the food. It tasted a lot better than the usual burger from the infield concession stand.)

The award for exceptional, extended efforts in executive editing goes to Bill Kentling, who spent endless hours editing, clarifying ideas, and debating the merits of the word "that." Thanks in this category also go to Aubree Foust, Glenn Hudson, and B. J. Matthews.

Thanks to those who were interviewed and provided information or details (in alphabetical order): Bobby Allison, Drew Brown, Joe Carver, Van Colley, Dr. Albert Gillespy, Jeff Hammond, Rick Hendrick, Tom Higgins, Tommy House, Larry McReynolds, Ty Norris,

David Pearson, Ed Silva, Ray Sk... Carolyn Waltrip, Michael Waltrip, Humpy Wheeler, Carolyn Waltrip, Larry Woody.

Thanks to Anheuser-Busch and Dale ... for giving me the "OK" to add this project to my usual ...ties. And a tip of the helmet to Richard A.te at ICM and Rob McMahon at Putnam. Second tin's a charm, eh!

Thanks to Mikki, for putting up with it all.

Oh, and by the way, special thats to my aunt Lindy, who took me to the Shawnee County Fairgrounds when sprint cars were still called supermodifieds, who let a nine-year-old kid help her with the weekly race reports for *National Speed Sport News*, who took me to my first Indy 500, and who appreciates the beauty and grace of loud, overpowered beasts sliding around a racetrack.

—Jade Gurss, coauthor

Darrell Waltrip won ree Winston Cup championships during his career, as ell as the 1989 Daytona 500. He is currently a commeator for FOX Sports' NASCAR coverage. He lives Franklin, Tennessee. Visit his Web sites at www.allwaltrip.com and www.dwstore.com.

Jade Gurss is the bestselling coauthor of *Driver #8* with Dale Earnhardt Jr. He lives in Huntersville, North Carolina.